GORDON KING (not to be confused with the singer/guitarist in Black Lace) is a musician and founder member of World of Twist (1983–92).

In 1994, he joined Earl Brutus, appearing on the albums *Your Majesty . . . We Are Here* and *Tonight You Are the Special One*. He is a member of the Pre New and also records and performs with his new group Quatermass III. On the days he's not being a rock star, he works as an archive producer in the TV and film industry.

Gordon left the north-west almost three decades ago and has since lived in the soft south with his partner, Jane, and two daughters, Jody and Dora. He still follows Manchester United and continues to listen to progressive-rock music.

WHEN DOES THE MIND-BENDING START?

The Life and Times of World of Twist

GORDON KING

NINE
EIGHT
BOOKS

NINE
EIGHT
BOOKS

NEB 006 PB

First published in the UK in hardback in 2022
This paperback edition published in 2023 by Nine Eight Books
An imprint of Black & White Publishing Group
A Bonnier Books UK company
4th Floor, Victoria House, Bloomsbury Square, London, WC1B 4DA
Owned by Bonnier Books, Sveavägen 56, Stockholm, Sweden

 @nineeightbooks

 @nineeightbooks

Paperback ISBN: 978-1-7887-0540-0
eBook ISBN: 978-1-7887-0539-4
Audio ISBN: 978-1-7887-0528-8

A CIP catalogue record for this book is available from the British Library.

Publishing director: Pete Selby
Senior editor: Melissa Bond

Cover images © James Fry
Cover background © Maryna Amediieva/Alamy
Typeset by IDSUK (Data Connection) Ltd
Printed and bound in Great Britain by Clays Ltd, Elcograf S.p.A

1 3 5 7 9 10 8 6 4 2

Nine Eight Books is an imprint of Bonnier Books UK
www.bonnierbooks.co.uk

CONTENTS

Cast

Gordon King – Your host and co-founder of World of Twist. A man whose glass has always been half empty with the bottle knocked over.

Jim Fry – Co-founder of World of Twist, missed his maths O level to go and watch David Bowie. A man who knows his priorities.

Tony Ogden – Original World of Twist drummer. The third hardest lad at Wood Lane Comprehensive.

Andy Hobson – World of Twist member from 1985. WoT member with the most winning smile. His favourite disco record is 'Pepper Box' by the Peppers.

Alan Frost, aka 'Adge' – World of Twist member from 1990. Inventor of the 'Pigeon Stroll', a dance for the ages.

David Hardy – World of Twist manager. The only adult in this story.

Julia Seppi, aka 'MC Shells, Julia Vesuvius' – The most glamorous SH-101 player in the history of rock.

Nick Sanderson – The second best Subbuteo player in this story (after G. King).

Chris Whitehead – World of Twist tour manager, former engineer, glam rocker, visionary.

Overture

'World of Twist were the Roxy Music of their time, I can't think of or give a better compliment than that.'

— Jeremy Deller, artist

Hanging on a wall in the ambassador's office at the British Embassy in Tbilisi is a picture entitled *He's a Rainbow*. The portrait, a screen-printed photograph on iridescent mirror card, shows the profile of a handsome male pop singer in his late twenties. He's wearing a fitted leather shirt and his black fringe falls lankly over his face. He is slightly hunched over and holds his microphone as if he's throwing a flighted dart. It's a striking image and easy to see why it might have caught the ambassador's attention. The singer pictured is Tony Ogden, vocalist with World of Twist, a Manchester-based group who enjoyed some popularity in the early 1990s. The picture is the work of Turner Prize-winning artist Jeremy Deller. A connoisseur of popular culture and World of Twist's most honoured fan, Deller has celebrated the group in art form on more than one occasion. His 2009 work *Procession* saw the group's original singer and their former manager parading a banner emblazoned with the legend 'We miss the World of Twist' through the streets of Manchester. I was the co-writer and co-founder of the group. I have a feeling that Jeremy may be slightly disappointed with this book. I think he would have preferred it if I'd printed the legend but if he bears with me he'll agree the reality of this strange tale far outstrips the legend. The World of Twist story began in 1983 in Sheffield, South Yorkshire, but the moment that will concern Jeremy and anyone who might have heard of us covers an intense two-year period in the early '90s when Greater Manchester's music and culture ruled the world – or a small part of it, fanning out from Salford to the north and Stockport to the south.

Two years after World of Twist folded, I joined a band called Earl Brutus. There were many similarities, both in personnel and in our respective MOs. The Earl Brutus story is worth telling in its own right and, in terms of excess, shouting and wanton destruction, is a far more disturbing tale than this one. Just as Earl Brutus were seen by some as an antidote to Britpop frivolity, five years earlier World of Twist became the house band for a raft of journalists who'd had their fill of 'Madchester', a media invention that to the smart observer had become a total yawn. It's perhaps ironic that they should have selected another Mancunian band to extricate themselves from the Manchester mire. None of this is to say that World of Twist didn't use the Madchester flag when convenient. We did so quite shamelessly. Some of us (particularly the one born in the south) broadened our accents a little to disguise our south Manchester origins and we were not above using our tenuous association with the city's more illustrious names to blag our way into clubs and concerts, but there is little I hold precious about the Manchester of that prefabricated era. The Manchester I pine for, the one that plays in my head on a scratched and faded 8mm film, is a distant cluttered memory that reaches way back beyond that pleasure-seeking, self-aggrandising decade. I see crumbling Victorian grandeur rubbing shoulders with daring post-war modernism. A city trying to camouflage its Howard Spring, Shelagh Delaney griminess with a radio telescope here and an urban heritage park there. A thriving city-centre pub standing alone in the middle of a demolition site. A fifty-fifty chance of getting mugged on a Saturday afternoon, a theatre housed in a giant lunar module in an old Victorian stock market building. I close my eyes and see football fans with long hair and wrangler jackets, satin scarves tied round each wrist and tartan scarves hanging from their waists. Electronics shops with fifty-year-old stock struggling to stay afloat. A huge decaying amusement park and zoo occupying 165 acres of land in one of the most neglected areas of the city. Head shops and tatty independent record shops where you could lose yourself for hours. The inexorable rain. Males young and old wearing platform shoes and trousers wide enough to double as ships' sails. Stockport's Merseyway precinct: Colvin Top Gear, Stolen from Ivor, Seven Miles Out, Nield & Hardy, On the Eighth Day, Mazel Radio, Shudehill, Virgin Records on Lever Street, Robinson's Records, Yanks, Johnny Roadhouse, A1, Reno's music store, the Peveril of the Peak, the Cyprus Tavern, Rafters, the New Oxford chippy, the underground market and the Stretford Paddock two hours before kick-off.

This is the Manchester that forged World of Twist, not an arbitrary moment in time between 1986 and 1990. World of Twist and Madchester arrived at the same time, but we had nothing or very little to do with each other. As the most erudite Mark E. Smith commented at the 2008 *Mojo* Awards, 'Don't believe what you hear about Manchester – it's all fantasy.'

Prelude: The Sons of the Stage

On 15 and 16 November 1991, World of Twist played the final two dates of their second and final UK tour – at the Town & Country in Kentish Town, London, and the Academy in Manchester. Both venues held over 2,000 people and both nights were sold out.

Selling out in London was a bit different than in Manchester; everyone would come out for us in Manchester. It was compulsory. Selling out the capital was a real endorsement. Admittedly there was very little on the box that evening – *Russ Abbott*, *Casualty* and an *Omnibus* celebration of Irish stand-up comedians.

I've never been on *Top of the Pops* or had a top-twenty record, which, in the currency of the time, was the yardstick by which success was measured, but in the entertainment business there is very little that beats playing to a full house, be it in the back room of a pub or at a 2,000-capacity venue. The performer can relax in the knowledge that most of the audience will be there because they like you.

The Town & Country concert was one of three World of Twist shows I played drunk. That afternoon, our publishing company had taken the songwriting team out for a slap-up meal and, with a free bar at our disposal, singer Tony Ogden and I were unable to show any kind of restraint.

We got back to the venue with maybe forty minutes to spare before showtime. Too far gone to do otherwise, we availed ourselves of the rapidly diminishing rider.

We went straight for the spirits. There were no nerves on my part as alcohol quickly vanquishes those, replacing them with a lethargic and self-satisfied confidence that evaporates the moment you realise your hand-eye coordination has abandoned you. Being drunk on stage – and I was never otherwise during my entire career with Earl Brutus – is similar to getting pissed at altitude: it hits you like a tram.

I was the guitarist in World of Twist. When we played live most of the backing was sequenced – a practice some would deem as 'miming'. From the stage, an Atari computer, piloted by the wonderful Pete Smith, fed into a number of sound modules that were mixed out front with the live drums, bass, guitar and vocals. Our drummer Nick Sanderson was one of the best in the business and would never drink much before a show. Tony Ogden was Mr Consistent and never gave a less than 90 per cent performance, even when under the influence. I, on the other hand, could not perform properly with any amount of alcohol in my system so would need to sit this one out – that is, turn my guitar down for most of the show. Nobody would know the difference.

The lights dimmed and our walk-on music, 'Ogdens' Nut Gone Flake' by the Small Faces, kicked in. For the benefit of any groups just starting out who may be reading this, it's worth noting that having an opening tune, or some sort of aural introduction, is an essential component to any successful rock show. Bowie in his absolute heyday would enter to Wendy Carlos's electronic interpretation of Beethoven's *Ode To Joy*; progressive-rock giants Yes would walk on to the climax of Igor Stravinsky's *Firebird* suite. In more recent times, Morrissey would whip his audience up with 'Imperfect List' by Big Hard Excellent Fish. The entrance is the most critical moment in any live show and to ignore this simple fact is to misunderstand the very chemistry of a rock concert. There is an electrifying drama to the walk-on, which left unexploited is robbing your audience of one of the biggest adrenaline rushes they'll ever experience. Detroit's MC5 had a dedicated rabble-rouser in Brother J. C. Crawford for this function. Crawford's introductions were biblical in scale, taking the spoken intro to almost Pentecostal levels: 'Brothers and sisters, the time has come when each and every one of you must decide if you are gonna be the problem or you are gonna be the solution . . . are you ready to testify? . . . I give you a testimonial, the MC5!!'

Back at the Town & Country in 1991, World of Twist waited in the wings with the Small Faces as the phased swirl of organ and strings reached its crescendo. Nick Sanderson walked out first, followed by the guitarist and our various synthesiser players. Nick launched into a furious drum solo, which I embellished with a deafening peal of feedback and wah-wah, out of which the gentle opening bars of 'Sons of the Stage' would emerge. Last out was Tony O, naturally, dressed in his trademark black leather shirt, white slacks with a jumbo belt buckle – Severus Snape restyled as Vince Taylor, Rigsby remodelled as Gene Vincent. World of Twist had been doing this for a year and a half and we were getting pretty good at it. True, our modest show was a long way from our wildest dreams. There were no girls swimming around in fish tanks yet, no Busby Berkeley-style choreography, no Peter Pan high wires, no scenery or costume changes. Of course, this would all happen once we'd achieved U2 status, blowing their tatty Zoo TV extravaganza into the next century.

The smoke machines were fired up and our slide show (heavily influenced by the Human League's) blinked into life. Our show was informed by multiple elements, all lovingly credited if anyone cared to enquire: *Selling England by the Pound*-era Genesis, the Human League, ClockDVA, Crass and just a soupçon of *Third Reich*-era Residents. But the main influence was definitely Hawkwind circa 1972. The brief was to excite, to astonish, to amuse, to uplift, but also to confuse, unsettle and disturb. This was high mass and we were the high priests. We were pretentious for sure, but it was a pretention borne of years studying and experiencing the finest exponents of rock theatre. And it *was* theatre. As far as we were concerned, we were here and the audience was way down there and never the twain would meet – which certainly explains why we never had many people visiting us backstage after the shows.

We didn't always get it right but on the nights we did, World of Twist were a stunning live act. If being in a rock band had merely entailed playing epic shows we'd probably still be doing this, but rock 'n' roll isn't that simple. Somewhere along the way you have to sell some product. And shifting product was never our strong suit.

1

Almost Cut My Hair

I should point out, before it's too late, that I am not a proper Mancunian. If pressed on my origins I usually say Stockport but I was actually born in Royal Tunbridge Wells, like Shane MacGowan. My dad is a proper cockney, although he doesn't sound like one, and my mum is a posh Stretford lass. They met in a field one afternoon sometime after the Second World War. I didn't reach Manchester until 1965. We lived in Urmston at my mum's sister's for a while, then found a house in Stockport, where we stayed until the end of the '60s.

I spent the summer after the Summer of Love learning to ride my bike. My family lived in Woodsmoor, Stockport, Cheshire, before it was absorbed by Greater Manchester in the great urban reshuffle of 1972. The Kings lived nearly opposite the Morleys, another north–south blended family. Their son Paul would grow up to be a pivotal figure on the Manchester music scene in the late '70s, new wave's finest journalist by some distance, a writer with a particular dislike of progressive rock. I'm fairly sure he once served me with some joss sticks and a fanzine in the book shop in Stockport where he worked, but aside from that our paths have never crossed. However, I feel a deep connection with Paul Morley. In his wonderful book *Nothing* he describes in vivid detail an attack of Bell's palsy. I read the passage just a few days after my partner Jane had suffered a similar attack. In a further coincidence, the subject of Paul's first romantic adventure was also the focus of my earliest prepubescent fantasies – Hilary Angel. The Angels were a pious family who lived diagonally opposite us. I can picture Mr and Mrs Angel dressed in full Salvation Army garb standing proudly at their front gate (although this is definitely my memory playing tricks). Their daughter Hilary was the stone fox of Flowery Field, so it was with some nostalgic envy that I read of Paul and Hilary's heavy petting in our local park sometime in the early '70s.

From 1976 through to the mid-'90s and beyond, Manchester has occupied a lofty position in this country's cultural canon. It is with some justification regarded by many as the alternative music capital of the UK. Back in 1968, however, the Hollies (with Peter Noone's Herman's Hermits in close attendance) were the best the city could offer. Riding the jetstream of the Merseybeat boom, their trademark harmony pop was trumped only by the Byrds and the Beatles and, despite the several leagues that separated them, these mop-topped Mancs had an uncanny knack of consistently turning out top-tenners. Our Hollies had even dipped a cautious toe into the world of psychedelia, but any real pretensions they had of outlasting the '60s were dealt a fatal blow when Graham Nash, their poster boy and spiritual guru, fresh from a life-changing Maharishi-inspired fling with Joni Mitchell, booked his seat on the Marrakesh Express and left our rainy city for ever. In those days, anything of any real consequence, pop-wise, happened south of Watford. Certainly, many rock and pop luminaries hailed from the north, but they all buggered off to London the moment they got a sniff of fame. Manchester was most famous for its two top-flight football teams, the nation's favourite soap opera and the country's worst ever plane crash. Psychedelia and the fag end of the Summer of Love would almost certainly be bypassing Manchester.

It was a hot summer holiday afternoon, as I remember, and I was getting in as many circuits as I could before tea time, head down, pedalling furiously. Down Palmerston Road, round the corner into Arlington Drive, past my house, past the Angels and the Morleys and the start of another lap. I was just turning left into Cromley Road when I saw something so disturbing I lost control and fell off the bike. Sitting there on a low garden wall (which is still there) were two beings who could well have been beamed in from another planet, wearing the strangest clothes I'd ever seen. Velvet trousers, frilled blouses, strings of coloured beads. Both were barefoot with very long hair, but one had a beard. A man with the hair of a woman. The man said something. I picked my bike up and ran home as fast as I could. But I couldn't get them out of my mind. Hippies. Actual hippies in Stockport. I didn't know it, but it was a moment that would shape my life.

Across the water around this time, probably that same month, possibly while riding their bikes, two young New York actors, James Rado and Gerome Ragni, had a similar epiphany, inspiring the counter-cultural Broadway smash hit *Hair*. My own hair has been of varying lengths since 1967, but I have enjoyed most inner peace when it has been 3 or 4 inches below my collar. The hair came before the music for me and its importance cannot be overstated. Was it H. G. Wells who once wrote, 'Whenever I see a young man with long hair, I do not despair for the future of the human race'? Or perhaps he was talking about bicycles.

I will die knowing I didn't experiment enough with my own mop. It troubles me now when I think of it. Yes, I've had very long hair and also very short hair – a no. 2 crop I got in the winter of 1984, which, believe me, is not the time of year to be going from long hair to virtually no hair. I've had perms, feather cuts, razor cuts, basin cuts, highlights, lowlights and even a short-lived Mallen streak. I've back-combed, straightened, curled and crimped my hair. The fringe has been short, long and way too long. I've worn a parting on the left, on the right and down the centre. I've slicked it back, slicked it forward and from side to side. I've used Brylcreem, wax, putty, gel, mousse and even KY Jelly to get it to go where I've wanted. And let's not even start with the hairsprays. However, my hair's never been blond. I've never had a Ziggy cut, a '70s Rod Stewart or a '60s Steve Marriott, a satisfactory quiff, a bob, a mohawk or, amazingly, a 1979 Phil Oakey. Given that I've been blessed with such a plentiful thatch, I do feel I've let it and myself down in some respects.

WHEN DOES THE MIND-BENDING START?

Though the mystery couple never returned to Flowery Field, in the next few months there would be further sightings of long-hairs in Stockport precinct, Woodbank Park and once outside our school gates. They began to appear in Sunday supplements and even on television. I returned to school that autumn with a new sense of purpose. At the earliest opportunity, I would grow my hair. I had always relished my quarterly outing to the barber – the dab of Brylcreem on request, the complimentary pack of football cards. At the end of my regulation medium back and sides, I'd ask for a 'John Connelly'. A couple of pumps of gentleman's lacquer and a deft flick of the barber's comb would achieve that late-'50s style worn with some aplomb by the Manchester United and England winger. The look would last maybe an hour before gravity took hold and it collapsed limply into the classic basin cut. Now, with my newfound ambition to join the enlightened long-haired throng, barbers became something to be avoided – to be feared, even, on a par with the dentist's chair, the nit nurse and our headmistress Miss Grant.

2

Molded, I Was Folded, I Was Preform-Packed

I can't remember if pop music mattered to me that much before the summer of 1968. Pop wasn't an ever-present thing in our house. We had the soundtrack to *West Side Story*, the Beatles' *Help*, Herb Alpert's *Going Places*, an album by Pete Seeger, a comedy record by Peter Sellers in which he 'hilariously' recited Beatles lyrics in the style of Olivier's *Richard III*. On occasion my mum would buy a pop single; something by Rolf Harris or maybe Gene Pitney. I recall her being quite sold on the Euro smash 'Guantanamera', a song that vies with Chicory Tip's 'Son of My Father' as the source material for Britain's most celebrated football chant. The rest of my parents' collection was classical, of which my favourite piece was (and maybe still is) the four *Sea Interludes* from Benjamin Britten's opera *Peter Grimes*.

At the age of six years and seven months, major musical events that had passed me by that summer were the debut releases by Family, Fairport Convention and the Crazy World of Arthur Brown. I was also sweetly oblivious to the release of the Velvet Underground's *White Light/White Heat* or Pink Floyd's comparatively tame follow-up to their debut album, *A Saucerful of Secrets*. Films I would have missed include Lindsay Anderson's *If . . .* and Kubrick's *2001: A Space Odyssey*. I would have shown little interest in the formation of a supergroup comprising former members of the Byrds, Buffalo Springfield and the Hollies, or even how the Beatles proposed to follow *Sgt Pepper*. What would have mattered most to me that summer was Manchester United's emotional victory in the European Cup Final, that Cliff Richard, dressed as Austin Powers, had been cruelly robbed of victory at the thirteenth Eurovision Song Contest, the launch of Gerry Anderson's new TV series *Joe 90*, James Bond's latest car and gadget (disappointingly a white Toyota and a gyroscope) and the forlorn hope of getting a Johnny Seven gun for Christmas.

In Woodsmoor in the late '60s, the sun always shone. It was, by and large, a happy period. My dad's company car was a Wolseley 6-110, a Rolls-Royce for the masses, the Beatles were on the telly all the time and Man United won the European Cup every year. Me and my polite gang of Flowery Field tearaways spent every minute possible outside. We hung about on an area of wasteland opposite the Mirrlees Blackstone Diesel Engine Company, now re-landscaped as a section of the Fred Perry Way. Our favourite spot was in the shade of a vast electricity pylon that kept watch over us as we strived to stem the flow of the River Goyt. Its radioactive emissions would galvanise us against any potential attack from the Hazel Grove gangs.

Invariably we'd encounter some hard lads from across the fields who, on pain of a good kicking, would liberate us of our pea shooters, cap guns, catapults, penknives, magnets and any loose change we might be carrying. On one occasion, one of our crew suffered the humiliation of having to surrender his Wayfinder shoes – the ones with the secret compass in the heel. I doubt he ever got over that.

In Michael Crick's book *Betrayal of a Legend*, written two years before Manchester United's second coming, he discusses how in the early '60s the Edwards family of Salford gained control of the football club by very underhand means. Louis C. Edwards & Sons supplied meat to most of the schools in the Manchester area in the 1960s. Their meat was reputedly shite and I must have eaten lots of it. As an eight-year-old I was a very poor specimen of Edwards-infused nourishment – stick thin, pigeon-toed and knock-kneed. Once a week I had to attend a physio class where a bunch of us would be encouraged to waddle round a gymnasium with a beach ball wedged between our knees. Footballers we certainly weren't. I also had to wear really crap shoes. Start-Rite Inner-Raise were the only footwear recommended for my condition – black or brown lace-ups (but mostly brown), with rounded toe and reinforced heel and strictly no gimmicks. How I'd dream of owning a pair of black Tuf slip-ons, some Clarks Commandos or, heaven forbid, the aforementioned Wayfinders. Not only was my body dwindling but my brains were turning to mush. I'd entered the infants a very promising youngster, but after three years' tuition had turned into a very cheeky and disruptive individual. Not yet delinquency material but not the sort of kid you'd look forward to teaching off the back of a night's go-go dancing. Back in 1969, there was none of your National Curriculum nonsense. Great Moor Primary School still adhered to the post-war concept of streaming kids entering secondary education. The idea was to weed out all the aggressive ones, the difficult ones, the thickos and the slow learners, and throw them together in a room so they could inspire one another to even greater heights. On hearing that my unruliness would ensure my place in the C stream, my parents decided to move. The first place they looked at was a bargain-bin Grade II listed manor house in Furness Vale, Derbyshire, called Yeardsley Hall. Once home of the pugnacious Jodrell family, after which the famous Lovell Telescope is named, the house was reputedly haunted, no doubt by those poor souls Roger Jodrell had longbowed to death on the battlefield at Agincourt. But the building was absolutely fucked and my dad, although skilled with saw and hammer, deemed its renovation a monster undertaking. He plumped instead for a more modest project not far from where we lived.

Bramhall was 2 miles down the road from Woodsmoor but socially speaking it was on another planet. It was a move slightly above our station and made possible by the condition of the house my parents were purchasing at 33 Valley Road. Mr Leahy, the former owner, had lost his wife several years earlier and to honour her passing had let the house fall to pieces around him. Consequently, there was not a floorboard that didn't need nailing down, a yard of pipe or wiring that didn't need replacing or a brick that didn't need repointing, and my dad, the Barry Bucknell of the north, elected to do every job himself under and above the flooring.

Bramhall was part of the Cheadle parliamentary constituency and a traditional Tory stronghold. You never saw a Labour poster stuck to a window or pinned to a tree. The closest the area got to progressive leadership was when the Conservatives lost the seat to the Liberals in 1966.

In the general election of 1970 it was once again a straight punch up between the blues and the oranges. In the event, Sir Tom Normanton ousted Liberal TV personality and future baron Michael Winstanley and so helped yachting fanatic the Rt Hon. Edward Heath take his position at the nation's tiller.

Bramhall as we remember it was Acacia Avenue writ large. Very presentable at first glance but you got the impression that something twisted and sinister was lurking beneath the surface – tarts and vicars and wife-swapping parties unquestionably, but possibly pagan worship and almost certainly satanism. It would come as no surprise to learn that the Brookdale Amateur Dramatic Society doubled as the north-west branch of the Hellfire Club – 'All fur coats and no knickers', as Bet Lynch famously described Bramhall on an episode of *Coronation Street*. It was with some hilarity that we discovered celebrated north London bass geezer Jah Wobble had moved to the village in the early noughties and apparently still lives there.

WHEN DOES THE MIND-BENDING START?

The youth of the village certainly liked their drugs at the time and you could always expect your medicine cabinet to get a full examination if you invited any stranger into your house. On one such occasion, an older friend, armed with a pharmaceuticals handbook, was rifling through our cabinet and discovered my bed-wetting pills. These were pills to make you stop, you understand. He helped himself to the vial of little red triangles and, while I'm uncertain if he managed to get trashed, I can guarantee he didn't piss the bed.

3

Get Down and Get With It

The Beatles notwithstanding, pop music for me started with the Seekers' 'Georgy Girl', shortly followed by the Tremeloes, Love Affair, the Foundations and Dave Dee, Dozy, Beaky, Mick & Tich. The '60s ended with the Paper Dolls, Harmony Grass, Jefferson, Barry Ryan, the Cuff Links and my newly developed penchant for baroque pop – a legacy of too much exposure to the classics in my infancy.

The new decade – pop's greatest decade – began with Chairmen of the Board, T. Rex, Rod Stewart and Slade, who were the first band I became obsessed with and the first band I saw live, supported by a little-known south London combo called Status Quo, who would give me a foretaste of the tinnitus to come.

July 1972. Most of the pop music in our house was owned by my elder brother Rob. I had some Slade and a couple of

12

inherited Beatles singles to bring to the turntable, but our collection was a bit thin. The only LPs we could afford were the ones they sold in our local newsagent for 99p: anything on the Marble Arch, Pickwick or Music for Pleasure labels or Pye's *Golden Hour of* series. At the very best, we're talking *Big War Movie Themes* by Geoff Love & His Orchestra and, at the worst, a *Golden Hour of Miki & Griff*. Of course we'd both been hoodwinked previously into buying a *Top of the Pops* or *Hot Hits* album. Their titillating covers promised a cavalcade of up-to-the-minute top-thirty smashes, only to reveal on first play that every song was a spectacularly half-arsed cover version of the listed hit. There were certainly some very amusing takes on the likes of the more distinctive singers like Noddy Holder, Marc Bolan and Bryan Ferry (apparently future Buggle Trevor Horn was the 'go-to' Ferry in the land of *Hot Hits*). But things were about to get distinctly more far-out. One afternoon, Mike, my mum's kid brother, called round leaving a pile of LPs for Rob and me to listen to. Strange records with strange covers by strange looking bands we'd never heard of: Family, the Nice, ELP and Yes. Family sounded pleasant but maybe a little too folksy for our unrefined ears. The Nice were more popular and ELP, too, with their Chicory Tip keyboard sounds, but our favourite was undoubtedly Yes. *The Yes Album* remained bonded to Rob's Fidelity HF45 multi-stacker for the rest of the summer. We'd never heard anything like it. I hadn't consciously been in search of the lost chord, but this exotic gateway would change my musical horizon for ever.

After this introduction, Yes became something of an obsession and I quickly absorbed myself in their back catalogue. I was thrilled to discover their next album, *Fragile*, was every bit as good as *The Yes Album*, benefitting from the arrival of the dashing Rick Wakeman. I'd not sidelined Slade or any of my more pop-orientated favourites, but from there on they'd take second place to progressive giants Yes and ELP, though 1973 saw them drift further down the pecking order with the discovery of Genesis, Focus, Hawkwind and Roxy Music.

Sunday 10 September 1972. Mike's got tickets for Rob and I to see Yes on the *Close to the Edge* tour. With only Slade to compare them with, I am totally unprepared for the impending fireworks.

Belle Vue, Manchester had at one time enjoyed the distinction of being the largest pleasure park in the British Isles. Now the place is a complete mess. The boating lakes have been filled in, the once proud zoological gardens are now famous for their threadbare collection of wildlife, and the funfair is probably the best place in Manchester to get mugged. However, as the city's largest venue with a seating capacity of 4,000, the King's Hall is still going strong. Earlier in the summer, it had seen rioting at an Osmonds concert.

For Yes, the place is packed. The audience are mostly in their early twenties. There is definitely more hair than at the Slade gig, fewer women and more Afghan coats. I'm feeling cool and confident in my new black C&A PVC snakeskin coat. I've got a damson shirt with one of the new rounded collars and a purple and yellow tank top. My mum's bought me some love beads and my hair is now touching my collar, so I'm blending in nicely with this bohemian company.

We watch a particularly uninspiring and no doubt hand-picked support act called Wright's Wonderwheel, then collect ourselves for the spectacle to come. In my rather limited theatrical experience – *Aladdin*, *Jack and the Beanstalk*, *Puss in Boots* – the activity of erecting the stage and supporting apparatus for the evening's entertainment usually takes place behind the curtain, but here we see the frenzied exercise unfold in front of us. Groups of long-haired young men in jeans and T-shirts stroll purposefully around the stage, stacking equipment and building drum kits. Mike tells me they're called 'roadies'. I make a mental note of this so I can tell the careers adviser when he asks what I'm intending to do in the future. I've been watching Rick Wakeman's tower of keyboards being assembled and haven't noticed what's happening stage left. The sight of Steve Howe's guitars all tuned and polished, sitting on their respective stands, sends a bolt of excitement through me. A huge, flat mirror ball disc has been uncovered above the stage, there's some last-minute fluffing, then the roadies disappear and we're staring at this rather grand set, awaiting the players.

The house lights dim and the stage is bathed in darkness, with only the lights from the amplifiers visible. Flashbulbs are popping all around the arena, illuminating the stage for fractions of a second. I'm standing out in the aisle so I can see. The opening music starts, the climax to Stravinsky's *Firebird* suite.

Just three months earlier, Status Quo had wandered on stage at the Free Trade Hall like a bunch of navvies returning from the

15

pub.* There'd been very little pomp, too, about Slade's entrance. But this is pure theatre. As the camera flashes intensify, we catch sight of new drummer Alan White and Steve Howe as they board the stage. Lanky bassist Chris Squire appears holding the most famous cream Rickenbacker in music, followed by flaxen-haired keyboard goliath Rick Wakeman, the flashes bouncing off his luxurious sequinned cape. Finally, the diminutive figure of singer Jon Anderson walks to the front, dressed from head to toe in white. Accrington's own prog-rock angel.

Wakeman attempts to blend his Mellotron strings with the last chords of Stravinsky. It's an awkward segue, but the lights finally come up and Yes are off, a jaw-dropping feast for my pre-teen senses. The all-gurning Steve Howe writhes around with his Gibson ES-175 like he's just landed a pike; Jon Anderson is all smiles, cheesecloth and maracas; but the eye is naturally drawn stage right – first to Chris Squire leaping like a salmon in his white frock coat and thigh-length boots, then to Wakeman, the undisputed star of the show, tall, blond and sparkling and playing two keyboards at once, his head thrown back in blind ecstasy. I have arrived. This is my church and the power of these gods compels me.

* The 'navvies' quote is shamefully pilfered from Nick Kent's famous review of Pink Floyd at Wembley in 1974. Reporting on the first of Floyd's four nights at the Empire Pool, Kent, who really didn't have a good night and found the band's appearance physically repellent, adjudged the current state of Pink Floyd thus: 'No other combine quite sums up the rampant sense of doomed mediocrity inherent in this country's current outlook right now.' The Floyd had obviously taken Kent's trashing to heart as, by the time they reached Manchester a month later, they were superb, although guitarist David Gilmour clearly still hadn't washed his hair.

I fully understand that, at this point, I've probably lost a good half of you – those who would regard a concert by Yes or their ilk as the most turgid experience rock has to offer.

I make no apology.

4

Flying Sideways Through Time

In 1971, Bramhall Grammar, our local secondary school, was turned into a comprehensive. For under-achievers such as myself, this was fantastic news. It meant I wouldn't have to sit the eleven-plus exam, which I would have flunked without question, or attend one of two notoriously rough secondary moderns in the area.

Bramhall High, as it was renamed, still had all the trappings of a grammar school. We were separated into houses, named after local stately homes. I was in Tatton House. Cricket and rugby were the favoured sports, alongside country dancing and cross-country running. If you wanted to play football, you had to stay after school and play in your own time, so consequently the school football teams were a bit of a pushover.

In 1974 the local aircraft manufacturer Hawker Siddeley gifted a number of decommissioned RAF Vampires to schools in the Stockport area. Bramhall's plane was displayed proudly behind the newly erected sports centre. While these sleek-looking aircraft still formed an impressive centrepiece in the forecourts of Cheadle Grammar and Cheadle Hulme School eighteen months later, Bramhall's plane had been smashed to smithereens – and I'd helped.

As one of the school longhairs, I was always getting hauled out of lessons and brought in for questioning when any drug-related incident occurred. On one occasion four ambulances were lined up outside the school after four of the school's leading drug enthusiasts had overdosed on barbiturates and collapsed in class. On that day I was treated as something of a celebrity as I waited outside the headmaster's office and was promised witness protection if I turned queen's evidence and grassed up the suppliers. Of course I knew bugger all about the incident except to say the drugs were likely to have been purloined from some hapless parent's bathroom cabinet.

It was still a major frustration that we didn't have more music at home. The 50p I got for my Saturday-morning milk round courtesy of Mike, the stingiest milkman in Cheshire, allowed me to buy a new single every couple of weeks or a new album every six weeks. I'd also joined the school record library, but they only allowed you to take an LP out every month. I'd even resort to Dial-a-Disc on occasion, a premium GPO line that played a single record over the phone every week. 'Hull Teledisc Service. Sydney Scarborough, under the City Hall, Hull, for television, radio and records presents "Burlesque" by Family': I must have dialled that particular selection about twenty times and doubled our phone bill.

I also enlarged my LP collection by joining the Audio Club of Britain, forerunner of the mighty Britannia Music Club, whose enticing and colourful adverts covered the back page of the quality Sunday supplements. The deal was you bought four albums for an introductory price of 49p each on the understanding that you would purchase another eight at full price over the following two years. Failure to respond to the monthly newsletters within the prerequisite time meant you would automatically receive and be charged for the 'Editor's Choice', which was usually the latest release by one of the giants of easy-listening (Mouskouri, Roussos, Last), for which you would be expected to stump up a premium £2.75. For my introductory selection I plumped for Quo's *Piledriver*, the Groundhogs' *Who Will Save The World?*, *Moving Waves* by Focus and, as a wildcard, Rory Gallagher's *Deuce*. My dad found out I'd joined and went berserk. When he finally cooled down he wrote to the company, explaining that as a minor I'd joined without his prior knowledge or consent, that my membership would be terminated henceforth and that my four introductory LPs were 'awaiting collection'. We never heard another word from the ACB. It was a fabulous scam and he must have been secretly rather pleased with himself, accidentally creating a free music-sharing system decades before Napster's Shawn Fanning was even a twinkle in his father's eye.

My dad worked in the ceramic tile trade, managing a showroom and warehouse in Manchester's Miles Platting area. One of his finest moments was to supply Sir Bobby Charlton with a few square yards' worth for his bathroom. My dad still talks fondly of the transaction. My parents occasionally socialised with the owner and his wife and both parties thought it would be nice if I got together with their son Steven, seeing as we were both 'pop mad'.

Steven turned out to be a nice enough lad, though a couple of years older than me. He looked not unlike the guitarist from Mud and the first time I clocked him I thought he was a girl. For a few months Steven became my new mentor. I first met him at his mum and dad's palatial pad in Northenden, south Manchester. Steven was granted unbelievable privileges, such as smoking in his bedroom, swearing in front of his parents and access to his father's quadraphonic hi-fi. Looking back, I get the impression he thought I was a bit of a prick, but for a few months I idolised the lad. Steven's bedroom was something else. He had his own hi-fi up there and a bass guitar and amp stack. He'd fashioned some spotlights out of empty catering cans of marmalade and coloured 60-watt bulbs, and the scent of joss sticks hung heavy in the air. I began dressing like him; long-sleeved fishtail shirts, Afghan coat, bush hat and love beads. Steven's twin music passions were Status Quo and Hawkwind (themselves a fusion of Status Quo, Fairport Convention and the BBC Radiophonic Workshop). Hawkwind were just about to tour their new album, *Hall of the Mountain Grill*, and Steven asked me if I fancied going to see them.

And so it was that on 10 December 1973 I was at Manchester's Free Trade Hall for my first unchaperoned rock gig. Hawkwind, still riding high on the back of their 1972 top-three summer smash 'Silver Machine', were following up their celebrated *Space Ritual* extravaganza. Sadly Bob Calvert and Dik Mik were no longer in the line-up; nevertheless, this promised to be an exciting night. Oppressively scary, rumoured to take drugs and renowned for playing at ear-splitting volumes, Hawkwind also featured rock's premier exotic dancer, Miss Stacia Blake, who, with the exception of my mother, would almost certainly give me my first glimpse of in-the-flesh adult female nudity.

Hawkwind's following were quite different from the Slade and Yes audiences – even hairier and a sight scruffier. They were more like the dudes I'd seen sitting on a wall six years earlier. There was an overwhelming stench of the alternative in the air. The aroma, later to be identified as patchouli oil, would adorn my wardrobe and school uniform for the next five years. I stood in the bar before the show, taking in this extraordinary assembly of freaks waging an intellectual war with their surroundings. The Free Trade Hall was the home of Manchester's beloved Hallé Orchestra and displayed proudly around the perimeter of the bar were marble plinths supporting bronze busts of the orchestra's most celebrated conductors: Hamilton Harty, Hans Richter, Malcolm Sargent and its favourite son, 'Glorious' John Barbirolli. Someone had stuck cigarette butts up Sir John's bronze nostrils. It was, I thought, a gloriously irreverent gesture and I'm very glad my dad wasn't there to see it.

Hawkwind played all the favourites. The sound was amazing, the lights flashed beautifully and I got to see the great Lemmy perform with them. However, Stacia – no doubt uncomfortable with being billed as a stripper – defied the bookies by keeping all her togs on throughout and, after many weeks spent listening to *Space Ritual*, studying every inch of its sixteen-sided fold-out cover, it was just not quite as mind-blowing as I'd imagined. Of course, that was not the version I told at school the following day, by which time Hawkwind's stage show had metamorphosised into a cosmic Busby Berkeley production.

After the Hawkwind show I started attending gigs fairly regularly at Manchester's two main venues, the Free Trade Hall and the Palace Theatre. The Palace, though compact, had one of the largest stages in the country, so any groups taking a big theatrical number on tour would usually play there. In the space of five months, from late '74 to April '75, I saw Pink Floyd, Genesis, Yes and Hawkwind (again) at the Palace. I had a rapacious appetite for these colossal extravaganzas. My preference was for a mix of pantomime theatrics and spectacular lighting and, in that respect, Genesis were way ahead of the field. But Hawkwind and Yes staged equally lavish productions, while Floyd had the benefit of their amazing quadraphonic PA system, which was a truly unnerving experience.

The sense of drama, theatricality and high pomp that I witnessed between 1972 and 1976 was a significant factor in the development of World of Twist's live show.

It was a massive frustration in the band's early years that we were unable to stage the sort of show we were visualising. From the very outset we dreamed of podiums, strobes, pyrotechnics, UV lights, dry ice, mirror balls, films, slides and sparkle – everything that was way beyond our budget. If we couldn't have that we'd mess around with the stage placements. The drums would come to the front, stage left or right, as they always appeared on vintage *Top of the Pops* performances, the singer would stand behind on a higher level, but not centre stage. Our objective was to try to create an unfamiliar and unsettling experience for the hundreds of people who'd visit the same venue several times a year accustomed to the typical rock band set-up. The Human League Mk I were massively important in this respect – proof positive that the classic rock band configuration wasn't necessary to generate excitement. In fact, with a few slides, some seductive lighting and the right tunes, you could remain totally inert and still project high drama.

Once World of Twist received some funding, we invested heavily in the show. Inspired by an *Avengers* episode, we got a 7-foot circular hypnosis wheel, a huge heavy beast that revolved on a big metal frame with an industrial motor. We wasted thousands on TriLite, a modular aluminium exhibition frame from which we could hang lights, screens, curtains and so on. The problem was that most of the venues we booked couldn't fit the structure on stage, so the rotating mirrored columns we'd had built didn't see much action. We bought two bales of fibre optics and a huge black backcloth. The idea was to clip the fibre optics into the material, creating a massive star-cloth. It would have been very impressive except that no one got round to finishing the job and the fibre optics were just draped over the backline like phosphorescent silly string. It looked quite good but it could have looked amazing. The slide show, featuring dozens of stylish cigarette adverts from the '60s and '70s, was driven by three carousel projectors. We had strobes, smoke (though sadly not dry ice) and UV lighting. At some point, we were on the verge of paying several thousand pounds to a north-west boat builder to make us a sparkly fibreglass pod for the computer equipment, a mini version of the Martian spaceship in *Quatermass and the Pit*. Another extravagance that never got beyond the drawing board were the

Atlas guitar amp stands fashioned out of fibreglass and sprayed gold. We would have two matching Atlas figures, both supporting a Fender Twin guitar amplifier on their shoulders. A pulpit for Tony Ogden was another idea mooted but never built.

It's a major regret that World of Twist never released a second album, never appeared on *Top of the Pops*, never toured Europe or the States, but perhaps my greatest regret is that we never got to use any dry ice. As a fan of Yes and Genesis and as a regular pantomime attendee, I'd been brought up on the stuff. It was a wonderful theatrical effect when the ice drifted in from the back like a rolling fog. It would cling to the stage and, depending on the amount used, come up as far as the guitarist's knees. Sadly we had to make do with smoke machines, which were a different proposition. If not used with restraint they could overwhelm you very quickly, to the point where you could barely see your hands on the fretboard. Tony loved the stuff and our crew was fairly trigger-happy, so just as the stage was clearing you could be engulfed by another veil of sweetly scented fog.

We always had very grand plans for the future. The revolving heads (more of which later) would get larger; they'd have laser-beam eyes and at some point would talk to the audience. Girls in fish tanks was something else we discussed, as was a full-size replica of the Mad Mouse roller coaster from Blackpool Pleasure Beach. Future gigs would feature a long line of guest musicians brought in for a featured solo – Patrick Moore would play vibes on 'The Spring', Roy Castle would play the trumpet introduction to 'Lose My Way', then he'd come back later to spin some plates during 'Kick Out the Jams'.

5

Bill Nelson's in His Tube

There are many ways to form a band but most – maybe over 95 per cent of those who try – get it horribly wrong. Not everyone who starts with this winning formula will succeed and a few who ignore it will prevail, but it's rare. So how do you do it? What's the secret?

One: Firstly you find people you want to form a band with. It sounds obvious, but it's not. It's so easy to find yourself two years down the line with a bunch of pricks you really can't stand and who prove impossible to shift without dismantling the whole thing. Your thing.

Two: One of the band, maybe you, but if not definitely your closest ally, has to be a ruthless bastard who can hire, fire, promote and demote without conscience. Without this you'll struggle.

Three: Decide who you want to sound like.

Four: Decide who you don't want to sound like (this is actually more important than #3).

Five: Have an idea what you want to look like (this is more important than #3 or #4).

Six: Choose your band name. This can take weeks or sometimes months. If it's being done by committee try to hold your ground. Don't settle on a name you quite like or the one that everyone agrees on. This won't work and it's worth leaving the band at this point if you can't get your own way. This will mean passing through stages one to five all over again but, importantly, that terrible or forgettable name arrived at by dreary consensus will not be associated with you for ever.

Seven: Get some instruments and/or equipment and learn to play and/or operate them to a fairly high standard. In the history of pop there's only been one period where this stage was deemed unimportant and most of the groups who followed that particular credo disappeared without trace.

Eight: Conceptualise. This is essential. Amazingly, it's the most neglected, overlooked part of forming a band, but you skip this step and you are doomed.

Nine: Write a song. If you've followed the first eight stages the songs should flow. If they don't, you need to retrace your steps, as you slipped up somewhere along the course.

On paper, World of Twist were formed very quickly in 1983, but the process took about seven years and started in the playground at Bramhall County High school. With Jim and me, the conceptualising never stopped.

Erroneously, perhaps, Wikipedia lists the only famous musicians to emerge from Bramhall as Sarah Harding and Martin Fry. I was fortunate to make Martin's sage acquaintance long before he became a musician, long before his band ABC hit the big time, but even more fortunate to meet his younger brother Jim.

It was inevitable that, as the two most pop-obsessed kids in the school, we would get together. We were pretty different fish, though. Jim was in the year above me and a bit of a trendy. He had a feather cut, Oxford bags and was popular with the girls. I wasn't. I wore my hair several inches past my shoulders and, being a bit of a short-arse, favoured platform shoes. Outside school I wore split-knee loon pants, an Afghan coat and stank of patchouli. We didn't move in the same circles – I didn't move in any circles – but we'd discovered we were about the only two kids in the school who actually went to gigs. As it happened, we had a fair bit in common: both born in Kent, within 10 miles of each other; parents all born in the first two years of the '30s. We arrived in Manchester at roughly the same time (1965) and we both bore the millstone of having academically superior elder brothers.

The first gig I attended with Jim was Be-Bop Deluxe in early 1976, a significant event not because of the headliners but because of the support act. Be-Bop Deluxe I'd badly misjudged, believing them to be a rock 'n' roll revival act in the style of Sha Na Na. I'd made the same mistake when I'd first heard Roxy Music.

Sadly Be-Bop Deluxe registered very low on the excitement scale that evening. However, the support act were hugely intriguing and of great importance. The Doctors of Madness were too early and perhaps too old to take part in the forthcoming punk revolution but it was definitely the first signifier for us that the wind was about to change. Their frontman was the cadaverous 'Kid' Strange, 6 foot 4 with blue hair and mirrored contact lenses. Bass player Stoner extended the 'undead' theme with his corpse-like make-up. Violin player Urban Blitz and drummer Peter DiLemma completed the line-up. Musically the Doctors were sub-Ziggy, sub-Iggy, sub-Dolls and sub-Velvets in every sense, but there was absolutely no one who sounded like them in February 1976 and to us (particularly Jim) it was the most original thing we'd seen or heard in years.

Four months after the Doctors of Madness gig, I encountered a very exuberant Jim between lessons. Did I fancy going to see a band called the Sex Pistols tomorrow night for 50p? Jim was particularly excited by the name, but it didn't exactly grab me and we didn't go. That was the legendary Sex Pistols Free Trade Hall gig #1, subject of a book and an ITV documentary and immortalised in the film *24 Hour Party People*. A few weeks later, Jim finally got to see the Pistols' return show with his brother. I did not attend. It was the Buzzcocks' debut gig and will forever be filed in my brain as one of life's historic missed opportunities.

Jim fully embraced the punk phenomenon that I was personally finding hard to embrace. Having been in a prog-rock bubble for the best part of four years, I found it tough to reconcile a musical landscape where most of my heroes were now public enemy number one, subjugated by and large by musicians who delighted in claiming that they neither possessed nor required any musical ability. And therein of course lies one of the major untruths propagated during the punk explosion – that musicianship was immediately dismissed as the devil's practice, when, in truth, it was mainly the bands who could actually play who managed to ride out the punk wave to the post-punk or new wave. Certainly in the case of guitarist John McGeoch (Magazine, Siouxsie & the Banshees), bass player Barry Adamson (Magazine) and drummer Budgie (aka Peter Clarke) from the Slits and Siouxsie & the Banshees, the superlatives were ringing out immediately. And let's not forget that the Pistols were one of the hottest and tightest combos in the business. There were actually very few of the great punk/new wave acts who couldn't play. The ones that sounded like they couldn't (Subway Sect, the Fall) – that was all affectation. Although I was an immediate convert to the Pistols and Buzzcocks, the first few months of the punk revolution was for me a phoney war. I retained my parallel love for dinosaur rock and still coveted the latest offerings by Yes, Genesis, Peter Gabriel and Hawkwind.

6

If the Kids Are United

May 1978. With the end of school looming and another hot sum
mer of punk approaching, I finally succumb to good taste and
part company with my now ridiculously long hair. It has never
attracted the ladies in the early-Genesis way I'd imagined and has
recently become a liability at gigs, whiplashing my pogoing neighbours with its wet, greasy tendrils. I'd love to say I got a mate to
do it with some old kitchen scissors, but in the event I went to a
particularly poncey joint in Cheadle called the Razor's Edge and
emerged with a ghastly shoulder-length mullet not a million miles
from the cut favoured by DJ Mike Read or pub rocker Nick Lowe.
What you might call the power-pop look. All I need is a skinny tie
and pastel jacket with the sleeves rolled to the elbows.

I'm resigned to leaving school without any qualifications but
go through the motions of sitting my O levels. I hate every subject – even art, which I'm quite good at (my six-year-old study of

George slaying the dragon was once displayed at Stockport Art Gallery). I've done no revision and haven't read any of the books for English. I entertain myself in the exams by shoehorning lyrics from punk songs into my heavily padded answers (*I wormed my way into the heart of the crowd* or *Fast cars they run me down*). I know the sixth form won't be an option, so there'll be no skiing trips to Aviemore or fell-walking in the Lake District. Oh well, at least I can enjoy the summer before it's all official.

I take a job washing up at Francesco's Italian restaurant in Underbank, Stockport and get very well acquainted with the soundtrack to *Saturday Night Fever*. The place is inconceivably popular and they don't have a dishwasher so the job is very hard. 'Pasquale, *svelta*!' The kitchen staff can't pronounce my name so they call me Pasquale. I refuse to believe it's an Italian Christian name and imagine it means 'shithead' or similar. Still, the job pays well and I spend every penny on more records and gigs.

For a while, I get sucked into that whole singles-collecting lark, which was a central factor in holding the punk/new wave industry together. Everything was printed and stickered as a limited edition. New releases had limited runs of coloured vinyl and picture covers, ensuring they sold out before they were deleted, thus generating a very competitive collector's market. Stiff Records were the main perpetrators, or certainly the originators of this selling technique, and their first twenty records were highly sought after, even if very little of their output was punk, strictly speaking.

Every minute not spent scrubbing dishes is spent in Manchester's underground market, hanging around the record stalls. For several weeks I earn a few extra bob selling bootleg records. The

WHEN DOES THE MIND-BENDING START?

Buzzcocks' *Time's Up!* LP sells like hot cakes, but I get seriously burnt trying to shift ten copies of *Night of the Iguana*, a Stooges bootleg that actually sounds worse than *Metallic K.O.* I make a little money back by painting the flat of the owner of my favourite record shop. His stereo and massive record collection is something to behold and the two weeks spent sloshing emulsion are a real education. It's here I first become acquainted with the Who and the Small Faces, early Pink Floyd and Todd Rundgren.

My new passion is Ultravox! I've been a fan since their first release, 'Young Savage', intrigued by their glam-influenced take on punk. As with Magazine, it was inevitable I'd like Ultravox! Both bands have a keyboard-led sound, so not a million miles from prog rock. But away from the violins, ARP Odysseys and pretentious lyrics, Ultravox! have a very abrasive edge to their sound, which I love. Guitarist Stevie Shears produces this incredibly violent tone from his Fender Strat, like nails dragging down a blackboard. Their second LP *Ha!-Ha!-Ha!* is my record of the summer and I'm desperate to see them live.

Ultravox (the ecphoneme no more) are announced as Friday's special guests at the 1978 Reading Festival, which boasts a pretty decent line-up, including Patti Smith, the Jam and, for old times' sake, Status Quo. With my newfound wealth it's definitely worth spending £8.95 on a weekend ticket and my dad will be delighted that his 1950s Camping Club tent will be getting another outing. It's also announced that Ultravox will play a five-night residency at London's Marquee the week before the festival so I plan to catch their final show, spend a day in London record hunting before travelling over to Reading. In the lead up to the show I'm horrified by the news that Stevie Shears has been replaced by some bottle-blond tart called Robin Simon, but in the event he turns out to be pretty good. At the famous Marquee Club, Ultravox are heart-stoppingly brilliant. Their new sound is more intense, more Germanic, their new look less glam and less gauche. This is not the same band later to be seen goofing it up with Midge Ure at the helm. John Foxx wouldn't have stood for that kind of moonshine. I hang around at the end like some stage-door Johnny and manage to get backstage. Foxx is a little stand-offish, but that's okay, he is the ice-man. Canadian drummer Warren Cann is the most chatty. Everyone signs my programme apart from the new lad, but I'm not too bothered about him.

The previous month, I'd been hoping to attend the Deeply Vale Free Festival on the dark side of the Pennines. ATV and the Durutti Column were appearing on Saturday plus a little-known north Manchester outfit called the Fall. If I stayed until Tuesday I'd get to see Crispy Ambulance and the king of gliss, Steve Hillage. My plans were thwarted, however, by a lack of funds, lack of transport and my parents' refusal to let me go. Nevertheless, Reading would not be my first pop festival. Two years previously I'd attended the first Chorley Wakes Folk Festival at Charnock Richard with Tim Hampton, cousin of Leeds United left back Peter Hampton and the only other boy in my year with long hair. I recall we drank a small amount of cider and were encouraged to join a conga line during Hedgehog Pie's set. That's about as exciting as it got.

I don't know what to expect of Reading. Chorley Wakes with better music, perhaps? I arrive around teatime on Thursday

WHEN DOES THE MIND-BENDING START?

and the first thing I see is a fight between rival caterers that results in a burger van being pushed over. So Woodstock it isn't. I pitch my tent next to a bunch of long-haired lads from the West Country. They tell me they're in a group called 'Heavy Tread' and give me one of their business cards, which reads, 'Heavy Tread will Rock the World'. They don't look much like rockers but they're very friendly and I keep their card for a long time.

The festival site isn't yet open so I join Heavy Tread for a beer and we watch some drunken lads push their mate in a shopping trolley into the Thames.

Reading '78 will be remembered as the year of the punk invasion and Friday was the day of the punks. I don't want to miss a minute. Sadly, the first four or five acts are a bit ropey so I go and grab a beer and a burger from one of the upright vans. Returning to the main field, there's a marked change of atmosphere. The punks and grebos who have been rubbing along quite nicely up until now have been joined by hundreds of skinheads and fights are breaking out all over the place.

The skins are here specifically to see Sham 69 and during their short visit will cause as much aggro as possible. The story is well documented on the brilliant ukrockfestivals.com website. Steve Swift's account is particularly chilling: '1978 was like a crossover year from the old-type festival-goers into the newer younger element, my clear memory is of a hippy having his acoustic guitar smashed over his head by some skins, while all the time saying, "I love you man, I love you." It sounds funny today, but was disturbing at the time.'

Most of the bands have been dodging beer cans and bottles all afternoon, but things move up a gear when Sham take the stage around 6 p.m. All the skinheads have pushed their way to the front so the safest place to watch is back near the mixing-desk tower. You have to love Jimmy Pursey – never has a rock star's heart been fixed so firmly in the right place. Pursey is wonderfully skilled at whipping his acolytes up into a frenzy and then will break down in tears when they inevitably start attacking each other. At Reading, he introduces the rabble-rouser 'Rip Off' with a lengthy rant about how 'the kids' have been hoodwinked and short changed by Malcolm McLaren and his Sex Pistols and ends with a snarling, 'Where are you now, Mr Rotten?' Of course, two months after Jimmy's tirade, Mr Rotten will be back on track with his new band PIL and the best single of 1978. Sham's set closes with Pursey's own anthem for doomed youth, 'If the Kids Are United', by which time most of his skinhead cortège have joined him on stage. To hammer home his point, Jimmy has invited the aforesaid Steve Hillage on stage to join the party. In orange boiler suit, the copper-curled Hillage adds some trademark space rock riffs to Sham's lumpen Morris stomp. For many years, I'll believe I've dreamt this until I see the film *Kids Like Me & You*, which recalls the whole Friday at Reading that year in all its messy glory.

Back in Manchester, it's time to face the music. My O-level grades are as bad as predicted with just one pass in English. Stockport Art College have offered me a provisional place on their graphic design course if I get a CSE grade 1 in art (equivalent to an O-level pass). I get a grade 2, so they place me on the standby list. If anyone drops out, I'll be offered a place. Fortunately, quite a few decide they have better options and bail before enrolment, so I get lucky. Not for the first time.

The three months I spend at art college are among the happiest times I can remember. It's a perfect opportunity to reinvent myself, from buck-toothed longhair to sharp new wave hipster in the blink of Gary Gilmore's eye. I get rid of my Nick Lowe mullet and get a proper razor cut and my first pair of Doc Martens. The other first years are a great bunch and very quickly we form a gang. Julia Adamson, later of the Fall, is in the year above alongside future World of Twist man Alan Frost, known to all as 'Adge'.

Gigs are our lifeblood at this time. We see Patti Smith and the Pop Group at the Apollo, the gig where Steven Morrissey first encounters Johnny Marr. A month later, I unwittingly get to meet the unknown Morrissey as he's taking the door money at Joy Division's gig at the Band on the Wall. It was A Certain Ratio's second or maybe third gig. This is the evening their new guitarist (and World of Twist's future soundman) Martin Moscrop hands his cards in with glam rockers Alien Tint (second on the bill this evening) and joins Flixton's industrial noise trio. Joy Division will eventually usurp Ultravox as my favourite band and this is the first time I see them. There's a scene in the Ian Curtis biopic *Control* where the singer arrives late on stage from the toilet and makes his entrance through the crowd. Unless this was a regular occurrence or part of the act, the incident happens at the Band on the Wall show. I remember Curtis politely moving me out of the way to get on stage.

Manchester appears to be at the very epicentre of the new wave. Bands are starting up left, right and centre and we're eager to get involved.

7
Noise Annoys

After *Tubular Bells*, possibly the most essential coffee-table album of the early '70s was *Scott Joplin's Piano Rags* by Joshua Rifkin. The ragtime fad, which had already kicked off in the US, spread worldwide in 1973 after Marvin Hamlisch adapted the catchiest of Joplin's rags, 'The Entertainer', as the theme music for a new Redford/Newman blockbuster, *The Sting*. For twelve solid months and beyond, every compilation of TV funnies, sports bloopers and pratfalls would be accompanied by the plinketyplonk of Joplin's cakewalk anthem. In south Manchester, Diana Gertrude King got bitten by the ragtime bug and bought the LP, the sheet music and a strange-looking piano to play it on. In next to no time, my mother was knocking out fairly accurate versions of 'The Entertainer', 'Maple Leaf Rag' et al. It was a surprise that she was actually an accomplished player since we'd never before had a piano in the house. Joplin was as pop as it got for our

Gerty, though. The rest of her repertoire comprised classical lollipops from her youth: Chopin, Mozart, Beethoven. She couldn't even play 'Nut Rocker'! For months, I remained oblivious to this strange piece of mahogany furniture, but, as my progressive bent strengthened and I fancied myself as rock's next keyboard wizard, or at the very least the new Bobby Crush, I began to tinker with it a bit. I discovered it was much easier to pick out a tune by using just the black keys (a dodge Bryan Ferry had been employing for several years with Roxy Music) and you could make a magnificent spooky racket by holding down the sustain pedal and bashing random keys at the end nearest the window. My prime achievement during this exploratory period was learning the opening bars to John Barry's theme from *The Persuaders*.

Hearing my crude but determined efforts, my mum sensed I might have a musical bone in my body and very encouragingly splashed out on some piano lessons. This hated ritual involved a forty-minute bike journey to visit a very large and jolly lady who clothed herself, in thrall to current singing sensation Demis Roussos, in various outsize floor-to-ceiling kaftans. A quick run-through my homework piece would reveal that I'd made very little progress in the preceding seven days. We'd then spend a further mind-numbing ten minutes on music theory before she selected another banger from her book of tunes for beginners. Squirming awkwardly as my teacher's chunky fingers expertly rowed her boat *gently down the stream*, I was finding it hard to make the connection between this weekly pantomime and becoming the next Keith Emerson. After a few visits, Mrs Mills' northern doppelganger sussed out that I never touched my pieces from one lesson to the next and suggested we stop wasting each other's time. So I stopped going and contented myself banging out the opening bars of the *Persuaders* theme ad infinitum.

Fast-forward to 1976. With little progress made on the piano but convinced my future lay in the realms of pop music, I heard there was a band at school in the year above who needed a bass player. So, on the promise that I'd wash the car, mow the lawn and clean the windows every month for the next five years, I convinced my mum to take me to the Rhythm House in Stockport where I could be kitted out with the requisite hardware. The staff saw us coming from several miles away and palmed me off with a Jazz Bass copy so cheap it didn't have a name on the headstock, plus a ghastly black and yellow 25-watt Boosey & Hawkes amplifier not suitable at all for bass guitars. I didn't even get a curly guitar lead. After a week's solid practice, I turned up at the drummer's house for the audition with my ersatz rig and high hopes for a rocking start to my music career. The guitarist spent ten minutes impatiently trying to teach me the bass solo from 'All Right Now', then he and the drummer spent the next two hours taking the piss out of my clothes. So I didn't join Effigy and would have to wait another two years until my next musical foray: Blackout.

Blackout were not, as our name suggested, disciples of the more established Lancashire Neo-Nazi band Skrewdriver but a punk/art school collective with a passion for early Siouxsie & the Banshees and a name lifted from a track on Bowie's *Heroes* album. However, attempts to publicise our first gig were dealt a hammer blow when the Anti-Nazi League followed us around Stockport ripping down our posters.

The band was formed at Stockport College sometime in 1978 by Jim Fry and ardent Clash fan Dave Connor who, as Dirtbox, had been busking around Manchester spreading the gospel according to Strummer. They recruited fellow graphics student Julia Adamson to play guitar and our south Manchester pal Tony Ogden to play drums. Fortunately they couldn't find anyone else to play bass so I got roped in.

I'd first met Tony the previous year as I'd occasionally hang out with his brother Tim and his hippy friends. They lived in this big house in Cheadle Hulme and had the run of the upstairs quarters. Tony had his drum kit set up there and would deliberately piss his brother off by playing it whenever Tim had company. Through clouds of dope smoke and alcohol haze, my first impression of Tony O was this hyperactive, overconfident whirlwind dressed in skintight leopard-skin pants. With a spikey blond crop, he was like Iggy Pop's younger, more irritating, brother. Tim and Tony squared up for a big shout-off. Both Ogden brothers had very loud voices, which was ironic as their mum June had probably the quietest speaking voice I've ever heard. Tony also had this weird, nervous laugh that was very unnerving. He never lost that. We started seeing more of him as he started going out with a girl in my year called Josie. Her brother Martin ended up fronting the Manchester band Laugh, who would morph into World of Twist's sister band, Intastella. Tony was one of the few people in our circle with a drum kit so if you came across a new band Tony was usually the drummer. The Void, Liquid Transit Van – the suburbs of Stockport were densely populated by fans of Hawkwind, Gong and all their bobble-hatted offshoots.

Blackout played their first gig at Hazel Grove Youth Club, supporting Xaverian glam rockers Alien Tint. The youth club was attached to Jackson's Lane Secondary Modern (aka 'Jacko's Jailhouse'), adding an element of danger to the proceedings, i.e. there was a fifty-fifty chance we'd get battered. For my first ever gig, I wanted to look the part so I took myself down to the antique clothes market on Deansgate and selected an outfit that would ensure I looked anything but the part. A sky-blue grandad shirt and a pair of huge overpleated pants (which I fancied looked a bit like David Bowie's *Stage* kecks) were topped off with a waistcoat and a cravat, lifted without permission from my dad's wardrobe. Proper new wave. Minutes after taking the stage, my new duds were coated with gob as our dynamic frontman implored the audience to spit on us. Spitting on bands as a mark of respect was thankfully a fairly brief phenomenon that developed around punk's middle period. This disgusting ritual was responsible, according to Joe Strummer, for the Clash's frontman contracting hepatitis. As far as I'm aware, Blackout's Dave Connor was the only frontman from this period who actually asked the audience to spit at him. Dave's request was taken up with some enthusiasm and seconds later all manner of internal and external fluids were raining down on us. Some smart alec at my side of the stage had found himself a plastic spoon and was firing Vimto-coloured spittle with great accuracy in my direction. This was not just saliva – great globules of purple phlegm were dripping from my guitar strap and, worse still, off my dad's cravat. For some reason, Julia and I copped the worst of the flak. But despite the flob-fest we'd endured, it had been a triumph for all concerned. We'd done a proper gig and it felt fucking brilliant.

We got a rehearsal space in Stockport next door to A Certain Ratio, who all looked like members of the Hitler Youth – that is, the emaciated ones who didn't make the poster. ACR were being courted by Factory Records at the time so there may have been a bit of professional jealousy on our part. However, they were all very friendly and we sometimes went for a post-practice pint with them at the White Lion. We were starting to take the band seriously and the music was developing a little. For our second gig (again at Hazel Grove Youth Club), I ditched the dressing-up box in favour of jeans and baseball boots, de rigueur for all budding new wavers in 1978. Of course we got spat on again but not quite so much and any gob that did land on me I'd teasingly rub into my shirt like it was part of the act. Dave Connor was developing into the consummate frontman. He was unfeasibly good looking and played the art school punk to the hilt. If there was any chance of Blackout taking off it would be down to him. But Blackout was doomed. Julia had already installed herself in a far more artsy quintet called Illustration, I was dreaming of joining Ultravox and Dave (sadly no longer with us) had ambitions to be a surfer. So our second gig was Blackout's last. The next time I picked up my bass it would be in the land of shoes: Northampton, Middle England.

8

Do Not Panic

December 1978. We're moving. Not just down the road this time, to the next town or county, we are properly moving. To Northampton, 140 miles down the M1, 38 miles from Leicester, 60 miles from London. The Midlands. No-man's land. Neither here nor there. I've been given three choices: move down to Northampton with my parents and transfer my graphics course to Nene College; stay with my gran and complete my course at Stockport; or leave college and get a job and a flat somewhere in Manchester. The third appears the best option. I don't want to leave college, but the social life is far more important than the course and Jim has transitioned very smoothly into the daily grind, so I'll follow his lead. He's found work as a paste-up artist in Wythenshawe, but I'm not so fortunate. A label-printing company in Edgeley is the closest I can find to anything artistic. However, my graphic skills are not required and I'm set to work on the hot-foil machine printing business cards. I can't get the hang of it and they don't have time to teach me at the moment so I'm relegated to the tie-hanger machine. This is a balls-achingly dull job. I load a spool of gold printing foil and a reel of brown plastic in at one end and an anvil-size block comes crashing down on to another once every three seconds and cuts out a tie-hanger with the word 'Tootal' printed on it. The machine has no guard and if you get your fingers in the way they'll be crushed. Once the machine has produced 200 or so hangers, I will bag them up and seal the bag with a plastic clip. Monotonous isn't the word for it. And it's fucking noisy. Ear protectors are provided, naturally, but they are ineffective and the metal machine din resounds in my ears for hours after every dreary shift.

The two lads I work with are nice. They live just round the corner from the factory and invite me round to their houses most days at lunchtime. We listen to records and they take the piss out of my clothes. They tell me they wouldn't be seen dead in drainpipes, but I figure one of them is softening. A week later, high on my supply of youthful DIY rebellion, he arrives for work in a pair of razor-straight jeans and, out of nowhere, I have another recruit to the cause.

My northern gran, Dorothy Pinchien, lives alone in Great Moor, round the corner from my old primary school, I'm staying here until I can find a place in town. Dolly, as the family call her (short for 'Dolly Bird'), is very accommodating and doesn't mind my comings and goings. The house is tidy and comfortable but very quiet. I love thumbing through my grandad's collection of old United programmes. There's a pristine copy of the United

v. Sheffield Wednesday FA Cup tie from February 1958, the first game after the Munich air crash, the United team lists eleven blank spaces.

In the evening, I've been meeting up with Jim to search for flats in Didsbury or nearby Withington. We're not having much luck and may need to broaden our choice of location. One particularly depressing evening, we visit a house where the advertised two-person flat turns out to be a shared room in a house run by a latter-day Mrs Danvers. The room has two single beds with floral counterpanes, a dressing table and an en-suite bathroom. We have use of the kitchen during set hours or for an additional fee Mrs Danvers will provide an evening meal. She won't tolerate any noise or guests. Some other people are very interested so she'll need a quick decision. It's a depressing journey back to Stockport. My job's shit, I'm skint, I don't have my own space and it doesn't look like we'll ever find a flat. By the time I get back to Great Moor, Dolly's asleep so I can't put the TV or radio on. The only thing to do is go to bed, but tonight sleep won't come. My mind's racing. On a global scale my problems are pretty small fry but right now they feel massive. *I should have moved south with my mum and dad*, I realise. *I'm just not ready for this. But then I'd probably feel just as shit leaving all this behind if I'd moved down there.* All my recent choices seem to have been bad ones; I don't feel I'm in control of anything. Thought chases thought as I sink into my homemade abyss. The bedroom is cold, dark and quiet. Back home I'd always go to sleep with my radio on a timer. When I was younger, I'd drift off listening to records, *Thunderbirds* adventures, *Hancock's*

Half Hour or Bob Newhart. I can't handle silence – I never could. In this acute quiet, I realise I can hear something very clearly. I can hear the pounding of the tie-hanger machine at Vista Labels like I was sat next to it. It's not the clang of metal on metal – more as though the two metal blocks have been wrapped in sponge. It's a steady rhythmic thud that I can't get out of my head until it's the only thing I'm aware of. I sit bolt upright in bed, my heart racing. It's pounding really fast and it's not regular. Shit! Am I having a heart attack? I switch the lights on and walk to the bathroom. I check the mirror and my pulse. I don't look any different – just a bit worried. I walk back to the bedroom, turn the lights off and sit on the edge of the bed waiting for my heart rate to return to normal. It calms down a little so I lie down. I'm feeling tired now but my head starts filling with negative thoughts again, this time they're more frenetic and harder to process. I can still hear that machine pounding in my head and it's been joined by what feels like a tight metal band circling my temples. The heavy irregular heartbeat has started again and I jump up and switch the lights back on. I don't know what to do. I'm walking around on the landing and I've woken Dolly up. 'Sorry, Gran. I can't sleep, I've got a headache, I was just going downstairs to get some water.' I'm trying to act normal but I'm shaking like a leaf. I don't think I've ever been this scared. There's nothing to distract me from the thoughts and feelings I'm experiencing. I want to put my clothes on and just run out of the door. Of course, what I'm experiencing is a severe panic attack, but there is no such thing in 1979 so I must be going loopy.

After several hours of this, my brain gives in to fatigue and I finally fall asleep. But I wake early, unrested. The events of last night are clear as day. My heart rate is normal but the metal band is still there and my face feels numb on one side. I'm a mess. I can't go to work like this.

Dolly is up and I try to explain what happened last night. It's impossible but she listens patiently. 'It sounds like your nerves,' she says. 'Nerves' was the general expression used for anxiety, panic, OCD, depression, insomnia, agoraphobia etc. before any of these conditions became common parlance. The trouble was, 'nerves', as I understood it, were the domain of neurotic housewives and very old people, jittery old dears who would jump out of their skin when the doorbell rang.

The treatment for 'nerves' was rest. If rest wasn't possible (as it isn't for most), then industrial-strength sedatives. There was none of your CBT back then. You got the drugs and you got them down your neck asap. The problem with sedatives is the body becomes tolerant of them very quickly so the dose has to be increased over a period of time and before you know it a prescription that could floor an elephant is being taken on a daily basis just to keep the patient upright.

I've rung in sick and managed to get an appointment with our old GP in Bramhall. I walk down to Woodsmoor Lane and wait for the bus. I've not been back to Bramhall since we left a few weeks earlier and it feels really weird – not like the place I'd lived in for eight years but more like a model village or a film set. Midwich, perhaps, and I'm the cuckoo. I don't know what I'm expecting from the doctor and he doesn't say much. I get the feeling he thinks I'm making this up. I'm sure he thinks I'm a drug addict, or one of those older lads at school who used to come over and raid your parents' medicine cabinet. He finally gives in and reaches for his pad, prescribing me 1mg of lorazepam under its trade name, Ativan, to be taken twice a day. That's it. No instruction to call back in a week or so, no leaflets about yoga, breathing exercises or coping with anxiety. Of course not – there is no such thing.

I wait until I'm back at Dolly's before I pop the first pill of the day. I'm sitting on the sofa in the rarely used front room. I've got a cup of sweet tea and a copy of the *NME*. I read the same Joy Division gig review over and over, wondering what's going to happen when this thing takes effect. Thirty minutes later, I'm engulfed in a marshmallow haze. It's not unpleasant but it feels weird. The metal band and the numbness have gone, but I definitely don't feel capable of operating machinery. I try to stand up but my legs feel like pipe cleaners. Jesus, is this the alternative to how I felt the night before? Dolly is very reassuring and promises that the effects will wear off after a while and I'll feel more normal. They do wear off but I don't feel normal – nothing like it. My new normal is like the world viewed through the visor of a snug-fitting crash helmet. Everything's slightly blurred, slightly dead.

'Yeah, it's been a strange few weeks. I've left college, left home, my family's moved down to the Midlands and I've started work.'

I'm trying to explain my predicament and yesterday's absence to my boss, but it's clear he has no idea what I'm on about.

'So you've had a nervous breakdown, then?'

'No, I don't think it's that. I'm not sure, I think it's nerve related. I've been to the doctor's and he's given me some pills, which seem to help.'

'But you'll be wanting some time off work?'

'No, I don't think so. If I could just have a break from the Tootal machine, maybe?'

'Yeah, well you'll need to learn to print, then.'

I climb up to the shop floor and the lads greet me with a knowing grin.

'So you got a bit pissed on Monday night, then?'

'No, not really.'

'Yeah, well a Tuesday's okay to pull a sicky but don't ever try that on Monday or you'll be out of here.'

'Ah, okay. Actually, I was feeling pretty crap and I don't feel much better today.'

'Just keep your head down, then. You're on the hot foil blocker, aren't you? Yeah, nice easy job, best place to be if you've got a hangover.'

I switch the machine on and it does indeed sound like the two metal blocks have been wrapped in sponge, but then it feels like my brain's also been wrapped in sponge. How long's this shit going to last, I wonder?

I meet up with Jim in the pub that evening and try to explain what's happened. He's not in a great mood and is about as understanding as my boss. It's natural. If you've never experienced anything like this, or been close to anyone who's experienced anything like this, you won't understand. You'll be blissfully ignorant of this condition, just as I was forty-eight hours earlier.

We finally strike lucky and find a nice bachelor pad in West Didsbury, midway between Didsbury and Withington. There's loads of great pubs and coffee bars and it's just twenty minutes on the bus to Stockport or Wythenshawe. It's fully furnished and my dad's donated our old hi-fi to the cause, the most important piece of furniture. We start hanging out with the two Alans – Frost and Keogh – and for a month or a couple of months we're a bit of a team and talk of getting a band together. In my heavily tranquilised state, I'm finding it very difficult to get up in the mornings and I'm late for work on more than one occasion. Finally, the boss calls me in and tells me it's not working out. I can't think of anything clever to say so I take his word for it and wander down to the DHSS with the first of many P45s. I spend a couple of weeks wandering aimlessly around West Didsbury, meeting up with Adge on occasion, but it's clear that without a job I can't stay in Manchester.

One evening, I find myself in Stockport Library trying to find out what's going on in my head. I'm leafing through the medical section and find a book called *Self Help With Your Nerves*. I'm not expecting much from a book with such an uninspiring title but in the first two pages the author has pretty much described every symptom I've experienced in the previous six weeks. The author is Doctor Claire Weekes and her little book, first published in 1962 with the deliberately trite title, is the most valuable essay ever written on the subject of anxiety and panic.

That Ms Weekes' revelatory studies weren't adopted overnight is astonishing. More astonishing is that you seldom hear anything of this wonderfully dedicated Australian research scientist, who died in 1990 at the age of eighty-seven.

9

A New Career in a New Town

I didn't want to leave Manchester. I mean, Northampton for fuck's sake. The only reason anyone had heard of the place was because George Best famously put six goals past their football team in 1970.*

I arrived in Northampton the week the Jam's 'Strange Town' was released. The song became my signature tune as I padded the streets of the town centre searching for something remotely like Manchester. Part Gothic revival and rather grand, part post-war functional and shit, Northampton was a strange old place and it took me ages to get my bearings.

---

* On his first day back from a month's suspension for knocking a ball out of referee Jack Taylor's hands, and on an apology for a football pitch, George (who never looked lovelier than on that chilly February afternoon) made a total monkey out of a hapless Cobblers' back four and, in particular, goalkeeper Kim Book, brother of the more illustrious Tony, skipper of high-flying Manchester City.

WHEN DOES THE MIND-BENDING START?

The enormous Greyfriars bus station, big enough to house two Saturn V rockets, was the foreboding gateway to the citadel. Dubbed the 'Mouth of Hell', in 2005 Channel 4 viewers voted it the third most hated building in Britain. There's a fabulous video online of the huge structure being demolished in a mere six seconds.

I ended up at ACME clothing, which was really the town's only 'alternative' clothes shop. The owner of ACME was a nice enough chap called Mick, who'd made his pile selling patchwork denim. Patchwork denim was everywhere in the mid '70s. The back pages of *Melody Maker*, *Sounds* and *NME* would be full of hand-drawn adverts for patchwork coats, loon pants, patchwork flared jackets, patchwork waistcoats and skirts, which could all be worn with your fringed moccasin boots or clogs, Afghan or army greatcoats, satin bomber jackets, beads, iron crosses and a dash of patchouli behind the ears. Mick, like many of his entrepreneurial ilk, believed that the kids would be wearing patchwork denim well into the next century and when his business went into administration he apparently had several garages full of the stuff. But you can't keep a good hippy-capitalist down and Mick had rebuilt his empire off the back of the punk explosion.

A year later I'd be on the ACME payroll but for the time being I was just a punter scouring the rails for some new duds and their noticeboard for some new friends. Most of what ACME sold was absolute shit: bum flaps in every hue, Dennis the Menace mohair jumpers, bullet belts, pirate-print drainpipes, ready-to-wear bondage trousers, jackets and boiler suits with de facto 'Anarchy' symbols, studded winkle-picker boots with too many straps. But among the crap, there was some nice stuff. I picked up a couple of cotton golf jackets, the type worn by Television's Tom Verlaine. You had to wear these zipped up at all times with the collar buttoned right up the neck or not at all. I also got a fabulous US Army raincoat, as favoured by the likes of Ian Curtis. I'd wanted one of these for ages. The trick was to pull the collar up gumshoe style, get the belt as tight as possible to effect that 26-inch waist look, suck the old cheeks in and parade around town looking as emaciated and as mis-erable as possible. This particular look was carried off best by the likes of Ian McCulloch, but there was one in every town. I first clapped eyes on Peter Murphy walking down Kettering Road. His mode was quite anti-fashion – an outsize harlequin sweater and skinny kecks, but with a head like that he could look as anti-fashion as he wanted. He definitely clocked me but there was nothing conspiratorial in his glance, more 'nice try kid but I look way weirder and cooler than you ever will'. He was right. He looked amazing, more Bowie than Bowie. The second time I saw Murphy, he was fronting Bauhaus at the Racecourse Pavilion in Northampton. Bauhaus 1919 (as they were called then) were Northampton's number-one punk/new wave band and the town's greatest musical export since Edmund Rubbra, Sir Malcolm Arnold or the Paper Dolls.

Bauhaus would do battle with sibling rockabilly act the Jets for Northampton chart supremacy in the early '80s. I was once in a record shop on Gold Street in 1981 when, fresh from their debut top-thirty success, the rocking Cotton brothers brought some signed Jets posters into the shop for the manager to give away to lucky customers. As soon as the Cotton boys departed, the manager and his assistant started laughing and put the posters straight in the bin. I don't know why but it always makes me sad when I think about that incident; I think it says much about the human condition.

Spring 1979, I'm in ACME, studying the noticeboard again, when I see that local punk band the Isaws are looking for a bassist. I've got a bass but no amp to plug it into. The Isaws haven't been inundated with offers from interested parties so joining is an easy process. I just need some equipment. I can't afford a whole new rig but if I can stump up for an amp and driver my dad promises to build me a speaker cab. A couple of weeks later I'm auditioning in the basement of a shared house in Grove Road in the centre of town. None of the band lives here but their mates do and they're all tireless patrons of the band. If I pass the audition it's win-win. Not only do I get four new mates from the band, but another four in the shared house. The Isaws – Alec, John, Rory and Pete – I note straight away are not a massively sophisticated outfit. Musically speaking, they're not a mile away from my former band Blackout. Blackout with a saxophone, perhaps. It's far too soon to start exerting any influence on proceedings, though, and I just learn the songs and enjoy some new company. They're an odd bunch. Alec and John (singer and guitarist) are the leather-jacketed Novak brothers of Yugoslavian descent. They're definitely the brains behind the operation but are rarely in accord. John manages the record bar at the local WH Smith, which makes my ears prick up. Drummer Pete Brownjohn is quite enigmatic and doesn't say much. He's a nice lad and a great drummer. I think he works in a lab somewhere. Rory Connolly is the sax player. He's great company: thoughtful, witty and loves Roxy Music. Rory is a computer programmer, in an era when none of us know what a computer is or does.

I find a job at a screen-printing company. Owner Vic is something of an enigma. He rarely smiles and you never knew where you are with him. He's okay, though, and gives me a lift into work most mornings. His neurotic girlfriend Cath is the one that warns me off Ativan. Like me, she'd started on 2mg per day, but now she's taking 20mg and still looks like she's on the verge of hysterics. I really enjoy the printing and get pretty good at it. I must be stoned out of my head most of the time as the solvents in the ink are so strong. Ironically, one of their regular customers is Hazchem (*Hazardous* Chemicals), who supply the warning stickers to the haulage industry. Vic trusts me to print the monthly posters for the new Theatre Royal productions. They're beautiful works of art and we have them pinned all around the workshop. Vic shares the space with a sign writer and graphic designer called Tony Tutchener. Tony is a veteran of Northampton's '60s music scene – a fact I wish I'd found more impressive at the time. He often runs me home after work and is kind enough to give me one of his old '60s band suits, a beautiful three-piece, Italian-styled number with ultra-thin lapels, no vents and extra narrow pants. I wear it continuously until it comes apart at the seams a few years later.

10

A Royal Interlude

My parents lived in New Duston at the northernmost tip of Northampton. After our house, it was all pretty rural until you reached Long Buckby. If you continued past Alpine Way for 2 miles you came to the Althorp Estate, for 500 years the home of the Spencer family and the final resting place of Diana, Princess of Wales. Of course, this didn't matter a fig to me or anyone else in 1979 and I'd have needed a fairly serious incentive to visit the place.

A miserable day out was improved considerably by the diligence of the 8th Earl's wife, Raine McCorquodale, who in 1977 following her marriage to Diana's father decided to open tea rooms and a gift shop at the stately home as a means of offsetting its astronomical running costs. Dubbed 'Acid' Raine by her unloving stepchildren, it was largely down to her efforts that her husband John was alive and well enough to walk Diana down the aisle on her wedding day, having suffered a massive stroke just three years previously.

Raine, 1947's 'Deb of the Year', was the daughter of cartoon socialite Barbara Cartland, whose outrageous wigs and omnipresent Pekinese became a well-known feature on British TV from the 1960s onwards. Cartland was a self-appointed spokesperson for the very rich and fortunate, although her personal fortune was wholly dependent on the patronage of consumers of the 'penny dreadfuls'. She wrote an astonishing 723 published novels during her lifetime. Ironically, the young romantic Diana had a voracious appetite for such titles as *Passionate Attainment*, *The Enchanted Waltz*, *A Virgin in Paris* and so on.

Barbara's daughter was a chip off the old block and one thing Raine learnt from her mother was how to handle a make-up gun. She must have got through at least five sticks of Rouge Hermès a week – double that if there was an ambassador's reception to attend. Margaret Thatcher's famous coiffure was clearly modelled on the Spencer thatch but in reality it didn't come close to Raine's magnificent bouffant, which must have required a good pint of Elnett to keep it in position. She must have got through gallons of the stuff.

After sacking everyone when she initially took command at Althorp (correctly pronounced Althrop), Raine began hiring again as the house started attracting more visitors. It was thanks to this recruitment drive that my mum came to work at the place, firstly as a guide and then, because she sounded quite posh, flogging overpriced jewellery and Althorp tat in the gift shop. Raine was very fond of her and wanted to employ her as a PA but my mum had a proper job with Northampton Social Services. She'd been there for a few months when she first mentioned John Spencer's daughter, the effervescent Diana. The future princess and my mum had bonded over their shared Christian name and Diana (our Diana) was absolutely smitten: 'You must come up to Althorp one Sunday and I'll introduce you to Diana. She always helps out in the shop and the café when she visits, she's a lovely girl, the same age as you, you'd really like her'; or, 'I was talking to Diana this afternoon, she's so bubbly, loves her pop music. I told her you were in a group and she was fascinated.'

It was Diana this, Diana that: 'Diana did the washing-up yesterday'; 'Diana helped us out in the gift shop this afternoon'; 'Diana was asking after you today, she said how's your son, when's his group playing?' Of course at the time I had no idea what the 'bubbly', 'pop-loving' Diana looked like, but what I wasn't looking for, to complement my Ian McCulloch stylings, was the attentions of some jolly hockey-sticks, deb of the week airhead from the upper echelons.

As history would reveal, in addition to jug-eared princes, Diana had a penchant for army officers, bodyguards and rugger types, so it's debatable whether she'd have jumped at the chance of a date with a pallid adolescent screen printer with indie pop star aspirations. Regardless, what I was looking for in a lady I'd be more likely to find down the Roadmenders, at the Paddock or playing bass guitar in Dolly Mixture.

One Sunday in 1980, my mum broke the sad news that the heir to the throne had been sniffing around at Althorp and it looked very likely that he was going to propose to young

Diana. This was a good month or so before it hit the papers, so everyone at Althorp was super discreet.

I have to say, I wasn't that impressed when I finally saw Di on the palace lawns the following February in that ghastly royal blue two-piece and a haircut from another century. *I've dodged a bullet there*, I thought.

So Diana and I never got together, but scarcely a day goes by when I don't ruminate on how I could have changed the course of history. In fact there's a very strong possibility that, had I acted on my mum's suggestion and in my country's best inter-est, instead of being obsessed with pop music and slightly more gothy women, we could now be living in a republic.

That's a heavy cross to bear.

11

The Path of Least Resistance

I popped into Grove Road after work one evening to be met by the sight of housemates Eric and John pogoing in the hall. The house was shaking to the sound of live music coming from the cellar, music a bit too syncopated to be the Isaws. It turned out Bauhaus were between rehearsal rooms and had offered to pay for the privilege of using the basement for a few weeks. So the Isaws found themselves temporarily homeless until my dad offered us some space at the tile warehouse he was managing. It was on an industrial estate about ten minutes from my new flat at Casuals Rugby Club, so suited me perfectly. I don't know if it was because my dad was enabling the band to rehearse or the fact that I'd felt I'd served my Isaws apprenticeship, but it was at Brackmills Industrial Estate that I initiated my takeover. It was quite simple from my point of view. We change the group name, write a whole new set, feed everything through echo units and fuzz boxes and try to sound as much like ClockDVA as possible. And so overnight the Isaws became Anémic Cinéma, named after a short film by Dadaist Marcel Duchamp. I still cringe when I think of that name – it's the kind of thing Nick Rhodes would have suggested. It's a wonder they didn't throw me into Hardingstone Dyke and leave me there, but no one offered any real resistance to my slow-moving coup.

We found a new rehearsal space above a garage a few hundred yards from Grove Road. The room was let to us by an Afro-Caribbean businessman called Vivian Allen. Viv had arrived in Northampton in 1956 armed with £500 in traveller's cheques and over time bought up numerous homes that he rented out to the town's growing Afro-Caribbean community, although judging by the peppercorn rent he charged us he was certainly no Peter Rachman. When not hiring out rehearsal rooms to Anémic Cinéma he was involved in car repairs, car sales, home removals, international shipping and Caribbean catering. If Viv was at the rehearsal room when we arrived, the first thirty minutes would usually be taken up by him strapping on John's guitar and playing a selection of reggae standards, almost oblivious to our presence. Ever the businessman, Viv made it clear that, should we ever play live, he wanted some part of it and regularly reminded us of the future rock 'n' roll and reggae extravaganza he had in mind. We were never ready to play live, though, never even close. Alec was the first to leave, clearly bored by the lack of activity. John gave it a little more time but eventually decided to form a band that wanted to gig every now and again. This left the power trio of Rory, Pete and me. We existed for perhaps another six months, maybe more. We might have been called the Royal Tourniquet (a name suggested by Martin Fry) at some point but we may as well have been called Work in Progress (Stage 3). We recorded every rehearsal and got some pretty good jams down on tape, but in truth we were treading water. We never wrote a song, never played a gig.

It was around this time I started travelling to London regularly on my own for gigs. It was an hour by train and if you missed the last connection back to Northampton then you could stay at Euston for a few hours or, if you got lucky, at some mystery destination in the capital. One of my first Friday-night forays was to see Joy Division at the Electric Ballroom in Camden Town. A company called Final Solution had started promoting some fantastic gigs in London and the Joy Division show was one of theirs. It wasn't until I moved there in the mid '90s that I lost the amphetamine-like buzz of arriving at Euston and disappearing down into the Underground for another London adventure. There wasn't another place in the country that could capture that sensation.

26 October 1979. It's the first time I've seen Joy Division outside Manchester and it's quite a shock. Emerging from Camden Town tube station there's winding queues of weekend post-punk kids and ticket touts are everywhere. They could have sold the venue out three times over. It's not something you expect to see at a Joy Division gig, which are traditionally cool affairs. A Certain Ratio and the Distractions make it an all-Manchester and Factory Records undercard. Joy Division's entry is so beautifully

understated: one of the crew wanders on stage with instructions to 'leave the lights on all the time', a precautionary measure should any over-excited lighting guy unwittingly trigger one of Ian Curtis's grand mal seizures. The band amble on bathed in green and blue spotlights that don't change during the entire set. They introduce themselves with a simple 'Good evening, we're Joy Division', before opening with 'I Remember Nothing', the least obvious opener in the whole Joy Division oeuvre. The breaking glass, fractured guitar and semi-operatic vocal ramp up the tension perfectly, faced with a crowd who've come to hear 'Shadowplay', 'Transmission', 'She's Lost Control'. They start a new song, 'Colony', and Curtis finally breaks into his spasmodic, ECT dance. It prompts an outbreak of similar movement at the foot of the stage and arms and fists are flailing everywhere. The crowd parts as a big fight breaks out but, rather than prompting any Jimmy Pursey-style intervention, Joy Division play on as if it's part of the act – I saw Joy Division in London three times and every time there were crowd fights. I cop off with a girl in tartan trousers who likes the cut of my US Army raincoat. *Tonight's the night*, I'm thinking, as we travel back to her pad in Balham. I wake up around six in the morning rather disorientated. I'm lying on a bathroom floor with my face covered in dried blood. My nose has been bleeding. My raincoat is still belted as tight as it had been when I left the Ballroom last night, so I assume nothing much happened. I poke my head round the bedroom door and the girl's in her pyjamas, sound asleep. It's too early to wake her so I step out into the south London chill and head for Euston. It's Saturday morning and I remember I'm getting the train to Manchester later to visit Jim. I love all this lone traveller stuff. I'll be eighteen in just under six weeks and I'm feeling very independent and free. And a bit wretched.

Two weeks later, I'm back in the capital for the greatest gig that ever was.

I'm still smarting from missing the Human League at the Marquee in June, so I was determined not to miss them on their forthcoming UK tour. The London show is another Final Solution promotion, with supports from the Teardrop Explodes, the Beat and the Flowers. A veritable post-punk spectacular.

The Flowers and the Beat pass without incident. They were okay but nothing special. I've been wanting to see the Teardrops for a while. The following year they'll release the mighty *Treason* and Saint Julian will begin to flower. Tonight, however, they're a little understated. They sound pretty good but with Julian Cope on bass they don't really have a frontman. Be careful what you wish for.

The stage is decluttered for the League's arrival, the riot shields (built to protect the League's gear from flying missiles during their formative period) are erected and the reel-to-reel tape machines are put in position. It looks more like the set of a Samuel Beckett play than a rock gig. Four big trapezium-shaped screens dwarf the three Leaguers who've arrived on stage under the cover of darkness. Based on the Kryptonian Council high court scene in *Superman I* and replicated on the inside cover of *Reproduction*, it remains the most stunning visual backdrop I've ever seen.

Phil Oakey, if not rock's greatest frontman then certainly in the top five, strolls on from the back of the stage. Tonight he looks wonderful – the asymmetric haircut is at its absolute peak, beautifully brushed and meticulously ironed. Clad in leather jerkin with jumbo belt, Phil's make-up is immaculate, but the whisper of a five o'clock shadow gives him the look of a 1920s matinee idol more than an unreliable cross-dresser. He's sporting a single dangly earring and in his special ladies' outsize high heels, he looks about 6 foot 6. Oakey arrives at the microphone just on cue: 'There's something in your soul that makes me feel so old, in fact I think I've died about 600 times . . .' This is wonderful, it doesn't matter that Martyn Ware has a moustache and Philip Adrian Wright looks a bit bland. Phil Oakey could perform in front of the Marshall Tucker band and it would still look and sound extraordinary. '. . . I'm moving back to the age of men.' You tell 'em, Phil.

For any kid who grew up in the '60s, their slide-show is a boys-own delight: JFK, Gerry Anderson, *The Man from U.N.C.L.E.*, Yuri Gagarin, John Wayne, Steve McGarrett, Kubrick's *Lolita*, Hitchcock's *Psycho*, lots of cold-war missiles emerging from silos. The near total lack of movement on stage is beautifully contrasted by the ever-changing wall of boomer nostalgia above.

The set ends with an ecstatic 'Zero as a Limit', a song that would, in some cultures, send its listeners into a whirling hypnotic trance.

So there you have it – the best gig ever. Every concert from this day forward will be measured against it and none – not Prince,

U2, Kraftwerk, not even the Human League themselves – have come anywhere close. Welcome to the future.

I finally got a job at ACME. I'd wanted to work there since I'd arrived in town. Printing pop group T-shirts seemed like the last word in reflected glamour. Now I had the necessary chops and after the tricky multi-colour prints I'd been knocking out for Vic, this was an absolute piece of piss. The atmosphere was fairly relaxed but it was clear that the whole operation had become slightly more professional since the company had occupied several ink-splattered units above a music shop on Kettering Road. There were no ink-fights on the shop floor and the management all had offices upstairs, which overlooked us, so there was very limited opportunity for larking about. Kevin from Bauhaus worked there every now and again when he wasn't rocking the provinces. He was usually on bullet-belt duty, which was nice and menial and involved no mess – he malleted fifty to sixty empty cartridges into clips with a buckle fastener to produce an approximation of something that Lemmy might wear. You could get about ten of those made in an hour if you got a wiggle on.

Kevin put me on the guest list for Bauhaus's London show at the Electric Ballroom on 20 March. They'd just released their second single 'Dark Entries' and were beginning to get quite a following in the capital. The previous month we'd seen them at a John Peel night at the famous Nag's Head in Wollaston. That evening Murphy had harpooned a biker in the audience with his mic stand and this very big bloke just stood there with his mouth open as if he was part of the show. Bauhaus were getting unspeakably good as a live spectacle and, though they'd never challenge Joy Division or the Human League for my affections, there was no denying that they were one of the hottest live acts of the post-punk era. In terms of theatre, there was really no one to match them and tonight's main act didn't come close. Backstage there was a proper new wave commotion going on. Sal Solo, the lead singer from headliners Classix Nouveaux, had been gargling with TCP to preserve his less than wonderful voice and had accidentally drunk a fair quantity of the antiseptic elixir. As Bauhaus packed away their gear, Sal was being shuttled out of the building into an ambulance. Solo's reputation as a post-punk Nosferatu took quite a hit that night but he was no way as evil as his image suggested. Today he gives Christian guidance in the USA. What prompted Sal Solo to drink so much TCP that evening is a mystery that will only be solved when the Classix Nouveaux story is written, but his band were hopeless and, having to follow Bauhaus, Sal would have been acutely aware they had no future in the pop game.

Jim was still living at home in Bramhall and working in the graphics place in Wythenshawe, but he'd had enough. He served his notice and headed off to Rotterdam for a couple of weeks to visit Martin's old mate Mike Pickering and his girlfriend Gonnie. Mike had been called back to Manchester while Jim was there to check out an old boat showroom with his friend Rob Gretton, with the intention of turning it into a nightclub. A year later the building was opened as FAC51 The Hacienda.

The band was going nowhere and it was starting to feel like Northampton might have run its course. I'd always had a shine for London and it seemed an exciting place to be at that moment. I got it into my head that I'd live and work in a big London hotel and spend the evenings out clubbing. It wasn't much of a plan but I let everyone know it was what I intended to do and that I'd be leaving at the end of the month.

Jim dropped by on the way back from Holland. He was as restless as me and wanted a change. He fancied moving to Northampton but I let him know that I'd already decided to head for the capital. Jim didn't fancy London and suggested Sheffield. I was loath to abandon my London dream, but Sheffield made perfect sense – it was the most happening city in the UK at that moment. We could kip on his brother Martin's floor until we found somewhere to stay. So Sheffield it would be.

Two weeks later and with great ceremony, armed with my one-way ticket to South Yorkshire, I entered the Mouth of Hell and boarded a Sheffield-bound National Express coach. Just north of Birmingham we stopped for a twenty-minute comfort break. My urethral sphincter was a fair bit tighter in those days so I opted to stay on the coach and carry on with my sleep, but there was a commotion down at the front so I wandered down to investigate. Some old bloke was in a bad way, struggling to breathe. The driver wanted to get him off the coach so we took an arm each and edged him down the stairs. As we were walking him across the car park, he just dropped and we were left supporting his full weight. We couldn't hold him, so we laid him down on the tarmac. He appeared to be breathing but I couldn't really tell. Another passenger appeared who had the necessary first aid skills, so I left them to it and went to grab a coffee. As we set off, I leaned over to the fellow in the seat in front and asked if the old man was all right. 'Aye, all right f' next life!' was his blunt Yorkshire response. Shit. I tried not to attach too much significance to the incident, but it was all a bit *Midnight Cowboy*. Was I doing the right thing?

12

The North Loop

There was nothing arbitrary about our decision to move to Sheffield. We'd had a fascination with the place ever since Martin had moved there four years earlier. From the home-produced cassettes he brought back when visiting his parents, we heard the likes of the Human League, Cabaret Voltaire, ClockDVA and Martin's own synth combo Vice Versa. None were as powerful as Joy Division, but this was much darker stuff. True, Martin would gild the lily a bit when describing how these people lived, but Manchester seemed very straight down the middle compared to its South Yorkshire neighbour. Sheffield was more like Berlin, or perhaps Dusseldorf or Sodom and Gomorrah. By the time we got to Sheffield, the Human League Mk I had been and gone and Mk II was about to take the UK by storm, ClockDVA and Cabaret Voltaire had both released LPs and Martin had moved out from behind his synthesiser to front a new band, ABC, formed from the ashes of Vice Versa. We couldn't have come to Sheffield at a more opportune time.

To compound all the aforementioned excitement, we had come to the most youth-friendly city in Great Britain. Under the Labour-controlled council, David Blunkett would ensure that Sheffield was far and away the best place in the country to be unemployed. Bus fares were capped at 2p and your dole card was dubbed 'your passport to leisure', with swimming pools and a smorgasbord of facilities provided free upon presentation of a current UB40.

Actually, there was nothing perverse about Blunkett's ideas and it's mystifying that they weren't adopted nationally. Unemployment was surging and the economic climate was demoralising enough without further penalising the electorate every time they wanted to take a bus ride or get some exercise. Blunkett also recognised that young people liked to enjoy themselves from time to time and that there was nothing criminal in earmarking a tiny proportion of the pittance received in benefits to pay for a night out. To this end the council promoted a series of concerts for the unemployed at Sheffield Poly. These weren't piss-pot gigs, either. They featured top names like New Order, the Damned, UK Subs and Bow Wow Wow. The scheme, dubbed 'Rock on the Rates', came in for some considerable criticism from obvious quarters. But it was a great idea and arguably did way more for morale than anything Mr Tebbit's bicycle-loving bureaucrats could have dreamt up.

The only thing preventing us from entering this New Jerusalem was the fact that Martin had given us exactly two weeks to find a flat or it was back to where we'd come from.

Barber Crescent, Crookesmoor was the headquarters of ABC: Radical Dance Faction. Here Martin lived with Disco John, Sheffield's premier alternative DJ, in a crumbling and condemned end-terraced house. ABC rehearsed in the front room every day from ten, so Jim and I needed to be out of the house by 9.30 and we couldn't return until late afternoon.

We found a one-bedroom flat opposite Crookes Valley Park and registered at the labour exchange so we could get our hands on one of their golden tickets. Any ideas of forming a band would be put on hold for the time being while we explored our new home.

Sheffield, we realised very quickly, was quite a militant city. It had every right to be. Few of its adult workforce were in full-time employment and the situation would only get worse once Ian MacGregor had finished dismantling the steel industry and got to work on the country's coal mines, of which South Yorkshire had many.

Sandwiched between Newcastle and Belfast, Sheffield was the ninth-largest urban agglomeration in the UK (statistic from *Threads*), but compared to Manchester it felt more like a village. You could walk from one end of the city centre to the other in less than ten minutes. There were lots of interesting bohemian types wandering about and you got the impression that something interesting was happening below the surface. But it soon dawned on us that we may have oversold the place to ourselves. The pop world loved Sheffield, but what we quickly discovered was the Sheffield production line was grinding to a halt. That's not to say that the people weren't having a go. Sheffield's music scene was as thriving as Manchester's, probably more so with the abundance of disused factories, warehouses and office spaces making finding rehearsal rooms relatively easy. The problem was, that having harvested a golden generation, Sheffield's B and C lists were painfully uninspired. It was as if the rest of the rocking conurbation had made a pact with itself not to ape the pop stylings of the Human League or anything that might be deemed commercial. The Cabs were an obvious influence, but a second-rate Cabaret Voltaire – and there were quite a few – was a very dismal proposition. It struck us as the ideal moment to put a band together, to let the brainstorming begin. We'd take the bits that had worked for the likes of the Human League, ABC, DVA and we'd weld it to the bits and bobs they'd forgotten to quote from. We'd take a good look at the alternative music Sheffield was currently producing and do the opposite. Sheffield was all about the future, we noted, so we'd lean heavily on the past, condemned to repeat it. 'To acknowledge the past is the best way of meeting the future' – Tony Wilson, 21 July 1978.

A lot of our ideas were merely ones ABC had discarded when they buried Vice Versa. In many ways, Vice Versa provided the blueprint for World of Twist. We loved the lyrics in particular ('Eyes of Christ in wrap-around shades'), which hinted at something very modern but sounded like B-52's meet Kraftwerk.

We loved the way the music business of the early '60s distilled the art of music-making into simple throwaway catchphrases, as though music were something disposable you bought from a vending machine: *teen; teen-beat; easy-beat; easy*. And *twist*. Not merely a dance craze but a whole pop genre – basically anything you can twist to, which is pretty much everything. If anyone asked what kind of music we intended to play, it was 'twist'. It meant nothing, it meant everything. We spent several weeks trying to come up with a name: Shake-o-tron and Binatone (my clock radio) were both popular.

One of our favourite albums of the moment was Decca's 1973 compilation, *The World of David Bowie*, essentially a re-release of the label's 1970 compilation of the same name but re-packaged with a Ziggy-era Bowie on the cover to hoodwink the uninformed into buying it. The first manifestation of Bowie is often identified by his cornball comedy hit 'The Laughing Gnome', recorded in 1967 but re-released in 1973 as a cash-in in the wake of Bowiemania. The first album (*David Bowie*) is a total masterpiece. It's clear the man put a huge amount of work into this release. I've often wondered whether Bowie would have preferred success with this era Bowie to his later achievements, which leaned so heavily on US influences. With his 1967 release, Bowie was playing straight into my hands with all its baroque flourishes, quotes from musical theatre and those Anthony Newleyisms. After his 1967 debut the rest of DB's oeuvre must have come comparatively easily to the man. As I arrived late to Bowie, this was probably the third or fourth album of his that I got to know intimately. So here we had another key influence.

Maybe it wasn't as key as the northern soul beats and James Bond themes but early Bowie (particularly 'She's Got Medals') was essential to the Twist mix. The *World of* series was part of a series of compilations, samplers and best-ofs released by Decca between 1968 and 1982: *World of Hard Rock*, *World of the Hammond Organ*, *World of Tijuana Brass*, *World of Lulu* (volumes 1 and 2), *World of Music Hall*, *World of the Cinema Organ*, *World of Ed 'Stewpot' Stewart*, *World of Easy Listening* (volumes 1 to 6). There were over 400 titles in the series. There was no *World of Twist*, but that's definitely where the name of our band came from.

Martin seemed quite excited by our small project, excited that his kid brother was finally getting his act together five years after seeing the Sex Pistols, five years after getting his *Licence To Rock*. One evening in the pub, Martin explained to us his 'Chelsea Boot in Face' principle, central to the ABC concept. As soon as your audience think they've got the measure of you, you change tack, you switch, you short circuit. Martin and his band were true to his word and, following on from the colossal success of ABC's debut album *Lexicon of Love*, the band mothballed the gold lamé, reverted to a trio and traded in the strings for some loud guitars. A third change of direction saw the band recreate themselves as Hanna-Barbera-style cartoon figures for *How to Be a . . . Zillionaire!* There's little doubt that ABC would have found Duran Duran-scale success if they'd towed the corporate line and released *Lexicon of Love* ad infinitum, but you have to admire them for not doing that.

World of Twist took the 'Chelsea Boot in Face' notion very seriously. However, our concept would be more brutal, destructive, stupid. We would deliberately fuck things up once we'd found success. The objective with World of Twist was not to see how many ways we could ride the rock horse around the course. We would deliberately fall at the first hurdle. We would crash head first through the first fence. Tony Ogden loved this idea. It was instrumental in his decision to join us and probably played a good part in the group's final demise.

I'd kept in touch with Bauhaus's drummer Kevin and looked forward to his regular hand-drawn postcards, which invariably featured beelike/Michelin men characters who would, later in the decade, come to life as Love and Rockets side project, the Bubblemen.

Kevin invited me on tour for a few dates. I met up with them in Nottingham for a Rock City sell-out, then it was down to Hammersmith Palais for the big London show. There I met a very beautiful girl called Catherine who called herself Angel and we kept in touch for a while. After the show we headed into central London and a very swanky bar full of up-to-the-minute London clubbing types. A group of Blitz kids who were polite and pretty came over to the Bauhaus table and introduced themselves as Blue Zoo. They'd just released a record and handed us all a copy. I was expecting it to be dreadful but it was actually very good. 'An epic, soaring ballad,' said *NME* of 'Love Moves in Strange Ways', making it their single of the week. Blue Zoo's Ziggy-fixated singer Andy O had the kind of looks A Flock of Seagulls would have murdered for. They went on to have a bit of a hit and released a couple of albums but the hard-boiled '80s had no use for Blue Zoo and they were returned to Essex, sold as seen.

Danny Ash, the Bauhaus member with the most hair and make-up, overheard me say that my old neighbour Paul Morley was sitting across the room. The faceless Morley was another critic of the band and Danny had to be physically restrained from confronting the journalist. I actually thought Paul would quite like them if he got to know them a bit, but if it came to blows, I didn't fancy his chances against the wind-mill arms of Ash.

The following night the band were playing Portsmouth at the city's fabulous Guildhall. The toilets were the grandest I'd ever used. The band had to do an interview at Radio Victory and they weren't very enthusiastic. Someone suggested I should do the interview as the unseen fifth member so we hastily concocted a story that I was Brilburn Logue, a pseudonym the writer Alan Moore had used for his *Mask* sleeve notes. We pretended to the interviewer that I was the brains behind Bauhaus, writing all their music and conceiving all their stage shows. The DJ looked a bit lost when he heard this; it obviously wasn't on the notes he'd hastily scribbled down beforehand.

I said goodbye to Bauhaus. They went on to worldwide popularity and eventually relocated to the US. I returned to Sheffield and my quest for the big time.

13

Casino Classics, Volumes 1 and 2

Up to now, Martin had been quite secretive about ABC but he finally let Jim and me hear a few tracks. We were stunned. They were really good. They'd completely torn up the Vice Versa songbook and there wasn't a synthesiser in sight. Their new rhythm section, Mark Lickley and David Robinson, had come straight out of the clubs. All the best musicians in the area had paid their dues in the working men's clubs of South Yorkshire. They were to Sheffield what early '60s Hamburg was to the Liverpool bands. Stephen Singleton had moved from synth to saxophone. He was yet to really get to grips with the nuances of the instrument but he looked good and was very animated on stage. Mark White's transformation was a revelation. I'd thought he was a great singer/frontman with the original band but he was a much better guitarist. And then there was the new singer. Martin had sung on the final Vice Versa tracks and had sounded pretty good but, Jesus, he'd come on. It was just a matter of time before the band was signed and they were already being courted by the majors. We followed them to their next three showcases at Leeds, Birmingham and London. Leeds was all cycling tops, floppy fringes and a bit too much on-stage dancing, but, by the time they reached Birmingham, it was a slick operation. Martin was in jacket and tie, his on-stage patter now honed to perfection. We were at the Holy City Zoo, the club co-owned by Aston Villa's Andy Gray. Also in the audience were footballer Frank Worthington and Brummie hopefuls Duran Duran. ABC were incredible.

In London they played a discotheque called Legends, which was pretty much the snazziest joint I'd ever been in. A shrine to 1980s interior design, Legends, a cock-stride from Savile Row, would host Elizabeth Taylor's fiftieth birthday party the following year, so tonight we were warming the seats for the likes of Burton, Nureyev, Bennett, Starr, La Rue and Frankie Howerd. We all felt fairly scruffy and northern as we entered the club full of elegant men and stunning women. London band Funkapolitan were handing out promo copies of their new record. They were beautifully presented in a film reel box with a very stylish band logo. They meant business and we were slightly nervous for ABC, armed only with their cloth-cap funk. But Funkapolitan had no songs and their beat was bovine and clumsy. ABC would dispose of them and their ilk so effortlessly it was almost cruel. We could afford about one drink apiece so we spent most of the night dancing. The elegant Londoners weren't much good at that, either.

If you liked your music alternative and fashionable, Sheffield nightlife was very simple. On a Wednesday night you went to Penny's on Eyre Street and on Fridays and Saturdays you went to the Limit on West Street. Life went on like this until the Leadmill got its alcohol licence in the autumn of 1982. The university, poly and art college would hold regular discos on campus, but Penny's and the Limit was where the locals and those students who were happy to mingle with the townsfolk would gather. Penny's was the big dressing-up night of the week. I'd never been to a club like it before or since. A sort of Poundland Legends, here the new romantics would rub shoulders with the goths, the raincoat brigade, the zoot-suited funkateers, the Numanoids, the yet to be christened gender benders, the early Bowie fans and some of the hardest-looking drag queens in history. Add to this the loyal patronage of Sheffield's premier pop acts the Human League, Cabaret Voltaire, Heaven 17 and the up-and-coming ABC and you had yourself quite a midweek scene.

The night was the creation of Martin's flatmate John Blyther, aka John Tracy but known to all simply as Disco John. John was very stylish, always immaculately turned out, like a cross between Napoleon Solo and *Marathon Man*-period Roy Scheider. He was well known around town and enjoyed the status of being Sheffield's top alternative DJ. It was John who introduced Jim and me to the wonders of Stephen Friedland, aka Brute Force, another corner piece of the World of Twist jigsaw. We talked records a lot and I mentioned I'd like to do some DJ'ing while

I was in Sheffield. John was in the final year of his degree and asked if I'd like to take over as DJ on Wednesday nights at Penny's until he'd finished his exams. So overnight I became something of a face. No match of course for Disco John and his Simon Templar stylings, but I like to think I brought a bit of youthful lemon-sucking charm to the proceedings. It was a seamless transformation: I basically played all the records John played, straying only occasionally from the path to play the odd new release or personal favourite. The evening was very formulaic; the core crowd pleasers were Japan, Simple Minds, Magazine, Banshees, Kraftwerk and Human League. Into this mix and depending on mood, we could blend some Echo & the Bunnymen, Teardrop Explodes and OMD, early Soft Cell, Bauhaus, Duran Duran, Depeche Mode and so on. Bowie and Roxy were staples naturally, as were Grace Jones, the B-52's, Talking Heads and Byrne & Eno. The club was hip to the new funky mood sweeping the land and would always feature some James Brown, Chic, Sister Sledge and Prince, blended with the Latin grooves of Kid Creole and Coati Mundi. If I ever went off road it would be in the direction of Iggy Pop, the Psychedelic Furs or the Postcard stable, but it was risky to drift too far from the Disco John remit. Two traditions John insisted I upheld was the early Bowie record and the Numan record. For the former I would play a track from Bowie's debut album, usually 'Little Bombardier'. As the opening notes sounded, the dance floor would obediently clear and two or three Bowie heads wearing loose-fitting shirts, enormous pleated trousers and ballet pumps would perform extravagant and very literal mimes as the regular dancing punters loitered impatiently around the edge of the dance floor. The Gary Numan fans always brought their own records and wore home-made imitations of *Replicas*-era Numan suits. The Numans were not tolerated to the same extent that the early Bowies were. On one occasion, one of the lads rushed up to the DJ booth after performing and asked for his records as some lads near the bar had threatened to hit him. The owner of the club was a cheerful Liverpudlian. He never really got what John was trying to do but he liked the fact that his club was always packed. Every now and again he'd donate a bottle of fizzy wine for the best dancer, the sexiest girl etc.

'So, Gordon mate, tonight I'm giving away a bottle of bubbly to the weeeeirdest-dressed person in here, okay?'

A few hours later, a fairly normal-looking young man with lots of eyeliner poked his head over the DJ booth. 'I've come for my champagne – I'm the weirdest person in here tonight.'

We both had a bit of a chortle and I was pleased to hand the bottle to Marc Almond, who was over from Leeds for the night and thanked me for playing his record 'Memorabilia'.

'That's you!! Wow, that's a brilliant song. Have you got anything else coming out?'

Marc explained how their next song was very poppy: 'We're going for the charts this time.'

'Tainted Love' went to number one on 1 August and went on to become 1981's best-selling single.

My newfound Wednesday-night star status had its perks and overnight Jim and I became more popular with the ladies. We were still sleeping in a single room at Harcourt Road, with the spare room reserved for record playing. It was more Ted and Dougal than Eric and Ernie, but it was an obvious passion killer and any girls who had the misfortune to come back with us invariably ended up sleeping on the sofa bed next door. One of our friends told us of a conversation she'd overheard in the toilets at Penny's one evening: Girl One: 'I quite fancy the DJ and his mate'; Girl Two: 'I wouldn't go back with them, you never get owt there.'

Of all the Sheffield bands, the one that intrigued us the most was ClockDVA. The Human League were my favourites, of course, there was no question about that, but for all their barmy lyrics, amazing tunes, fantastic haircuts and the odd splash of Dada, the League were not a complicated group. They were the electronic Monkees. DVA (never ClockDVA), on the other hand, were preternaturally dark – confusing, frightening and fascinating. They had songs called 'Time and the Female Mirror', 'Film of Our Death', 'Somnambulists', 'Lomticks of Time', 'The Pop Hell'. I'd have paid for just the titles. Their singer was Adolphus 'Adi' Newton and they had group members called Veet, Tyme and Quail. Their synth player was called Simon Elliot-Kemp, a name that suggested some cold-hearted science type who develops the world's most functional killing device, or maybe an occultist, a member of the landed gentry with unspeakable sexual perversions and an Orgone Accumulator in his bathroom. I first saw the band at the fabled Sci-Fi Festival promoted by Final Solution at the YMCA on Tottenham Court Road. That evening they did little to dispel my fantasies that they lived together in a Crass-style commune with leader Adi Newton controlling their every twisted thought like an indie Jim Jones. The show began with a sordid and deeply disturbing piece from their dance/performance art wing Prior to Intercourse (PTI), a boy and a girl in gimp suits with strobe lights. This was not for the impressionable and easily shocked like myself. It was followed by an introduction from Samuel Beckett's *Ghost Trio*, which is probably the most unsettling walk-on sequence I've ever witnessed. Then came DVA themselves, gaunt, leathered up, menacing but surprisingly polished. Their new drummer Quail looked very presentable in an *Unman, Wittering and Zigo* sort of way. He probably lived in a room with no furniture and just his collection of Hitler Youth side drums.

DVA were a scary bunch, make no mistake. How did they speak, I wondered? Like Christopher Lee, Bela Lugosi, the Invisible Man, Captain Black, the Hood, Surface Agent X-20, Titan, an Ice Warrior, an Aquaphibian? Or perhaps they had their own made-up language, like Christian Vander's Magma. Maybe they didn't speak. Of course the spell was broken when they opened their mouths and sounded like the Eric Olthwaite Gang.

ClockDVA had sort of split up by the time we got to Sheffield, or at least the band I saw at the YMCA were no more. Within months, Adi Newton had regrouped with a new DVA, who were mostly session-musician types, many of them plucked from clubland. John Carruthers was the new guitarist, who would add Cure-type, Bunnymen-esque colourings to the funky palette blended by bassist Sean Ward and drummer David Palmer. John would go on to replace Robert Smith in Siouxsie & the Banshees, Sean Ward would end up in Simply Red. David Palmer would join ABC, the start of a stellar pop career that would see him thumping the tubs for the Yellow Magic Orchestra, the The, Sting, Al Green and Rod Stewart. Adi Newton would play with DVA until they were no more, then form the Anti-Group.

One man who didn't feature in the new DVA was their original bass player and Adi's right-hand man, Stephen 'Judd' Turner. Judd was a legendary character for Jim and myself and always the face you were drawn to if you saw any photos of DVA. If you were putting together your ideal post-punk band based on looks, you'd have to include Judd with his Iggy Pop smile and Louise Brooks haircut. He looked like he'd just stepped off the set of a 1920s German expressionist film. For a few short weeks Jim and I got to know him and even discussed putting a band together. He was off heroin, he'd cut his hair and he looked happy and healthy. We didn't see Judd for a couple of weeks and the next we heard he'd died accidentally from a huge overdose. He was twenty-four.

ABC decided they could go no further with their drummer Dave Robinson. He sounded pretty good to me but not to their new London producers, so he was destined to become their Pete Best without even a Hamburg visit (or equivalent) to soften the blow. ABC didn't need to look far for Robinson's replacement and ClockDVA's drummer needed little arm twisting to jump ship. David Palmer's decision to leave DVA turned out to be the fifth most significant event in the World of Twist story and perhaps the most significant event in the personal odyssey of Jim and me. Nick Sanderson of London via Bristol answered an advert in *Melody Maker* to join ClockDVA as their new drummer.

Bonfire Night 1981. ABC are on *Top of the Pops* for the first time with their debut single, 'Tears Are Not Enough'. This is a massive moment. The show has entered its third decade and lost none of its pop cache. Unbelievably, it is still the UK's only weekly pop show, occupying the same 7.30 Thursday evening slot it's held since our early teens. There are a few more balloons in the studio and the audience are encouraged to 'whoop it up' on cue, but the format is basically the same; the company are still employing presenters of dubious character and the performances are nearly all mimed. The following day, Martin is in the pub with Jim and Adi Newton regaling them with tales from the Television Centre. Adi has brought along DVA's new drummer, Nick.

'Didn't I see that bloke on *Top of the Pops* last night?' Nick asks Jim incredulously.

A week later, Jim catches up with Adi on a tuppenny bus ride through the city centre.

'That drummer seemed like a nice bloke, Adi. Was he any good?

'Really good. We're offering him the job. He's moving up here but he needs somewhere to live.'

As luck would have it, Jim and I have just moved to a new shared house at the foot of Brocco Bank in the shadow of Sheffield's Botanical Gardens. Steadman, the landlord, has threatened to fill the vacancy with the first person he finds unless we can get a sixth housemate. Jim suggests Nick and the light-travelling Sanderson arrives the following week with just a holdall, a box of 7-inch singles, two Casino Classics northern soul LP compilations – one blue, one red – and a copy of Tom Jones's *Live at Caesar's Palace*. He moves into the attic room next to mine.

We all fall under Nick's spell very quickly. We're enchanted by his louche ways, his great company, his leather trousers and his industrial-strength acne cream, which everyone in the house will soon be using – a nightly ritual that sees everyone's faces covered in white Tipp-Ex blobs that will burn through our blemishes as we sleep, removing both the white head and several layers of skin. Nick introduces us to the genius of Tom Jones, B. J. Thomas and Acker Bilk. It's via Nick that I first hear northern soul, the legendary 'Troggs tapes' and Buddy Rich berating a hapless Australian trombonist. Nick remains with us for the next twenty-six years until our lives are dismantled by his cruelly premature death in 2008.

This is my first time in a shared house and the only house I've ever been in with a carpeted kitchen. During our time at Everton Road, we will consume 500 tins of chicken and bacon Toast Topper and get through 300 litres of Country Born setting gel. I will be accused of using too much toilet roll and the Breville sandwich maker I bequeath to the house as a gift will be rendered unusable when a sleepwalking guest pisses in it. During his tenure, Nick places a pint glass over a small barnacled poppet that someone has brought back from an overseas trip. If the pint pot is removed, Nick assures us, the evil will be released. It's an oath we all take very seriously and the glass remains untouched above the fireplace.

Everton Road turns out to be quite the artist's hub. On the ground floor resides Bracknell's own Ian Anderson, student and former bass player with the Infra Red Helicopters. Ian publishes his own fanzine and will go on to found the massively influential Designers Republic. Ian's room is infinitely more stylish and tidy than the rest of the house. He has jazz blinds on his windows where the rest of us have bed sheets and old blankets. Ian is visited regularly by Darrell D'Silva, sax-playing future member of the Anti-Group. Darrell will go on to acting success with the Royal Shakespeare Company.

On the first floor lives Dave West, a writer with a trumpet. He, Nick and Ian bond over his Steely Dan albums. When Dave moves out, another Dave moves in – Dave Bloom, student and drummer with Sheffield band the Junk. Dave hails from Felixstowe in East Anglia, he's the first person in Europe to own an REM record and he goes out with the most beautiful girl in Sheffield.

We return from the pub one evening and, horror of horrors, the pint glass has been removed. The grotesque shell-encrusted souvenir from the Balearics sits there on the mantelpiece, grinning at us with its button eyes aglare. As promised, the Evil engulfs us all.

The following day I get a call from Northampton. My mum and dad are splitting up. Everyone is in a state and could I come home that weekend? For twenty years, no matter how unsettling life gets, no matter how fucked up things appear, I've been able to rely on that small oasis of order to reset my buttons. That notion vanishes in an instant. Perhaps I make more of it than I should – after all, it's just two people deciding they don't want to live together any more – but I'm still a jumble of neuroses, a complete bag of nerves. I've stopped taking Ativan but I rely on an irregular supply of Valium and too much booze to keep myself on keel – even or otherwise. I check my diazepam stocks and make an appointment with my GP.

I get home to find everyone eking as much drama from this depressing situation as possible. My dad is sleeping on the couch and going out for walks in the early hours. I can't sleep so I go with him, weaving around the country lanes of Harlestone and beyond. We usually end up near Lady Di's old house in Great Brington. The walks are the best thing about this messy episode; we talk as we've never spoken before. Dad talks about growing up within earshot of Bow Bells during the Blitz; the brick fights between rival gangs in the bombed-out remains of the surrounding streets; how his mum got him evacuated to 'beautiful' Walton-on-Thames and his dad brought him back to the chaos of Clerkenwell; the terror of the V1 attacks in the final years of the war; the nauseating buzz of the doodlebugs followed by the chilling silence before the bombs detonate, hopefully some distance away. He talks emotionally about the deaths of nameless childhood friends who'd perished during the Blitz. It's difficult to comprehend that he's speaking of events that had happened less than forty years earlier. *What in fuck's name does my generation have to worry about?* Always with the new dawn the spell is broken and silence returns. My mum makes plans to return to the north-west, while my dad will stay in Northampton until the house is sold. I realise that for the time being I won't have a 'home' to return to. Christmas will be very different from now on.

ABC are undaunted by the comparatively poor performance of their November debut 'Tears are Not Enough', as up their sleeve they have the Glengarry leads – the new Trevor Horn recordings. Their next single, 'Poison Arrow', is extraordinary. Disco John plays it to me at the new house he and Martin have moved to following the bulldozing of ABC's Barber Crescent HQ. This isn't the kind of record English bands make. It sounds like uptown New York, East Coast Motown, the Bee Gees, Diana Ross, Hall & Oates. In fact, it's pure Hollywood. It's difficult to see ABC failing now. 'Poison Arrow' is predictably a top ten hit and, for their *Top of the Pops* appearance, Martin has planned his 'Starman' moment, performing in a gold lamé suit. If history forgets his name, the band's name or the name of their records, everyone will remember the suit.

For J. Fry and G. King, things aren't moving quite so swiftly. We watch, we listen and we absorb but we don't do much music making. We talk a lot, we conceptualise and we dream. We will choose our moment.

14

Tomorrow I'll Buy Myself a Dress

Before Morrissey there was Edwyn Collins. The fact is, if Edwyn's eye had been anywhere near the ball between 1981 and 1983 and had his co-writer Malcolm Ross been anywhere near as prodigious as Johnny Marr, there is a very real chance there would have been no room or need for the Doyen of Davyhulme. Orange Juice arrived fully formed in November 1980, or as early as February if you were ultra-hip. Their third Postcard single 'Simply Thrilled Honey' was the release that had the critics cooing. If we needed an antidote to post-punk misery (personally I didn't), then Orange Juice and their engaging singer were just that. With his slightly awkward phrasing and not quite in the centre pitching, Collins was the anti-pop star we'd all been dreaming of. As clever as Cohen, as cute as Cassidy and with a fringe rarely out of his eyes, he even had the audacity to smile in photographs. On 2 March 1982, Jim and I went to see Orange

Juice at Sheffield University. Jim and I had bought into all this Postcard tweeness: we saw Edwyn Collins as being our sort of pop star and we were feverishly awaiting OJ's debut album, due to be released later that month. The gig was half full and Edwyn, who was as charming and witty as we could have ever dreamed, thanked those who had come out to watch his band in favour of staying in to watch David Bowie make his small-screen acting debut in Bertolt Brecht's *Baal*.[*]

After the show Jim and I went in search of our new heroes. With absolutely no security at the venue it was impossibly easy. We found Edwyn and the boys green-rooming in a lecture hall far too big for their needs. They were extremely friendly, especially Edwyn, who gave us 2p apiece to cover our travel costs. I promised myself there and then that if I ever become anything approaching a pop star I'd meet and treat my fans with the grace and warmth Edwyn had shown us that evening. And if I've ever fallen short of that pledge I apologise sincerely. As for Edwyn, we met him a year later, after he'd had a hit with 'Rip It Up'. I'd love to say he was as lovely as on our first encounter but he wasn't. Not rude or anything, just a bit self-assured and star-like. I promised myself there and then that I would never be famous. I was true to my word.

It was the autumn of 1982. We tentatively got started with the band. Jim had his old matt-black Strat-shaped guitar and his 100-watt HH combo – the 'Wilko Johnson'. His brother had

---

[*] Notwithstanding Bowie's real small-screen acting debut in either a 1969 commercial for Luv ice lollies or his 1970 showing opposite Lindsay Kemp in the risible *Pierrot in Turquoise*.

lent us a couple of keyboards to get the thing going: a Wasp synthesiser, a relic of Martin's Vice Versa days, and a Casiotone MT-40. The Casio had a built-in drum machine so we were up and running from the off. The first song World of Twist wrote was 'Space Rocket' (aka 'Space Rock-It'). It was, we fancied, a bit B-52's, a bit Barry Gray, a bit Human League. We were overjoyed. Neither of us had written a proper song before and we'd composed an instant trash smash. We followed this up quickly with another self-penned piece of post-punk abrasion titled 'It's OK'. By the time ex-Isaw Rory Connolly had travelled up from Northampton to join us, World of Twist had three whole songs and a clear vision for the future. Rory would play sax, Jim would sing, I'd alternate between guitar and keyboards and, if necessary, we'd find ourselves a drummer.

Tony Ogden was still in south Manchester. With his old friend David Hardy he was co-director of a delivery and freight company called Alligator Express. They had a very flashy pickup truck and a good-looking receptionist but Tony was not convinced the venture would be a success: 'There's just something about our faces that makes people think "cowboys".' Ogden got wind that Jim and I were finally putting something together and wanted in. He loaded his drums into the pick-up and headed for Sheffield. With no motorway links between the two cities, the motorist had a choice of two main routes crossing the Pennines: the desolate Woodhead Pass or Thomas Telford's legendary hairpin-bending Snake Pass. Tony would make this journey once or twice a week for the next twelve months, often driving back along the Snake without his lights on for the thrill of it.

Alligator Express had folded and, with its assets stripped, Tony was forced to make the 80-mile round trip in his mum's old Renault 4.

We found a rehearsal space a couple of doors down from the Limit Club above Chubbies sandwich shop. We entered through the shop to access the rehearsal room and the Chubbies husband-and-wife owners let us help ourselves to refreshments and snacks if we left some cash on the counter. The pre-cooked fried eggs, bacon and sausages for the following day's customers were laid out in big metals trays and covered by tea towels. We assumed the Chubbies were au fait with health and safety regs. They were a nice couple and took an interest in our endeavours. They couldn't make our first gig, heat four of the 1984 *Star* rock and pop contest, but they came to the final and looked genuinely incensed when World of Twist didn't win.

We needed some outfits. We were heavily influenced here by the Letraset rubdown transfer catalogue in which the men all looked like they'd stepped off Madison Avenue in the early '60s – the sort of casual wear favoured by the Tracy brothers as they relax between international rescues. All John Smedley polos, quilted waistcoats and fitted slacks. These styles, we discovered, were heavily out of fashion and not even available in charity shops, so if these were the clothes we wanted we'd need to get them made.

As an extension of Jim's photographic labours, he got a job as driver/roadie and lighting man for a Sheffield club band called Geisha. I can't swear that things aren't the same now but it may be necessary to explain how the South Yorkshire working men's club scene operated in the early 1980s. Sheffield, as we know, is a great northern city born of a proudly industrial past. During our five-year stay, we would witness the final breath of that industrial past with the collapse of the coal industry, the closure of the steel mills and the resultant mass unemployment. But Sheffield would rise again by necessity to become a new modern city, a city of commerce, a city of design, a city of learning. For Sheffield's satellite towns – Rotherham, Doncaster, Barnsley, Worksop, Stocksbridge, Dinnington, Dronfield, Wombell, Mexborough, Hoyland – recovery would prove much more of a challenge. These were fiercely working-class districts built on industries in rapid decline. The working men's club, traditionally the Labour club, had always been the social hub of these proud communities and family members young and old would congregate here in their hundreds at the weekend. The tradition was alive and well in 1982. For the musicians and entertainers in the area, there was plenty of work if you were any good – and that was the key. After a hard week's graft, in return for their monthly dues, these people expected cheap beer and blue-ribbon entertainment. Amateurs would not be tolerated. The field, for bands in particular, was extremely competitive. All 'turns' (the words 'band' or 'group' were not recognised in the clubs) would be required to play a set of cover versions of well-known songs. Any act playing current hits would find themselves at an advantage as they'd attract a younger beer-drinking crowd. All acts would need some sort of visual gimmick. For the female artist an absence of clothes and an excess of hair and make-up would suffice but the male acts required a far stronger pitch – lasers, strobes, smoke machines and projections were basics; clothes, hair and make-up would all need attention. High camp was surprisingly popular and the most popular act of that era, Radiation, were a riot of lipstick and backcombed hair. It was said that they were making upwards of £700 a booking during their heyday, nearly five times the average weekly wage in the UK. Geisha's shtick was not very sophisticated by Radiation standards. They all dressed up in kimonos and judo kecks and wore lots of make-up, even the mustachioed lead singer. Where Geisha scored over their competitors was that they were all exceptional musicians and, with a line-up of just guitar, bass, drums and vocals, they skilfully emulated the songs of Haircut 100, ABC and even Soft Cell. Their very pretty bass player Andy Hobson (not *our* Andy Hobson) was destined for better things and wound up in the Pretenders a few years later. For the rest of the guys and for all their unquestionable talent, they were merely treading water until oblivion beckoned.

Nick had fallen behind several months with his rent payments. He could bluff himself out of the situation no longer and Steadman wanted him out. Nick didn't actually leave, instead sleeping on my floor, on Jim's floor, on whatever floor would have him. But Steadman caught him in the house one afternoon and escorted him off the premises. Nick had never come to grips with the idea of paying rent, not when there were far more important things to spend his money on – booze, fags, leather trousers. He'd spend the rest of his time in Sheffield couch surfing.

Nick's place at Everton Road was taken by Andy Robbins, a cousin to the comedy Robbins Kate and Ted and therefore distantly related to Paul McCartney. Andy, a skilful keyboard player, had come up from Southampton to replace the guitarist in Geisha, who were going in more of a Depeche Mode direction. Andy was a dead ringer for Heinz Burt, bass player with the Tornados and unrequited love object of Joe Meek's carnal desires. Apart from the synthesiser, Andy's twin passions were Ultravox and the music of John Barry, so it was inevitable we'd start chatting. He played us a recording of a number of instrumentals he'd written and it was clear he'd inherited the Robbins' 'variety' gene. We were particularly taken by one track called 'The Big Theme'. We asked him to join World of Twist in his spare time and, surprisingly, he agreed. Our new signing made an immediate impact. Tony's drumming had brought us on massively but Andy's chops enabled me to play more guitar and we could start getting more adventurous. 'The Big Theme' immediately went into the set and we attempted a very ham-fisted but quirky version of 'Thunderball', the James Bond theme.

15

53 Miles West of Venus

Everton Road wasn't what it used to be. There was a lot of arguing about Toast Toppers and toilet rolls and I moved back to our old rooms at Harcourt Road, sharing the flat with Disco John's affable younger brother Alan who, prior to my arrival, had nearly destroyed the building while cooking chips. I remained with Alan in the charred apartment for a couple of months until my number came up at the council. Jim and I had been on the council list for a flat since we'd arrived in the city and had been warned we were so low priority it could be more than five years before we got offered something, so our ship had really come in. Or maybe not.

Broomhall Flats backed onto the derelict Viners cutlery factory. Ten to one you'd have wound your spaghetti round a Viners fork if you'd dined in the UK in the 1970s. A once flourishing outfit and one of Sheffield's prestige companies producing steel-made goods, it had fallen victim, like most of Sheffield's steel companies, to cheap imported steel. The huge factory was empty and derelict. Every window had been put through and every clue to suggest this was once a thriving manufacturer, the largest cutlery factory in the UK, was gone. Viner's demise was mirrored in the deserted walkways and empty, boarded-up dwellings in Broomhall.

A brutalist, mid-rise 'streets in the sky' design built alongside Sheffield's Hanover Way, Broomhall Flats, home at one time to Stephen 'Judd' Turner and the scene of his fatal overdose three years earlier, was the inspiration for the ClockDVA song 'White Cell'. The name of our block, High Petre, basically translated as high rock. Built in 1967, this sprawling complex numbered 619 two- and three-bedroomed flats. By the time we moved in, fewer than fifty were still occupied. The lifts worked intermittently and a ride in one of them was invariably taken in the company of a freshly laid human turd. I was fortunate that the only time I got stuck in one for any period of time I had a bottle of sweet Thunderbird wine to calm myself down.

The flats were a wonderland for the young West Indian community, who would host regular 'blues' parties in the unoccupied flats. A steel security door could be jemmied off in a matter of seconds and a double flat was easily large enough for a party of fifty to a hundred. Every Saturday morning the lads would turn up on the landings building these monolithic PA systems constructed out of recycled 1-inch chipboard. After the parties they'd rip out the 15-inch sub-bass speakers and leave the wood on the landings. I loved lying in bed while the blues parties went on, even though sleep was out of the question because the whole flat would be shaking. The windows would visibly tremble and you could feel your bed moving across the floor. In the wake of the inner-city rioting that had shaken many major cities, the police had learnt not to initiate any confrontation and the blues parties were left to run their course. They usually wound down at around five in the morning.

From construction to demolition, Broomhall Flats lasted twenty years. A similar complex in Leeds built by the same company was demolished less than fifteen years after its construction.

I'd been seeing a student from Maidenhead called Janet. I first saw her playing synthesiser in a local band and thought she looked like Cindy Wilson of the B-52's. In the cold light of day, she looked nothing like Cindy Wilson, but she was very nice and we hung about for a few months. She was used to going out with rugby players so I was her first excursion into the world of skinny, pasty-faced types. Janet was doing a French degree and ominously spent her second year out in rugby-playing Clermont-Ferrand.

Jim was flying out to America to flash the lights and carry the bags for ClockDVA, who had a couple of New York shows. I'd never been to America. In fact, I'd never been anywhere apart from England, Scotland, Wales, the Isle of Man and a week in the Costa Brava. I wasn't complaining. I knew there were kids who'd never seen the countryside or the seaside. However, I was jealous beyond belief. New York, eh? The Big Apple. I'm approaching sixty now and still haven't been. Fuck it. I'd rather go to Llandudno, to be honest. However, the thought of spending a week on my own in Broomhall was a bit depressing. Things hadn't been so intense that I was falling apart without Janet, but it would have been nice to see her. I didn't know if we were still going out technically, but I decided to sell all my punk records to finance a trip to France. I hung on to a few gems, like the first issue of Buzzcocks' *Spiral Scratch* and Joy Division's *An Ideal for Living* (I'm still convinced I got the first commercially available copy of that, fresh out of the box at Virgin Records, Lever Street, Manchester, 1978). Judging by present-day vinyl prices, I seriously undervalued my collection when I sold it to the fledgling FON records, but the sale paid for a great trip.

I'd written to Janet a week or so before my departure to let her know I'd be coming but she never received the letter. So I turned up at her apartment rather unexpectedly. She was out when I arrived and with my very limited French I tried to explain to her flatmate why I was there. I finally found some photos and she let me in. When Janet got home, she was more than a little shocked to see me and not the tall chiselled fly-half she was perhaps expecting.

The plan was to visit Janet, spend a couple of days in Clermont, then meet up with Jim and Tony in Paris, still working for ClockDVA. Janet hadn't visited Paris before so wanted to come along. ClockDVA were playing at a famous French nightclub, Le Bains Douche (literally 'baths and showers'). Janet and I turned up at the venue after 7 p.m., having missed most of the fun. ClockDVA had arrived for their load-in and sound-check mid afternoon to be told that they wouldn't be able to get access to the venue until five o'clock because some filming was going on. They asked if they could at least see the venue and were told they could come in but would have to stand at the back. All became clear when, once inside the venue, through the haze they recognised the Rolling Stones, who were recording a video for their new single. Obediently, they all hung about at the back of the room until the director clocked them, all sunglasses, leather jackets and trousers, and demanded they take part. Check out the video for 'Undercover of the Night' and they're all there: ClockDVA, Nick Sanderson, Jim Fry and Tony Ogden. After the shoot, the band hung around on set and exchanged road stories with the Stones. It was possibly one of the coolest afternoons on record and I missed it by two hours.

ClockDVA were performing in support of their new LP, *Advantage*. Tony was doing the driving so Jim could concentrate on the lights and they were looking cool – a backdrop of venetian blinds and harsh white light, all very film noir. The band were sharp and very together. Paris was surely theirs for the taking. DVA hit the stage to the incessant throb of 'Beautiful Losers' and the young Parisians nodded approvingly. Nothing suggested what was to follow, but at one point Dean accidentally hit the sax player Paul with the head of his bass guitar and nobody was smiling. Singer Adi tore off stage a couple of times. It was a bit edgy, a bit dark but very DVA. The audience lapped it up. After the show the room cleared quickly as the punters retired to the various discos in the building. I was still standing in the auditorium when Adi walked out of the dressing room holding aloft his crumpled trumpet. 'Who's done this?' he screamed. There was a scuffle and DVA guitarist John emerged with blood pouring from his head. It was clear things were not tickety-boo in the DVA camp. John departed for the nearest hospital, I helped Jim and Tone pack up, then we retired to the upstairs reception bar. Everyone was conscious that something serious had happened but we all had a beer and the mood was a bit more relaxed. A couple of hours later John returned from the infirmary with his head stitched and bandaged and he was seething. He confronted Adi in the bar, giving him half an hour to leave the building. Adi didn't stick around to play Gary Cooper and left immediately. Tony, Jim and I were sitting around with our mouths open. We'd just witnessed the death of ClockDVA. The most iconic of all Sheffield's post-punk groups – and possibly the main reason we moved to Sheffield – had gone up in flames over a bent trumpet.

DVA sans Adi limped on for a few months before calling it a day. Nick returned to London and found himself playing drums in a reformed version of Jeffrey Lee Pierce's Gun Club. It may not have been his dream gig but they toured all over the place and he had some money in his pocket. Travel, beer, cigarettes and company were Nick's four primary requirements in those days.

16

There's a New Sensation

19 September 1984. Sheffield's Top Rank suite has been renamed the Roxy. Its owner is a Northumberland entrepreneur called Barry Noble. His catchphrase is 'Is that all right f'yuz?' The place comes to be known as Barry Noble's Roxy and it's here that World of Twist will make their live debut. City newspaper *The Star* is in the second year of sponsoring an annual rock and pop contest, giving local bands the chance to bag a cheque for £1,000 and a considerable amount of talent show-winning cache. World of Twist are appearing in heat #4 of this year's contest. We consider our involvement both witty and ironic.

World of Twist couldn't be more ready. Our fellow contestants this evening are Katowicz, the Actors, the Peter Cushings, Secret Noise and Fiction. We know we're pretty good, well drilled, well turned out and look nothing like the other five bands, but we aren't expecting to win and don't give a shit whether we do or not. The pop gods have other ideas, however, and we do win. According to an insider, we're comfortable victors. The judges, he tells us, were particularly impressed with our ectopic stage placings.

It's a little less than three weeks until the final and we're on the horns of a collective dilemma. Tony and I, in accordance with our unwritten manifesto, want to fuck the whole thing up by swapping instruments on the night. Rory and Andy think maybe we should go for it. Jim is on the fence. Of course the prize money will come in handy if we win and we might get something out of it – a write-up in *The Star*, perhaps, a support slot at the Leadmill, a summer season in Prestatyn?

Three weeks later we're back at the Roxy for the grand final. The straights have prevailed and we've decided to go for it. The venue is packed and there's a little nervousness in the camp. Even so, we are convinced of our genius. Everyone's told us we'll win so surely we will. But we don't win. World of Twist come third, behind Madness tribute band the Anthill Mob and an early incarnation of Mumford & Sons called Maison Rouge. It's embarrassing. Coming last would have been okay; winning would have been okay. Coming third is pretty much the worst-case scenario. *Very promising, but not quite ready*. We'd entered as a joke and the joke had backfired badly. It was important that we didn't play live again, didn't leave the house again until everyone had forgotten that shit.

World of Twist needed a demo so we booked ourselves into the Music Factory studios in Rotherham, infamous now as ground-zero for the short-lived Jive Bunny phenomenon/pandemic of 1989. We recorded two songs as a possible A- and B-side, 'Skidding in Love' and an instrumental called 'The Sausage'. This was hugely influenced by northern soul sell-outs, Wigan's Ovation, and featured samples of saucy socialite snapper Cecil Beaton, causing the song in some circles to be known as 'Cecil's Sausage'. Years later, 'The Sausage' would be released by Bob Stanley on his Caff Records imprint (CAFF 16) with new versions of 'Skidding in Love' and 'Space Rocket'. The 7-inch record came in a pink sleeve with a photo of Andy Robbins, bearing the legend, 'Engineered by Jive Bunny'. I can say now that this wasn't true.

We got a gig at Hero's nightclub in Manchester. We'd added a slide show and a few embellishments to the presentation. It was all pretty wacky and tacky but it was quite unique for the period. Some of our Manchester friends came along and seemed impressed by our progress. Martin Wright brought along an old school mate who, by coincidence, lived in Sheffield. Andy Hobson, a politics, philosophy and social economic history dropout from Bramhall, was a good five years younger than us. We found him very personable, very smiley, very our kind of guy. He was knocked out by the Hero's show and a recent performance at Sheffield University and offered his services if we ever needed a bass player. We later learned that Andy had had a premonition of joining World of Twist. He'd encountered us in a dream one night and was told, 'Our bass player's had a terrible accident!' It was literally his dream job.

The band had outgrown Chubbies and moved to new premises at Ponds Forge near Sheffield Station. Now an international swimming complex, then it was a warren of pre-war indus-trial units and home to ABC's Neutron HQ. Nick Phillips had replaced Andy Robbins, who'd elected to leave both Sheffield and World of Twist after the break-up of Geisha. Nick had brought with him a double console organ and a Leslie cabinet, giving us a new, big sound. We took a vote and decided to get Andy Hobson involved, losing our only fan in favour of a new member. We didn't need anyone to remind us that we now had exactly the same line-up as Roxy Music Mk I.

Tony O had taken the plunge and moved to Sheffield. He hadn't worked since the freight company had folded and he didn't sign on. We wondered what he was doing for money, but we never asked. Soon enough, he'd end up selling pop posters like the rest of us. He'd bought a Fostex Portastudio, which was *the* new must-have musician's gadget. It was basically a four-track mixer and tape recorder that allowed you to record up to four tracks on a chrome cassette tape. By bouncing (or re-recording) two or three of the tracks together down onto the fourth, you had a mini multi-channel studio. It was the way the Beatles used to record. You could only bounce the tracks down a finite number of times before the sound started to degrade but the concept was ingenious and enabled us to demo some quite ambitious new songs as soon as they were written. Tony's tech-nical nous added another paradoxical layer to this most com-plex of personalities. Tony was a blizzard of nervous energy. He didn't look as if he'd have the patience to boil a kettle, yet he had infinite tolerance with instruction manuals and operating protocol that the likes of Jim and I were never able to endure.

However, Tony's biggest surprise was still up his sleeve. On one of the few occasions the secretive Ogden invited us round to his flat, he played us some tracks he'd been working on alone. The standout tune was 'Icerink', on which he'd played everything: drums, bass, guitar, keyboards and vocals. It was terrific, very much in the style of World of Twist but streets ahead of anything we'd attempted so far. It was the first indication that Twist might be destined for greatness. That evening there was an unspoken power shift in the band.

It was over a year since I'd last DJ'd in Sheffield. Disco John had completed his degree and taken back the reins at Penny's, but we rarely went there these days. The Leadmill was where the action was now and John had a night there, too. He also DJ'd at the Hacienda once a week, Factory Records' new space-age nightspot in Manchester. We loved clubbing and we loved dancing, but there wasn't really anywhere playing the music we loved – '60s pop, psychedelia, northern soul, the odd Motown track, Bowie, Roxy, a splash of glam, a dash of '70s soul. Everywhere we went it was all Grandmaster Flash, Was Not Was and the Tom Tom Club. They were okay for a toe tap, but you couldn't slide around the floor easily to that stuff. The only solution was to start our own night.

Someone tipped us off about Mona Lisa's, a pocket nightclub attached to the back of Maximillions on Charter Row. The place was owned by Nigerian nightclub supremo Max Omare. Max, whose surname meant 'what God says', drove a Rolls-Royce, liked white suits with big lapels and had a penchant for a bit of chrome and smoked glass. With a lavish £250,000 refit, he had just launched Maximillions from the ashes of his former club Genevieve's. Thankfully, he had not spent a penny on Mona Lisa's and its original '70s decor remained crudely intact. You entered up some stairs past a wall of pink and orange Perspex panels overprinted with topless models with Afro haircuts. Once inside, this 'exotic' theme was repeated throughout the club, the centrepiece of which was a small sunken circular dance floor.

We couldn't believe our eyes when we first saw it – it was perfect. Max seemed a bit ashamed of the titty pics and offered to take them down but we told him we'd find another venue if he did. We pinched an exploding arrow logo from the cover of a Marshall McLuhan book and had it printed over a roll of white satin that I'd pilfered from ACME clothing but had never found any use for. We draped this around the dance floor and bought a liquid wheel projector to complete the Mojo club look. We called the night the Wigwam and got some Jackson Pollock-style posters printed bearing the legend 'Music, Dancing, Flashing Lights'. On the opening night, to our utter delight, we discovered the female bar staff were forced to wear ridiculous orange babydoll outfits that they must have been air-blasted into. Tony stepped up to the plate to be our meet-and-greet guy. All those crap London clubs, like Le Beat Route, had one in an effort to create an exclusive Steve Rubell/Studio 54 sort of vibe. Obviously in Sheffield on a Saturday night, this was totally unnecessary, but Tony, dressed to the nines and tens, regarded it as his duty to usher in the clientele. On a typical night, he'd be wearing his Tom Jones suit, a blue velvet waistcoat with bow tie and cummerbund and bright red lipstick. Grinning manically and speeding off his head, Tony would pretty much shout the punters in. It was a curious approach to the art of hospitality, but surprisingly effective. The Wigwam took off quickly and before long we were getting a decent wage from the night.

The Sheffield nightclub scene of that time was fairly gangsterish and, if your club was a success, a rival club was likely to send some droogs down to try to ruin it by picking fights and nicking handbags. That was how the Wigwam eventually went downhill. I remember folding up the satin screen one evening to find it was covered in blood from a bottle fight a few hours earlier. Eventually, Jim and I couldn't face the night unless we were totally anaesthetised. The vodka run every Saturday became an essential component of running the club. At its height the Wigwam was a superb night out and the stuff of legend but, perhaps mindful that our South Yorkshire sojourn was coming to an end, we abandoned our Saturday spot late in 1985 to a new club called the Jive Turkey, an up-to-the-minute hipster's paradise run by future Sheffield hitmakers Funky Worm.

Notwithstanding the comparative riches the Wigwam generated, none of us had been particularly flush since we'd been in Sheffield. Jim, Tony and I had all drifted into the black economy. Our primary income up to the point we left the city came from the sale of unlicensed pop posters. Snappy Pop Pics was run by two former students Kane and Charlie, who had made a modest killing buying unposted billposters and selling them at universities and colleges. For a young, shy, student, an A0 sized poster of Whitesnake's *Slide It In* or the Undertones' *All Wrapped Up* displayed a certain independence and measured sexuality and would easily cover up two-thirds of your bare student accommodation wall. As Jim and Tony could both drive, they got more work than I did but I was enlisted if they needed a poster-seller's mate, essential at the fresher's week bazaars. I paired up with former Everton Road housemate David Bloom for a number of these, the two puniest members of the squad in one sizzling black-market poster-selling organism.

In Liverpool one morning, after we'd set up our wares in the student union, we encountered the feared Manchester poster mafia, who encouraged us to pack up and leave.

'Lads, there's been a change of plan. You can't sell posters here today.'

I realised instantly that this was a polite but firm invitation to fuck off, but, even so, Dave bravely (or naively) attempted to argue our corner.

'We've driven here from Sheffield. We've bought a sales permit from the office so we're authorised to trade here today.'

'No, you don't understand, mate. You won't be selling any posters here today so it's time to leave.'

We left the Manchester boys to exploit our very lucrative pitch and buzzed off back to Sheffield.

'We need more muscle,' we told the owners.

We were full of adrenaline and misplaced bravado, but secretly pleased not to have taken a kicking over a carload of bootleg Cocteau Twins posters.

17

The Titan of Cirencester

A group of us were in a pub discussing our ideal band, visually-speaking, made up of non-rock music personalities. Suggested notables were the Investiture-period Prince of Wales, possibly on rhythm guitar. Actor Derren Nesbitt, as he appears in *Victim*, would play lead. On bass guitar, *Sparrows Can't Sing*-era Murray Melvin (who actually looks a bit like Certain Ratio bassist Jez Kerr). The vocalist had to be fleet-footed interceptor pilot, Mr Triple Threat himself, the one and only Peter Gordeno, and, if you don't believe me, check out his super-sexy Spanish TV performance of 'Fever' on YouTube: Anton Chigurh meets Pan's People – it will leave you weak at the knees. The drummer was a tough one, until someone suggested David Hemery, Britain's Olympic gold-winning hurdler of 1968, twice winner of TV's *Superstars*, 6 foot 2 of sinew and muscle and possessor of the greatest ever nose in the history of professional sport.

So began a brief but intense fascination with David Hemery. The discussion prompted Tony and me to join a gym on West Street. For 1985 we would shape up, we decided. For Tony, who was a muscly guy, it was all about body sculpture and toning. For me it was about introducing some muscle where hitherto there'd been none. We both bought vintage-style tracksuits, as close to the kind of thing Hemery would have worn in '68 as possible, and we got down to business. Unexpectedly, endorphins were unleashed into our respective systems and we kept at it for longer than a few weeks.

Continuing what could only be described as a 'health kick', once a week we started playing football in the recreation blocks beside the flats. I stopped taking the lift and ran up and down the stairs several times a day. It was the fittest I'd been since I was ten. Paul Bower of Sheffield's first proper punk band 2.3 offered to bring a team down to play us, so we set up a fixture for the following week. Annoyingly, Paul's team didn't show up – they were punks, after all – so after a thirty-minute wait we gave in to some local kids who were desperate for a game. We'd been playing for about ten minutes and the local kids were running rings around us, when I challenged for a fifty-fifty ball with a lad who looked about twelve. He missed the ball and scored a direct hit on my left knee. I hobbled around for a minute. Under the tracksuit, my kneecap didn't seem to be where it should have been – it had been displaced by 180 degrees to the back of my leg. I managed to pull it back to the front and sit down on the asphalt. There was no pain but my leg seemed to have gone into shock, flapping about like a landed kipper. After a minute, I was helped to my feet. I tried to apply some weight to the left leg and immediately my kneecap disappeared around the back again.

The game was stopped and someone called an ambulance. A crowd had formed around me. My assailant, a little nonplussed but not overly concerned by what he'd done, caught my eye and shrugged his shoulders. To be honest it didn't feel as if he'd kicked me that hard – he must have hit the sweet spot.

At Sheffield General, they sorted me out with a full-on *Terry and June* plaster cast, crutches and painkillers. Back at home, Jim kindly set my bed up in the lounge so I didn't need to get upstairs. Despite my recent fitness blitz, I realised I was no Superman. The pain was unremitting. At first it was a steady throb, then a more focused stabbing. I couldn't talk and everyone started to look uncomfortable. Tony offered to go up to the hospital to get some stronger medicine. He came back with some morphine that clearly wasn't on the NHS. The morphine didn't work and I was starting to hallucinate with the pain.

Twelve hours later I was back at Sheffield General, where a technician ripped off the cast. He tutted and shook his head. The night staff who'd applied the pot had done so before allowing the knee to fully swell up. Apparently there could have been serious, possibly fatal complications had he not interceded. A nurse drained several pints of fluid from my melon-sized knee and they wrapped it up again in a rigid padded bandage. The relief was unbelievable.

The dislocation was a bloody nuisance. The band was on an enforced hiatus, the gym membership had gone up in smoke and the pain was still excruciating. I needed to keep moving to stop myself from getting constipated but getting around Broomhall Flats on crutches was a nightmare. The landings were always wet, the lifts rarely worked. Even when they did it wasn't worth chancing it, as they were likely to break down between floors. My leg recovered but the knee, although front-facing at least, never really did and the injury put paid to any ambitions I held of becoming a real northern soul dancer.

The council would begin the process of demolishing Broomhall Flats over the next few months. It was only a matter of time. The place was now scarily derelict. There were twenty to thirty 'white cells' still occupied – all single men, 'lost of sense and of will'. The housing department advised us that they had a new flat available on Campo Lane, S1. Ironically, the block of refurbished council tenements in the city centre was built in 1903 and is still standing to this day. Thus Jim and I entered the final phase of our Sheffield experiment. If Julian Cope's *World Shut Your Mouth* LP is the record I associated most with High Petre, for Campo Lane's it is Sigue Sigue Sputnik's *Love Missile F1-11*, which Jim had on a never-ending loop. Two hundred yards from the headquarters of the NUM, sixteen months earlier this would have been the most super-charged area of the city. The miners' strike had ended six months before and now, despite its close proximity to the city centre, the area felt dead and forgotten.

Nick visited Sheffield with the Gun Club, who were playing at the Leadmill. It was great to see him again. After the show everyone piled round to our flat. Jeffrey Lee Pierce, the Gun Club's head honcho, was quite rock-starry and we weren't. He wanted to hold court but found it difficult with Tony and Jim in the room. It was apparent he wasn't used to the shouting. We were all ultra-pissed and Jeffrey didn't find the transatlantic banter divide easy to cope with. There was a scene of sorts and Jeffrey locked himself in the bathroom. After hammering on the door, Tony Ogden, international negotiator and diplomat, was let in and they tried to bash out a peace settlement. Ten minutes later Tony emerged bowed and broken: 'Guys, I've got rock star problems in the bathroom.' It always struck me as a good first scene of a play.

Our friend Stuart Boreman and business partner Charlie were keen to finance a World of Twist single. They booked us into the Slaughterhouse in Driffield, the studio where the Happy Mondays recorded *Bummed*, long since burnt to the ground. We recorded three tracks: 'Icerink', 'North South East & West' and an updated slower version of 'Space Rocket'. Stuart arranged a show for us in Bridlington, his home town. It turned out to be World of Twist Mk I's final bow. We were as good as we'd ever get – tourniquet tight and impossibly well presented. Andy Hobson had 'Strakered' his hair for the event. (In tribute to Commander Ed Straker from the TV series *UFO*, Andy occasionally dyed his hair silver or at least blond and combed it flat and forward. It was a winner every time.) After the show Stuart introduced us to Club 61 above the Winter Gardens, which was quite possibly the greatest nightclub in the history of the British Isles. It was thoroughly debauched in the most pleasant way possible. The Twisted Wheel, Wigan Casino, Pips, the Hacienda, Cream, Shoom, Fabric, the Ministry of Sound, Turnmills, Stringfellows, the

Talk of the Town: compared to Club 61, sadly long gone, these were merely posing as nightclubs. As a prelude to the release of our new single, Stuart printed some great posters of the band, with a special photograph of me and the legend: 'The north's number-one vocal group'. A showcase gig was set up at Penny's and Stuart and Charlie planned to release an EP shortly after. For some reason, lost in the mists of time, when the gig came round Tony and I didn't want to do it. It wasn't the first gig we'd pulled and it was starting to piss everyone off. Jim especially.

On 1 February, World of Twist had a gig at Manchester Polytechnic. February 1986 was one of the coldest months on record. Heavy snow had been forecast and we were wondering if it was sensible to be doing the gig. We could struggle to get there or back. Jim drove us over in a hired van; keyboard player Nick and our new roadie Dan were going by car. We got to the venue late afternoon and unloaded but by six Nick and Dan still hadn't shown up. Eventually, the venue got a phone call to let us know they'd been in a crash. A car full of underage joyriders had broadsided them seconds after they'd set off and both were in Sheffield General suffering whiplash. The predicted snow arrived, layering their injury with further insult. The show most likely wouldn't have gone ahead anyway because of the weather and we were stranded across the Pennines. We wound up sleeping in the van on a desolate Hattersley station forecourt, deep in Moors Murders country. The following morning, Jim attempted to get us back across the Woodhead Pass. It was a scary crossing with the snow still coming down and the van sliding all over the place.

The aborted Manchester gig was World of Twist Mk I's final call to action. Weeks later, we knocked it on the head and plotted a course away from Sheffield. Tony was the first to go. Sheffield had never really done it for him and since Nick had left the fun appeared to have been drained out of the place. Tony missed the madness of south Manchester, or rather his mad friends in south Manchester.

Since moving to Ponds Forge there had been a power shift in the band. Tony and I spent a lot of time rehearsing on our own. It was usually me at the keyboards, Tony on drums, but on occasion he also played guitar. He was miles better than me.

Jim was starting to feel marginalised and irritated by our lack of activity. We'd been offered gigs but Tony and I had a capricious knack for pulling them. A few months earlier, an invitation to play a graduation ball at Sheffield's Cutlers' Hall had been a huge humiliation for us. We'd had our reservations about the booking before arriving and playing to an indifferent audience of pissed-up, posh teenagers in ball gowns and tuxes. We might have swung it in front of a captive audience, but instead of putting us on the main hall stage, where they'd installed a swing orchestra, they stuck us in one of the ante-rooms on the way to and from the bathrooms. It was like playing on a float at the back of the Lord Mayor's parade. Tony became particularly cautious after this night and would up sticks at the slightest suggestion things weren't right.

Nick had asked Jim if he'd be interested in fronting a band he was getting together with Soft Cell's Dave Ball. The three met up in a pub in Notting Hill and ran through the plans for Big White Dwarf, a sleazier version of DAF, who would eventually record as the slightly more acceptable English Boy on the Love Ranch. While they're there, they notice Johnny Rotten sitting at the next table. The glamour is too much to bear . . .

I actually left Sheffield three months before Jim did. The poster work had dried up and I was absolutely brassic. Tony and Andy were already back in Manchester and there was no point in me staying. Sheffield? It had been an interesting experiment – I definitely didn't regret moving there – but I'd achieved very little in five years. Regrets? As John Betjeman said shortly before he died, I wish I'd had more sex.

18

Take Me Back to Manchester When It's Raining

We arrived back in Manchester to find the city in self-congratu-
latory mode. Factory Records were marking the tenth anniversary of the Sex Pistols' first gig in the city with a week of concerts,
exhibitions and music seminars – all very Factory – climaxing
in a big jamboree at the newly opened GMEX centre. This was
formerly Manchester's Central Station, a beacon of nineteenth-
century railway architecture and the gateway to the world's first
industrialised city. In reality, Manchester's music scene was
in a bit of a lull and the emphasis of this gala event was very
much on glories past, with only the Smiths representing any
sort of future. Still, in April 1986 the city instantly and effortlessly felt more cultured than Sheffield, although there was no
suggestion that anything exciting was just around the corner, or

even whistling down the river. The preponderant musical trend was 'jangly' guitar bands, floppy of fringe and fey of feature. Manchester had some very good ones (the Smiths, the Bodines) and lots of bad ones.

There was no Castlefield, Northern Quarter or tram network. Canal Street was not the LGBTQ+ Mecca it is today and the few clandestine clubs and bars were subject to regular raids and police harassment. The city was still under the law-enforcing stewardship of James Anderton, who later that year would air his famous comment about AIDS sufferers 'swirling in a human cesspit of their own making'. Manchester's biggest musical export during this period was Simply Red. In truth, we hadn't moved back to a very happening city.

Tony and I were both back with our mums, Tony in Cheadle, me in Marple, a picture-postcard town with a canal and sixteen locks just inside the Greater Manchester boundary. The decision to keep World of Twist going wasn't immediate and the first priority for me was finding work. The world of counterfeit pop posters had been very good to me in Sheffield but here in Stockport I was back on the starting block. Twenty-four years old with an extremely poor employment record, no qualifications and no contacts, my only option was one of those government-funded work initiatives. The Youth Opportunities Programme had been launched on the premise that it would offer the jobless individual meaningful short-term work as a route to full-time employment. But the wages were crap: it was basically working for your dole money.

The Community Programme offered slightly more interesting jobs with better pay but again on fairly short contracts. A friend of mine had recently completed a four-month placement repairing dry-stone walls in the Goyt Valley for £90 a week. Apparently the work was piss-easy, his co-workers were 90 per cent ex-students, so not a grafter among them, and, at even the slightest suggestion of rain, the supervisor would order everyone back to the minibus for tea and pontoon. Working in the Peak District with a better than 60 per cent chance of rainfall, the job obviously didn't involve much hard labour. A similar position caught my eye in Marple Job Centre. A team was required in New Mills to renovate the Torrs walkway on the side of the River Sett. New Mills was a town in north Derbyshire, home of Swizzels Matlow, a confectionary firm responsible for possibly two-thirds of the nation's pre-teen cavities in the 1970s. The job was for six weeks at £80 for what amounted to a four-day week with a half-day on Fridays. I signed up on the spot. It was only 4 miles up the road from my mum's place in Marple. An easy cycle and not a pub in sight, so I wouldn't end up pissing all my wages away during those inevitable wet lunchtimes and late afternoons. As luck wouldn't have it, the spring of '86 proved to be glorious and rain didn't stop play once, so we were grafting for most of the six weeks on site. I say 'we', but in fact there was a strict hierarchy established from the word go, which decreed that anyone under twenty-five, especially those with funny haircuts, would be up and down the ramp fetching bags of cement or shunting the stuff down to the 'hole', while the more experienced members of the team enjoyed a more relaxed pace, leaning on their shovels and supervising 'the mix'. The dry-stone wall I'd been dreaming of was actually a massive sinkhole, where most of the embankment had fallen into the river 50 feet below. There was no earthly way we were going to fill it in six weeks, but that didn't seem to worry the foreman or site manager, who turned up for a few minutes every week to shout encouragement. And there wasn't a student among us. I was probably the closest we got with my smooth hands and weird taste in music.

The next entry on my CV was in the graphics and publicity department of Stockport Social Services. My finest piece was a poster for the Kennedy Swinton Brass Band. During this time, I got reacquainted with the 78 Record Exchange on Underbank. Run by the two most miserable sods ever to enter retail, I somehow found out they sold 7-inch singles, even though they never had any displayed in the shop. They had thousands of them, most in mint condition in the original record company paper sleeves and still at 1974 prices. You had to leave a list with them and they'd sort out the ones they had and have them waiting for you when you next popped by. Since most of the stuff I was looking for was late-'60s bubblegum pop and early-'70s pop obscurities, the kind of stuff nobody was interested in around them, the hit rate from every list was about 75 per cent. I was spending most of my wages there. I'd buy maybe twenty-five singles each week. It wasn't a fiercely contested field but I'd say I had one of the most comprehensive late-'60s–early-'70s junk-shop pop collections in Manchester.

The next step was to get a flat in town. I'd been living a semi-rural existence out in Marple at my mum's since arriving back from Sheffield and could only afford to go into Manchester at weekends, so a new, well-appointed bachelor pad was essential. I found something suitable on Everett Road in fashionable

Withington, a couple of miles out of the city centre. The house stood opposite the birthplace of the great British actor Robert Donat, aka Richard Hannay, Charles 'Mr Chips' Chipping and Sir Robert Morton KC. His 1948 film *The Winslow Boy* vies with Mike Leigh's *Naked* and Michael Bentine's *The Sandwich Man* as my most watched film. A colossal actor who's moved me to tears on many occasions.

Tony Ogden had started writing again. He played us a few tracks and they sounded ace – far better than the stuff he'd been doing in Sheffield. Once again, Tony played everything and we were left wondering why he needed anyone else, but he was ultra-keen on getting World of Twist going again and over the next few months the band shifted personality. Now the direction was – to us, at least – simple. As our default groove we would take the beat from Mr Bloe's 'Groovin' with Mr Bloe'. The music would steal elements from northern soul and late '60s sunshine pop (both UK and US), melded with the Stooges, MC5 and *Space Ritual*-era Hawkwind. The lyrics would be frivolous, contradictory and stupid.

My glass knee aside, dancing was our favourite pastime and if the spirit of Twist was forged anywhere it was on the dance floor. Andy, Tony and I all liked the same stuff and our dancing was of similar style. Most of our moves originated from the cult horror film *The Creeping Terror*, widely considered one of the worst films of all time. Our go-to DJ was Dave Booth who played a cooking mix of northern, psychedelic, rockabilly and '60s pop. Be it at Berlin (formerly George Best's Slack Alice's nightclub), Isadoras or The Playpen, Dave played the best music in Manchester without question. The Hacienda became the place of legend but the music by and large was rubbish. If you wanted the sounds you simply had to follow Dave Booth.

We needed a singer. The truth is I'd always wanted to be the frontman. I looked the part: I was the tallest of the three of us; I had the most hair; I liked dressing up; I could move a bit and I was quite comfortable wearing a dab of make-up from time to time. Most importantly, I didn't mind looking a complete cunt for the sake of art. And if I was the singer I'd definitely go for it – there'd be none of this bent-knee bobbing and head-nodding nonsense favoured by some of the leading frontmen of the day. I'd give them the full, high-kicking flamenco floorshow, a touch of Jagger, a splash of Pop, a hint of Mercury, a slither of Gabriel and a dash of Tyner. My frontman would be easy and a little seedy, his clothes would be fitted and a little flared, a bit John Curry, a bit Donnie Burns.*

So in my head I was the singer before I got the job. The only caveat was the voice. My voice is awful; not flat or tuneless – in fact my pitch was much better than Tony Ogden's – but jarringly

---

* Around this time, I became semi-obsessed with ballroom dancer Donnie Burns, who, with his partner Gaynor Fairweather, would go on to become a fourteen-times world Latin dance champion. Although I had nowhere near the grace of this super-sleek Lanark, his jive in particular was the dance I aspired to. When the acid-house revolution broke a year or so later, I found my moves were a bit redundant in popular clubland, so I drifted further into the northern scene where such distasteful steps, though not strictly northern soul, were tolerated. I'm delighted to report that Donnie has grown old thoroughly disgracefully and still looks as flamboyant and camp as he did in his heyday. Donnie Burns, I salute you.

dull. I knew this when Tony and Andy suggested I take over the vocals.

'Look fellas, I'll give it a go but if you think for one moment it's sounding crap, please tell me straight away.'

Tony and I had started writing together round at his mum's place and we rehearsed once a week in Chorlton. I practised religiously. We tried some very ambitious northern soul covers: Tony Clarke's 'Landslide', Lou Pride's 'I'm Com'un Home In The Morn'un'. Tony had written his first ace of our second phase, 'She's Out of My Life', a fuzz-emblazoned slice of bubblegum magic that we never used for some reason. I'd written what I considered my finest tune to date, the never-to-be-heard 'You Never Get Used To Love' (our titles were deliberately corny before you ask). In the tradition of MacAuley & MacLeod, Cook & Greenaway, Howard & Blaikley etc., Tony and I discussed forming a songwriting partnership under the name of Lovecraft & Love. Tony would be front of house as the mystical romantic Tony Lovecraft, while I'd be the enigmatic Jason Love. The idea was borrowed from a proposed Ogden business venture, Wedding Dreams, a video production company fronted by the unctuous Anthony Love, always immaculately dressed in a white suit with carnation and sporting a Vandyke beard: 'Your dream wedding captured forever.'

I was starting to build some confidence as the singer. I had this creepy falsetto, which Tony seemed to like, while my baritone croon was not a million miles away – so I thought – from *Fried*-era Julian Cope. Things were really starting to fall into place when Tony and Andy pulled the plug one night after rehearsal.

'Err Gord, we've been thinking . . .' Being told you can't sing, particularly after you've spent two months really going for it, is humiliating. It's like being told you smell, except there's absolutely nothing you can do about it. I'd been the singer for about six weeks but that evening I was 'promoted' to guitar. Tony became Tony O, and World of Twist Mk II was born. The surprise was it ever took that long to happen. From that moment, Tony took control of everything. He certainly had more time on his hands than Andy or me but his drive was formidable. He'd been left a fair amount of cash in his dad's will and he splashed out on a home studio, which ensured we'd get to the next level in some style. Getting his old mate Dave Hardy in to manage us was an obvious move. Dave (the other half of Wedding Dreams and co-director of Alligator Express) was a mainstay of Tony's old Cheadle Hulme gang, the Mad Fuckers. A supreme blagger, affable, cheeky and tireless, Dave would talk to anyone and was friends with everyone. And he loved the band. Manchester's fabled band managers were some of the biggest twats on the planet so we were extremely fortunate to have Hardy on board. A lovely, lovely, lovely man.

Back in Cheadle Hulme, Tony had got to grips with the new rig very quickly. Again, it always struck me as a paradox that someone with a boredom threshold as low as Tony's could become so engrossed in learning to operate such a complex system. Marijuana certainly aided the process but I had to take my neophyte hat off to the lad as it took me weeks to catch up with him. But we'd now entered the futuristic binary world of midi sequencing with its unique language and its capacity to create

Left: Tony Ogden
(drums) with the Void,
Bramhall, 1977.

Right: Blackout's final
gig, Stockport, 1979.
The printer does us
no favours.

HAZEL GROVE YOUTH CLUB
NEW WAVE NITE

EVERY WEDNESDAY at 7 p.m.
Come early   Members 30p, Visitors 60p

February 7th
BLACK OUT   THE ACCELERATORS

February 14th
JOHN BISSELL with GROW UP
OüTTA TUNEZ

February 21st
THE SYSTEM   VIBRANT THIGH
plus F.T. INDEX

February 28th
STUPID STEPHEN   FAST CARS

Printed by F. Turner and Son, Stockport Road, Marple

The Star
Hofmeister
ROCK & POP
CONTEST • 1984
GALA FINAL

at
THE TOP RANK SUITE, SHEFFIELD
WEDNESDAY, OCTOBER 10.
7 p.m. until late.

Admission £1 which includes
a souvenir programme.

FINALISTS
★ WORLD OF TWIST   ★ ANTHILL MOB
★ THE NIGHT SHIFT   ★ MAISON ROUGE
★ DEPTH IN METRES   ★ CAIRO

Left: World of Twist
go for gold, Sheffield,
1984.

Left: World of Twist Mk II first photoshoot, relaxing at Upper Chorlton Road, Manchester, 1989.

ISADORA'S
69 HANGING DITCH · MANCHESTER

Experience the New sound

WORLD OF TWIST

In concert

Friday
7th July

£2·00

£1·50
before 11pm

"They came in my mind"

9 - 2·00am · FEATURING ANDREW BERRY'S MUSIC

THE DOME DISCO

Right: Flyer for World of Twist Mk II first show (actually 15 February 1990).

WORLD OF TWIST

WORLD OF TWIST

Demonstration cassette

Above: World of Twist sign to Circa, July 1990. Caroline Elleray and Dave Hardy (left and centre) with Ray Cooper (far right).

'The Leader', Dave Hardy, Withington, 1990.

Team Twist, Leeds, 1990. Left to right: GK, Mark Coyle, Viv Dixon, Jim Fry, Dave Hardy, Mike Hardy, Pete Smith, Julia, Tony, Adge, Quent, Martin Moscrop. Plus Angela (hidden) and Stuart Boreman (photographer).

Martin Hannett and Liam Mullen, Strawberry Studios, Stockport, October 1990.

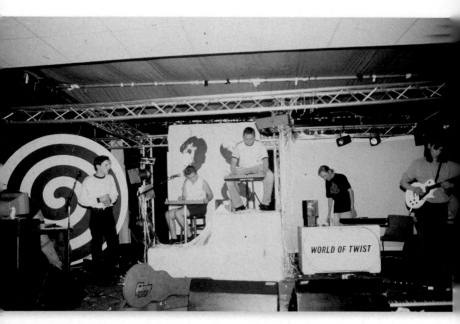

World of Twist get ready to rock, International, Manchester, August 1990.

Andy, Tony and Julia, the Ritz, Manchester, 23 December 1990.

Right: WoT a drag!
Recording 'Sons of
the Stage', Brighton,
January 1991.

Left: Glad to be sat in
a giant papier-mâché
oyster shell. 'Sons
of the Stage' video
shoot, February 1991.

MC Shells.

Men of Twist, Withington, 1990.

Captain Troy and Bathsheba hit the sales. Tony and Julia, Tunbridge Wells, 1991.

Early Victorian commotion in a record shop. Angela, Adge and Tony, Tunbridge Wells, 1991.

Constable Sanderson gets to grips with the new technology, Tunbridge Wells, 1991.

Adge, Wandsworth, 1991.

Julia, Tony,
Adge, Angela,
Wandsworth, 1991.

Tony O, 'Man of the
Month', *New Woman*,
1992.

Above: Tony Ogden calls time. World of Twist's final show, London, 1992.

Right: Jim Fry and Dave Hardy lead the parade. Jeremy Deller, *Procession*, Manchester, July 2009.

soundscapes we couldn't have dreamed of in Sheffield. Gone was the need to actually learn to play. With a click of the mouse, our most ham-fisted keyboard performances would correct itself. We could create impossible rhythm patterns, bass lines and arpeggios. Pianos now sounded like pianos, strings like strings. Okay, the thing couldn't write a tune, but we had the means to produce the kind of orchestration found on a Keith Mansfield Love Affair 45. We could speed up, speed down, transpose, transition and it dawned on us early on that if we could find a way of safely transporting the equipment we could turn our live performances into a virtual mime and concentrate on the dance routines.

The job at Stockport had come to an end and I'd joined the growing ranks of casual shop staff at Affleck's Palace, a clothes market just off Piccadilly Gardens in the centre of Manchester. This was where most of Manchester's young alternative and student population got kitted out. The student outfitting was particularly lucrative and very simple. The main requirements, regardless of sex, were: 1 x suede jacket, 1 x pair of Levi 501 jeans (a little ragged at the knees), 1 x pair of 'greasy' Gibson Doc Marten shoes in black or brown, but mostly black. Josie Wright our old friend from Bramhall, managed Wayne Hemingway's Red or Dead stores on the first and second floors and all the Doc Martens came from there so they were super busy. Any day of the week you'd find one or two of our gang on the shop floor. Tony even worked Saturdays at one point, which was unheard of. Andy worked on the second floor in an antique clothing store, whose biggest line was dinner jackets for student balls.

Josie needed to leave her flat in Didsbury and, since she'd had to put up with most of us kipping on her floor every weekend, she looked for somewhere we could all live. We moved into a house on Upper Chorlton Road on the edge of Whalley Range and Chortlon-cum-Hardy. The house was opposite the Army Reserve Centre, where at weekends enthusiastic cadets would take turns to patrol the gates with their wooden guns. Andy Hobson lived on the ground floor with his massive Belinda Carlisle poster; Josie, her brother Martin and I were upstairs. Spencer Birtwistle, drummer in Martin's band Laugh, managed to turn a 6-foot-square cupboard into a bedroom and was soon living there with his new girlfriend Stella. The move to Manchester had felt quite disjointed up to this point but the fun was about to start.

19
Experience the New Sound

We started clubbing fairly regularly and we'd catch the occasional band. I remember we were all very taken by a pre-Tom Hingley version of Oldham's Inspiral Carpets when we saw them at the International and, when Andy heard they were looking for a bass player, he thought he'd give it a punt. World of Twist hadn't really got going again and if he got the gig he'd be joining a really exciting 'working' band, so it was hard to begrudge him the opportunity. Even back then, the Inspirals, all basin haircuts and loose-fitting duds, were sporting the new 'Manchester' look, so what possessed Andy to go to his audition dressed like a member of the Bullingdon Club is a mystery. Andy was a great bassist and the Inspirals' setlist certainly wouldn't have presented him with any problems. Surely he had only to plug in his Mustang, flash his winning smile and the gig would be his. However, in addition to his ridiculous outfit, he'd taken it upon himself to jazz up the Inspirals' bass lines, adding unnecessary flourishes that were very World of Twist but didn't impress the Carpets one jot. So we got our man back and the Inspirals got theirs. In truth, it would be difficult to picture the band without Tupac-lookalike Martyn 'Bungle' Walsh.

1987 was the year I went northern-soul bonkers. While the rest of the crew were out in central Manchester at the Hacienda, the Boardwalk or one of Dave Booth's nights, Saturday evenings for me were spent at old village halls and ballrooms in Lancashire and Yorkshire – Tony's Empress Ballroom in Blackburn, the Empress Rooms in Mexborough (both possibly named after Queen Victoria, the newly crowned 'Empress of India'), Hyde Botanical Club, Hyde Town Hall, Failsworth Cycling Club. I always went on my own as the others would have been bored shitless. With my talcum powder and the half-bottle of vodka I'd smuggled in, I'd spend the whole night on the dance floor before being ejected onto the streets of some grim northern backwater at 7 a.m. the following day. I loved it. I loved the self-righteous, slightly miserable feeling arriving back in Piccadilly Gardens at nine o'clock on a Sunday morning to catch the bus back to Chortlon. It felt like I'd worked hard for my Saturday night out. World of Twist had always been attracted by the trashier end of northern – the plastic soul of Wigan's Ovation, the Spark label, the Casino Classics compilations (although they both contained bona fide '60s northern soul gems). We'd always tried to shoehorn northern riffs and hooks into the songs. We'd attempted extremely ham-fisted versions of Steve Karmen's 'Breakaway', the aforementioned 'Landslide' and our third single 'Sweets' began as an attempt to recreate a Freda Payne B-side. We covered the Jerms' 'I'm A Teardrop' for a Peel session, not because it sounded much like a northern soul record (it didn't) but because it sounded like a Tony Ogden lyric.

One Saturday night, I was stuck on my own in the house. Andy and Martin had gone to the Hacienda but I was a bit skint and settled for *Match of the Day* and a few cans, followed by an old black and white film on Channel 4. At around two-thirty, the boys burst in and they were both beaming. We hadn't been to the Hacienda for a while – we were usually in search of the music and the Hacienda didn't really play our kind of stuff – but apparently there had been a revolution on the dance floor.

'Gord, you've got to go, it's fucking hilarious. All these lads with bowl haircuts and baggy clothes smiling and doing these stupid dances . . . it's brilliant!'

What they didn't appreciate at the time was that they'd just witnessed the birth of a cultural shift and that the smiles and dances were all chemically induced. Ecstasy: we hadn't heard of it then but six months later it would be front-page news.

Whatever you may have been told or read about the Hacienda, the greatest nightclub in Manchester during the early '90s was without question the Tropicana. It started life as the Plaza under the odious stewardship of Jimmy Savile, changed its name to Tiffany's in the '70s, then underwent a total rebrand – although not a refit – as the Tropicana in the '80s.

On the evening Andy and I were shown around with a view to starting a new night there, World of Music, we noticed a used Tampax draped over one of the fibreglass water features dotted around the club. On the night we opened, a month later, it was still there. It was that type of place. Faded glamour. We had grand ideas that World of Music would be to World of Twist Mk II what the Wigwam had been to World of Twist Mk I. But disco dancing central Manchester had other ideas and our club was doomed to fail on its first night. When no punters turned out, Tony headed down Oxford Street and shouted some people in for us. He brought back a bemused couple who – God bless them – stayed and danced until the end of the night. Probably out of fear, but even so . . .

I'd fallen in love with a girl I kept seeing riding around Chorlton. I called her 'Chorlton Bike Girl' and she replaced 'Chorlton Bus Girl' in my hopeless affections. I eventually got to meet her and we went out a few times but it ended as soon as it had started. She did, however, introduce me to the joys of cycling and I bought a new racing bike from Harry Hall Cycles. I've still got it. Two to three times a week I made the 15-mile round trip to Tony's to work on our songs. Since Tony had got to grips with the new equipment, the songs were sounding unbelievable. I remember listening to one of his demos on a train to London around this time. It was an instrumental version of the song 'Speed Wine', which appeared on World of Twist's *Quality Street* album. I couldn't believe I was involved in anything that sounded so polished. At that moment, I realised we'd be huge, absolutely no question about it. Tony played me one of his new songs, 'The Storm', which was loosely based on two Iggy Pop numbers nailed together. It was a staggering piece of work and the demo in my opinion was never bettered.

You may be asking what I did in all of this? My role, I think, was to enhance, to colour in. Equipped with my box of musical felt tips I'd add a lyric here, an organ solo there, the odd mock-baroque brass arrangement. And credit where it's due, I wrote most of 'Sweets' and 'Sons of the Stage', of which journalist Simon Reynolds wrote: '. . . after this camp bacchanalia, the final coda – a fake orchestral fantasia of phased guitars and babbling Moogs – is a plastic apocalypse worthy of Prince, at once tacky and sacramental. Awesome.'

The only song I remember that was a straight collaboration was 'Blackpool Tower'. However, even with the writing splits weighted very heavily in Tony's favour, he was generous enough to offer a fifty-fifty split on the writing credits when we signed our publishing deal. With hindsight it was a mistake, as it became a source of resentment on his part, particularly as our personal then working relationship deteriorated.

The Berrys of Wythenshawe are very important to the World of Twist story. Cathy sang on our early recordings (including 'Jellybaby'), she was our girl Friday on tour and my regular dance partner at the discotheque. For the Manchester pop scene, Andrew Berry was the hairdresser to the stars. As Tony, Andy and I had always been fixated with our respective hairstyles, we became acquainted with Andrew soon after we returned to Manchester. He became redundant for a few years when I cultivated the Zodiac Mindwarp look that saw me through my early days of stardom, but was back again to give me a late '60s George Best in the latter days of Twist – a haircut that made the gossip pages of the *NME*. Andrew had a high-calibre clientele and would attend to the likes of Johnny Marr and Chrissie Hynde when requested. Andrew was a central figure in the Smiths story as confidant to both Marr and Morrissey ('his hair never looked as good when I stopped cutting it') and was one of a very few allowed into the inner circle. My mum got into a conversation with the late Johnny Rogan at a dinner party while he was writing his much-maligned Smiths book, *The Severed Alliance*, and for some reason he contacted me to try to get an interview with Andrew Berry (neither Marr nor Morrissey would contribute). Rogan was a bit of an oily character, as I recall, and although I got a credit in the book – probably grounds for a Steven Morrissey fatwa – I thought he was a bit of a plank, but perhaps undeserving of death by conflagration, which was Morrissey's dream outcome for the treacherous scribe.

Apart from his tonsorial flare, Andrew was an all-round Manchester 'face'. He was a respected DJ and a fine solo musician. Tony and I were recruited into Andy's backing band to perform a number of gigs around Manchester. His previous band was called the Weeds. I don't know if that was the name of the band we played with but, if so, in my case it was very fitting. The first date was supporting Suicide at the International, which was worth it just to share the dressing room with these two greats of electro pop. Alan Vega was the friendly one – he said 'hi' a lot and wore a big puffer jacket and massive trainers. Martin Rev was hunched over in the corner looking like Abraham Lincoln with heartburn. He seemed very anxious as I recall, as though he'd never played live before.

WHEN DOES THE MIND-BENDING START?

Our second show for Andy was a Cog Sinister showcase at the Brickhouse in Manchester, an evening I remember only as the first time I encountered Mark E. Smith. I met the legendary Mark E. on numerous occasions. I've been thrown out of a dressing room by him, invited back in seconds later and offered a beer, I've witnessed him being punched to the floor by a member of Intastella, I've seen him in a face-to-face argument with Nick Sanderson, I've witnessed his drunken attempts to record a B-side. The Cog Sinister night was the only time I saw him sober. I always recall that gig when anyone's telling me what a cunt he was, as we found him really friendly and encouraging – but then it *was* a showcase for his label. I should also note that Intastella's Spencer Birtwistle (who wasn't the member to attack Mark E.), who later drummed for the Fall, would not have a bad word to say about Smithy, even after the great man sacked him and the entire band on a US tour. I think it's fairly safe to say also, that Mark E. Smith has been responsible for entertaining me in a live situation more than any other artist living or dead.

It was at Andrew's suggestion that World of Twist Mk II should be unveiled at the launch of his Dome Disco at Isadora's nightclub on 15 February. We'd been putting off our launch for a few months now. We didn't want to open as someone's support and it would be difficult to get a headline without promoting it ourselves. After all this procrastination, Andrew's suggestion was a perfect fit. We'd have a captive audience – Andrew's events were always well attended – and we could dress the stage to our requirements.

Tony had been chewing over the problem of how to house our midi keyboards and sound modules without displaying them to the audience and thus alerting them to the fact that our live performance was for the large part an elaborate mime. The solution was a hand-made backless shelving unit, painted white and fitted with castors. I painted World of Twist on the front in Grotesque No. 9 Italic, which was our go-to font until we switched to Compacta Light once we'd hit the big time. Finishing off the fascia with some Christmas tree lights, we had our centrepiece. Once the monitor was in place and Andy was sitting behind it with his SH-101 synth in position, the whole ensemble looked like a newsreader's desk. We'd knocked together a crude slide show and bought 6 metres of slash curtain for a backdrop. I'd bought a new wah-wah pedal and Paul Brotherton, my old friend from the Bodines, lent me his Peavey amp. Tony wore the first of many sparkly shirts and, with an artisan flourish, Andy was sporting a coloured denim suit. I misjudged the dress code badly and opted for a turquoise drape coat with a paisley imprint. It was a birthday present from Jim but it was a bit on the large side and robbed us of that sleek and fitted look we'd always sworn by.

Our old mate from Laugh, Martin Mittler, provided the sound for us and provoked the wrath of Ogden during the first song.

'Where's the D10?' shouted Tony from the stage. Our opening number was sounding a little sparse due to the absence of the Roland keyboard in the mix. 'Get the fucking D10 up.'

There was still no D10, so Tony jumped off the stage and marched over to the mixing desk to turn it up himself. It was quite dramatic but it served to get the crowd on our side. We went down really well with an enthusiastic melange of friends, work-mates and Berry-steppers who were 100 per cent in the mood for some noise and confusion. I was reminded of the first ever World of Twist gig five years earlier and how that had started on a high, too. The evening ended on a quiet note for me as I left the venue to get some cigs and they wouldn't let me back in.

'But I'm in the band.'

'There's no bands on tonight mate, it's a disco.'

Andrew Berry was also responsible for possibly the second most embarrassing episode in this tale. Andrew's currency was people. He was forever networking, gossiping, recommending this person to that, introducing him to her, her to him and he to thee. A thirty-minute Berry haircut would be a whirlwind trip through Manchester's smart scene, where everyone and every-thing was 'cool'. Like his equally affable sister, Andrew was very likeable. It was during one encounter that Andrew had some 'really cool' news for World of Twist. He had been speaking to New Order's Stephen Morris and bigging up World of Twist, naturally. Apparently Stephen was really interested in meeting us with a view to producing the band. 'You've got to follow this up, guys, he's really into it.'

And so it was that Dave Hardy and I drove out to the Morris estate somewhere in rural Macclesfield one afternoon to follow up Andrew's lead. My memory of how this came about is a little sketchy but we had Stephen's address and assurances that he was expecting us to call by on this particular date. Stephen must have been out in the fields with his flock when he saw us approaching and gave us a cheerful wave as we approached his front gate.

We mentioned Andrew (who he seemed to know) and after a few minutes we were sitting down in his big modern studio conversion with Gillian serving us tea.

'Sooo . . . who are you then?'

It was abundantly clear that Stephen had never heard of World of Twist and wasn't expecting us to call by. But he was immeasurably polite. He played the tape Dave gave him, tapped his fingers and made some encouraging noises, but, as far as producing us, the subject was never mentioned. He waved us on our way as cheerfully as he'd welcomed us and we drove back to Stockport knowing that we'd just seen whatever 'cool' the band may have had evaporate in the Derbyshire hillside. Nevertheless, Stephen Morris is my favourite living Joy Division member and my favourite New Order member outright.

20

Strawberry Fare

Even without New Order's patronage, doors were starting to open for the band. Dave had been helping out a band called Rig, who were based at Strawberry Studios in Stockport, and the studio manager Caroline Elleray had shown a lot of interest in World of Twist. Caroline later set up an office in Manchester with Dave, co-managing World of Twist and Intastella. It was through Caroline's Warner Chappell contacts that we got some recording time at Strawberry. This was really exciting news. Outside London, Strawberry was arguably the most famous recording studio in the country. Its reputation was founded on the work of 10cc, who owned the studio, and their groundbreaking multi-track techniques on songs such as 'I'm Not in Love'. As well as 10cc, Paul McCartney, Cliff Richard, the Moody Blues and even Neil Sedaka had recorded there. Producer Martin Hannett had a long association with the place, starting with his legendary work on Joy Division's *Unknown Pleasures* in 1979. In the late '80s the studio again became a hub, this time for the Stone Roses and the Happy Mondays, with Hannett once again at the controls.

Caroline got us an after-hours session in the main studio, which was okay by us as we were all-night people. We were paired with a young engineer called John Pennington who had assisted Martin Hannett for the mixing of the Mondays' *Bummed* LP. The bare bones of those sessions formed the basis for the single version of 'Sons of the Stage', but overall we were a little bit underwhelmed by the results. I think the issue was Tony's demos were recorded to such a high standard that the jump in audio quality was only minimal once we were in the studio. We never got over that hump. The World of Twist sound was so multi-layered, most songs would be running to twenty-four tracks of drums and sequenced sound before we'd even laid down a vocal or guitar track. It took a very fine ear to unravel that level of detail. It was a task that Tony would spend days working on with total focus. In the studio we were always up against the clock and Tony would lose patience very quickly. To my mind there were only a handful of producers with the ability to produce large-scale, multi-tracked, multi-sequenced material such as ours. In the US there was Bob Ezrin and Todd Rundgren, but they were sort of out of the question. In the UK we had Trevor Horn, Clive Langer and possibly Ian Broudie. It was suggested at some point that Broudie might be interested in working with us but Tony scotched that idea immediately. It was a shame, as I think it could have worked. Similarly, Langer was judged on his artist roster before he'd even been approached. I think Bob Ezrin would have been my absolute first choice but I doubt contact was ever made.

The Warner Chappell demos certainly did the job. Everyone who heard them suddenly predicted a big future for us. A label called Sheer Joy got in touch and asked to include 'The Storm' on an LP compilation of new Manchester bands called *Home*. We'd be rubbing shoulders with Mark E. Smith, the Paris Angels and Peter Hook's side project Revenge. The record came out in April and got us a lot of attention, with many reviewers citing 'The Storm' as the standout song.

Our first gig had sold out, but Andrew Berry had definitely been the draw as we played the same venue a few weeks later and it was only half full. Between gigs 1 and 2, we acquired a new member, Alan Frost, known to all as Adge.

Adge had what Tony would describe as 'a good head'. Other examples of good heads would be Slade's Don Powell, T. Rex's Mickey Finn, John Cale, Charlie Watts (a large proportion of drummers had good heads). A good head meant some sort of extreme feature, usually the nose, a gaunt bone structure and a manic stare. Having a less interesting head (myself, Andy Hobson, Nick Sanderson) did not preclude you from joining the gang but with a 'good head' you would be awarded instant membership. I can't think of any band from history made up entirely of 100 per cent good heads. The Stones are probably the closest but are let down in their earliest incarnation by Keith Richards, then later – following Keith's infinitely more good-headed 'Keef' transformation – by the pitifully ordinary Mick Taylor.

I'd known Adge since Stockport Art College and the months we hung around together before I left Manchester. He introduced me to the B-52's, raincoats and yachting pumps. He was a very cool dresser. We wanted someone to come on board and help with the visuals and we knew Adge made films, so we had a notion of him being our Philip Adrian Wright, our Mike Leonard, our Liquid Len. But like anyone else who joined, he had to play synthesiser on stage, too. For the second gig, in addition to our slide show, we now had the revolving head screen. Large cut-out heads of the band members, shot *With The Beatles*-style, spun round on geared motors stuck to a large screen supported by a hangman-style scaffold, onto which swirly oil patterns were projected from a liquid wheel projector. Despite endless upgrades, which eventually saw the heads suspended from the ceiling on metal rods that went up and down, we could never get the motors to spin in tandem.

Most significantly, the second gig was attended by an envoy from Circa Records, who were up from London on a scouting tour of South Yorkshire and the north-west. Their decision to catch the Twist gig was a serendipitous afterthought and their decision to pursue the band was based more or less on a Trans-Pennine snowball fight that had put the party in a very good mood.

In the first six months of our existence, World of Twist were a roadie's dream. We had hardly any equipment – the news desk, a computer monitor, the SH-101 synthesiser, a small guitar amp, a guitar, a cassette recorder a slide projector and a wah-wah pedal. The rotating heads rig took up the lion's share of the space, but in the early days, all our equipment fitted easily into the back of a Transit. It was all very Heath Robinson – *For want of a PP3 battery and some Blutac, the show was lost* – but the first few months after the first gig were a happy time for the band. We played several more Manchester shows, including the Hacienda and an aborted appearance at the Band on the Wall, where they pulled the plugs on us for not adhering to strict show-schedule protocol.

31 March 1990. There's revolution in the air. Protestors take to the streets in opposition to the hated poll tax. Julian Cope, dressed as a 7-foot alien (Sqwubbsy), joins the London protest. His account of the day's events, 'The Capital Explodes', is published in the *NME*.

The day after the poll tax riots, inmates at HMP Strangeways in Manchester started what would be the longest prison riot in British penal history, lasting twenty-five days. Our future book-keeper was among their number, though not in an accounting capacity, I understand. It did feel at times that World of Twist had a secondary function as an employment service for ex-lags and petty criminals, but it helped foster some nice vibes, a sort of gang atmosphere. We never really had any outsiders working for us. Some of our contemporaries may have been better organised but that industry wankiness thankfully never invaded the World of Twist set-up. We lost some good people to Intastella along the way (and vice versa) but we were very happy with our team. If you were a part of Team Twist you were an unsuccessful lifer.

21

The Scene

'The scene' was very important to the World of Twist concept. We even had a song called 'On the Scene', which, despite taking a massive rise out of ourselves, celebrated our perceived 'Factory' on the outskirts of Stretford. It was all cobblers, of course, but there was always something fascinating about those bands whose existence merged lifestyle, art, politics and living arrangements. It was a concept that started with the Velvet Underground but had more gnarly transatlantic appeal in the freeform theatre of Hawkwind, Gong and later Crass, bands who didn't look capable of tying their own shoes but whose stage productions were lavish, hi-tech productions calling on a collective dynamism that rarely came across in their photos. This was how we'd like to have been perceived by World of Twist's young fans.

As a teen pop fan, bands like Yes, Genesis and ELP had all made perfect sense to me. You spend several years getting really good at playing your instruments then nick the best bits from the Beatles and Simon & Garfunkel and fuse it with baroque-era classical music, get some impressive lights, lots of satin, some expensive rugs and pay a visit to the BBC theatrical wardrobe and away you go. The likes of Hawkwind and Gong were more problematic. How do these people stand up, let alone play their instruments? How do they persuade all these uninhibited sexy women to join their dark metaphysical circus? Their songs are full of sexual references. Are they having sex all the time? Is it normal sex? They're off their heads on drugs, that's clear from all the drug references on their album covers. What are the logistics of their chosen lifestyle? Where do they come from? How do they live? Do they keep in touch with their parents?

Our first video, *Jellybaby*, was an attempt to introduce the wider world to our fabricated 'scene'. Adge and his partner Angela Riley filmed it in black and white and colour on 8mm cine-film. Partly shot in Isadora's nightclub and Andy Hobson's new flat and showcasing his wonderful collection of thrift-shop art, *Jellybaby* features a pre-Intastella Stella Grundy with Cath Berry and our friend Lindsay, who had been earmarked as potential backing singers for World of Twist. This notion was scotched because, according to Stella, their voices didn't 'gel'. *Jellybaby* depicts a World of Twist gathering, by turns glamorous and wild, then chaotic and squalid. Here, make no mistake, is a drugs band – ugly, beautiful, aimless but focused, clever but stupid. I knew that had I seen that video as a fifteen-year-old I would have been hooked. I would have fallen in love with the women and wanted to be spiritually guided by the men.

On the morning of Sunday 27 May, the Madchester knocker-uppers were out in force. I didn't know anyone who wasn't going to the big concert at Spike Island in Widnes that day. I'd always been a bit indifferent to the Stone Roses. I liked the idea of them and they looked great, but I thought they came across as a bit humourless and I wasn't super keen on their music. 'Waterfall' was a good song and I liked 'What the World is Waiting For', but the rest was all a bit anthem in search of a tune. It was difficult to ignore them as their limited catalogue was played on a virtual loop in Affleck's Palace, along with the Happy Mondays' *Bummed*. Of the two I definitely preferred the latter.

But Spike Island promised to be a day of significant festivity. It was apt that the event was being held on the site of a Victorian chemical factory as chemicals were very much order of the day. Tony and Julia hooked up with Stella and Spencer, who were not enjoying the greatest of times, having scored some bad acid. I, on the other hand, had been delivered to the island courtesy of Dave Hardy and we had availed ourselves of some very good speed. I remember we all had a big game of football as soon as that had kicked in. It was an unholy wait for the main event and despite conflicting reports I can say with absolute clarity that the sound was bloody awful. This was thanks, I was told, to a vastly underpowered PA and the strong winds whistling in from across the Mersey.

Mercifully, the weather gods had smiled on the event and it was a bright, sunshiny day. And even with the appalling catering facilities, everyone looked very happy. I'm sure I saw a very tall man on the Island with small hooves instead of feet, although I've never been able to get anyone to confirm this.

To be fair, the Roses played pretty well. I remember being particularly jealous of John Squire's virtuosity as he solo'd away for all he was worth – at times with little regard for the song the rest of the band were playing. His chops were quite outstanding and something I could only dream of.

I think what killed Spike Island as an event was the absence of a supporting cast. If it had been our gig I'd have wanted the bill to be full of that era's big-hitters (particularly our Manchester colleagues), but with ourselves placed firmly top of the pack. The fact the Roses chose to entertain the crowds for nigh on six hours with DJs and African drummers smacked a little of self-doubt. Perhaps someone remembered Lynyrd Skynyrd blowing the Stones off stage at Knebworth fourteen years earlier, or maybe not.

For me and anyone who attended, the true high-water mark of the Madchester era was Intastella's free gig on the beach at Southport the following year. Intastella were seen as World of Twist's sister band. They were a few years younger than us but we would all hang around together, live in each other's houses and share the same management and road crew. Our success, when it inevitably happened, was going to be their success and vice versa. If World of Twist got there first we'd make sure we left a clear path for Intastella to follow. There was no animosity. We all wanted the same thing and it appeared to be in reach.

As it happened, it didn't quite turn out that way and, if Intastella had been as big as they should have been, that gig would definitely be remembered as an era-defining moment.

The band were in Southport to shoot the cover of their debut album *Intastella and the Family of People*. The cover photo was inspired by a sleeve from Andy Hobson's record collection. The 1910 Fruitgum Company – along with Ohio Express and the Shadows of Knight – were big Twist favourites. Their LP *Hard Ride* had a fantastic cover featuring a 1969 biker gang. It bore no relation to the music therein, which was a sort of Mike Post, free-jazz, sunshine-pop, garage band mash-up. Intastella, who at the time looked like the cast of *Scooby Doo*, recruited some UK biker types during a recce to a biker's pub in Derbyshire. They didn't quite get to recreate *Hard Ride*, as not many bikers turned up and the ones who did were a bit awkward, but they got to shoot a video and the evening's gig was fantastic and probably Dave Hardy's finest moment.

Nick always insisted that, in the World of Twist biopic, I would be portrayed by John Le Mesurier in the character of Sergeant Wilson. Dave Hardy's closest screen relative was Phil Silvers' Sergeant Bilko. Dave was more ready for success than any of us and I'd have loved to see how he'd have handled it. My guess is a non-violent Peter Grant. His carbon footprint would have been massive, that's for sure. The cars would have got very big, the ladies would have been omnipresent, he'd have been dripping in bling, but fundamentally he wouldn't have changed. If he'd lost the lot overnight he'd have been in the pub the following day laughing it off.

Dave loved everything about World of Twist and it must have been very painful for him to see us fucking it up so comprehensively. Dave could do all the manager things: he could locate mandolin strings in Austin (or he could have if we'd ever played there), or organise scale models of Stonehenge, but it really wasn't why he was there. Dave was the good-vibes man. The errant father figure, the life and soul. He could be forgiven for recruiting employees from his circle of friends rather than individuals with a particular aptitude for a given task, as it ensured we were always surrounded by good people.

A week after the Roses Spike Island debacle, World of Twist hit the big time. Penny Anderson wrote a little feature on the band in *NME* and we were listed on the front cover under Prince, Betty Boo, the B-52's, Steve Earle, Karl Denver, the Would-Be's and Saint Etienne.

Our first gig outside Manchester was in Notting Hill, London. It was hugely exciting to be taking our show to the capital, though not so thrilling to be travelling in a van with no seats. Subterania was an ancient but recently modernised venue built under the Westway, just down from Ladbroke Grove station. It was formerly the Acklam Hall, where just over ten years earlier Madness had played their first gig (as the Invaders), and, before that, the All Saints Hall, where Hawkwind (as Group X) had played their first gig twenty years before. A good omen, perhaps? We were supporting Paris Angels, another Manchester band. They were a bit more straightforward than us. Their brand of psychedelic dance music easily straddled the indie/dance crossover market and they had some great tunes, of which 'Perfume' was probably the standout. A nice bunch of people from our side of town, their guitarist Paul Wagstaff would eventually find a berth in Black Grape with Shaun Ryder. The last time I saw him (circa 1995), he definitely looked the worse for wear, which was perhaps understandable given the recreational exuberance of his new bandmates, Bez, Kermit and the aforementioned Shaun William Ryder. We felt sure we'd encounter our art school audience in London and they'd surely take us to their creative bosom. But after forty-five minutes it became clear that London didn't really know what to make of us: just another bunch of oddballs from up the M1.

The absence of any real alternative offers made it inevitable that we'd sign with Circa Records before the end of summer. We'd been down to see them in London and we liked the people, even if we weren't crazy about the other acts on the label. The fact that they had no other bands on their books made us imagine we might get some attention. Circa had only been going a few years but had enjoyed a lot of success in a very short period. Their two big earners were Massive Attack and Neneh Cherry. They operated like an indie label but they had the full Virgin machine behind them, so it never seemed like they were short of cash or had to cut corners. With World of Twist, they didn't until near the end. Circa was the brainchild of big-time operators Ashley Newton and Ray Cooper (not Elton John's percussionist). I never got the impression Ashley was that sold on us but Ray certainly was. Ray was a real personality and probably the nicest person I've ever met on that side of the industry. He enjoyed major successes at Island Records in the early '80s with acts such as U2 and Frankie Goes to Hollywood, but his greatest achievements – launching the Spice Girls, reviving Virgin America (with Ashley) – were still ahead of him. I think it was a measure of Ray's confidence in the band that prompted Circa to launch us in mid-November 1990, just before the Christmas stampede, which in retrospect was probably not one of his greatest strategies. On the day we joined Circa, we all piled into Ray's top-of-the-range soft-top Audi to head to the signing party. I mentioned to him that it was the best car I'd ever been in and without blinking he said I could have it if 'The Storm' got into the top twenty. He was as good as his word. After a fashion. My much-coveted soft-top Audi was eventually gifted to Definition of Sound after they'd had a hit with their second single. Ray sadly died in 2018, aged sixty-nine. A wonderful, funny man.

After signing, I stayed in London and went on a bit of a shopping spree. I tried to buy some trendy clothes – I bought a white, red and black top from Duffer of St George. A few months later Richey from the Manic Street Preachers was photographed in the same shirt, except he'd stencilled 'Kill Yourself' on his. I'd had the thumbs-up to get a new axe so I took myself down to Denmark Street armed with £700, which in 1991 could buy you pretty much any guitar on the racks. I really liked the guitar I owned. It was a 1973 Framus Sorento 6 that I'd browbeaten Rory Connolly into lending me the money for in Sheffield. For £90 the owner had thrown in a Selmer drum machine so it was quite a nice deal. When I bought the Framus it was a sort of cherry red with painted-on black f-holes and a really crap tremolo, which ensured that the thing was impossible to keep in tune. I stripped it of any remaining value by replacing all the original hardware with bits of a Gibson Flying V ClockDVA's John Carruthers had smashed up. I also got the guitar resprayed white. It looked brilliant and Jim christened it the Virgin Mary, while his black Strat copy, which looked tiny beside the Framus, was dubbed the Baby Jesus. The Framus sounded pretty good. I'd used it for all our recording and gigs up to now but I'd convinced myself if I ever wanted to get anywhere near John Squire's level then, rather than practising a bit more, I'd need a new instrument – something solid. I toyed with getting a Gibson SG (in honour of Pete Townshend and Zal Cleminson) but once I'd set eyes on the white Les Paul Studio with gold pick-ups, bridge and machine heads, I was only ever going to get one of those. Two neighbouring stores had the Les Paul for sale. In one of the shops they'd been quite arsey with me when I asked to try out different instruments, so I bought the guitar from the shop next door, then with my new Gibson in hand I walked back into the arsey shop and bought a plectrum.

Circa put us to work straight away recording a new version of 'The Storm' for a pre-Christmas release. We recorded the basic tracks at Strawberry then for some reason did the rest at a studio round the corner from Chelsea FC. The sequenced drums were replaced with a real drummer who was very flash but perhaps not quite us. The tune was embellished with some heavy flourishes. Ultimately we still preferred the version that appeared on the *Home* LP, but Circa appeared happy with the results.

An annoying factor during this period was the multiple remixes demanded of a particular single release to satisfy: a) dance-market potential; and b) repeat sales potential. The remixes, which were contractual, were by and large horrible and farmed out to a growing support industry of remix specialists, some of whom were very dedicated to their craft; others who simply saw it as a means to turn a buck. The trend really began with ZTT's formatting of the Frankie Goes to Hollywood tracks 'Relax' and 'Two Tribes', but where those mixes (there were about seven different mixes of 'Two Tribes') were done with wit and imagination, by the time of World of Twist, it was just another industry sausage factory.

Circa knew what they were doing, though. Their go-to press agency were Hall or Nothing, run by the indomitable Philip Hall. It's fair to say our press went through the roof the minute Philip got involved. It's also fair to say it went down the pan once he'd started devoting more time to the Manic Street Preachers, the band he co-managed with his brother Martin. Philip was an utter gent and invited us to his wedding reception, arguably the poshest do I've ever attended. Only four years my senior, Philip died at the tragically young age of thirty-four in December 1993. He was a constant reminder that the music business is not totally populated by twats.

I was introduced to Circa's graphics team, Michael Nash Associates, who would be designing our artwork. I loved hanging out at their Newman Street office. They seemed happy to have me around making collages and flicking through the Letraset catalogues. Anthony Michael and I got on really well and he seemed genuinely intrigued by our aesthetic. The release of 'The Storm' was accompanied by a bunch of totally random images. I think some of them – the Russell Hobbs appliances – might have been out of the slide show but there was nothing tying the rest of the pictures together. The cassette sleeve featured a delightful woolly snowman that we'd lifted from the cover of an old knitting pattern. It might have been a toilet-roll cover. I could hardly contain myself when this image was blown up to A0 size and posted all over London.

I loved being in London and would have moved there if it had been practical. There was an excitement that Manchester, with all its 'In The Area' vibes, just couldn't match. Being in London also neatly disguised the reality that as a creative unit World of Twist had stopped doing what we were being paid to do. Unless you're Prince or that strange breed of artist who prefers writing and recording to partying, or unless you have the bulk of the songs written before you sign up, it's unlikely you'll get a chance to write much in your first year.

Dave saw we were floundering in that department and early in 1991 found us some writing premises in Stockport just a few hundred yards from Hopes Carr, where in 1967 a Canadair C-4 had crashed, killing seventy-two holidaymakers returning from Mallorca. The area didn't look much different to how it had in the '60s – a maze of demolished factories, condemned slums and scrap-metal yards. It was by tradition the headquarters of Stockport's rag-and-bone trade. Our spartan premises comprised a workshop on the first floor of an old Victorian two-up, two-down, with loads of character but not much security. We were only there for one evening before we moved out. We'd just set the gear up when some local lads burst into the room 'looking for their mates'. They'd obviously clocked all our gear so we had to move out immediately. Our second rehearsal space was infinitely grander – a brand new warehouse in a railway arch a few hundred yards from Manchester's Piccadilly Station. It was big enough for a full stage set-up, two offices, running water and a flushing toilet. We had bought a lot of new equipment and staging, which needed storing somewhere, but as a writing and rehearsal facility it was criminally underused. 'The most expensive tool shed in Manchester,' as Nick Sanderson referred to it.

22

Hannett

Wary of being labelled the next Candy Flip, we were very reluctant to release 'She's a Rainbow', particularly as the record company seemed to be pairing it with 'The Storm' as a double A-side. We'd always liked the Mellotron-drenched Stones album *Their Satanic Majesties Request*. Far from regarding it as the band's '60s nadir, it was the only album of theirs that we all owned and stood alongside the Small Faces' *Ogdens' Nut Gone Flake* as one of our favourite servings of cod psychedelia. 'She's a Rainbow' was a largely forgotten Stones song when we did our relatively straight cover in 1990. In recent years it's been used in various high-profile commercials and television series, so to the younger reader it might seem a fairly dumb choice of cover.

Martin Hannett and Strawberry Studios had a long association. He'd first used the studio in 1979 for Joy Division's *Unknown Pleasures*, after which it became his studio of choice. Even when meagre working budgets didn't allow him to record there, he'd try to book the place for mixing. After an acrimonious split with Factory and a drawn-out battle with heroin addiction, Martin spent several years in decline until the release of the Happy Mondays' album *Bummed* went some way towards restoring his reputation. More recently he'd been working with Manchester bands the High and New Fast Automatic Daffodils. Caroline (our other manager) was still running Strawberry and asked Martin if he'd be interested in working with World of Twist. I'm not sure if Martin was ultra-selective at this point in his career, but he asked if he could meet us.

I was a little nervous for a number of reasons. Hannett had been out of the limelight for a good few years but his legend was still writ large in Manchester folklore. He was a cantankerous sod who didn't suffer fools at all. He was also responsible for soundtracking the latter part of my teens, so he was something of a hero. Caroline assured us that he was an absolute sweetie and we'd really like him.

Martin lived in Chorlton, which was familiar territory, so we arranged to meet in a local pub, a dangerous environment for Martin. Tony and I had never met him before and had no idea what he looked like. Fortunately he was the only person in the pub that lunchtime. I don't know what I expected him to look like but probably not a cross between John McCririck and Giant Haystacks. Martin clearly wasn't in the best shape but he turned out to be a charming and very funny man. He carried a notepad with him and had this endearing habit of repeating and writing down what you'd just said if it tickled him.

Strawberry paired Martin with one of their stars of the future, Liam Mullen. Liam was about eighteen at the time but could have easily passed for fourteen. The last time I'd seen Liam he was being thrown out of the control room at Strawberry by the Fall's Mark E. Smith, who'd mistaken him for a ligger. When Smith demanded to know why the session hadn't commenced he was informed that he'd just thrown the tape op out of the building. So Smithy, in a ritual he was no doubt familiar with, had to go and apologise to the poor lad.

The 'She's a Rainbow' sessions were surprisingly conservative. There was no setting my guitar rig up on the studio roof and the famed Ursa Major Space Station never made an appearance.

Liam was really the captain on the 'Rainbow' session. He told us later that Martin would call out for this and that effect and Liam would obediently patch them in, listen on headphones to see if they worked or not, then remove them accordingly. Martin was none the wiser. On one occasion I was sitting at the back of the control room listening to the playback and whatever they'd done (or whatever Liam had done) suddenly sounded mega.

Anxious not to lose the moment, I called out: 'That's it, Martin, it sounds really good.'

Nothing.

'Martin, it's sounding great, leave it like that.'

Still no reply.

'*Martin!*'

I jumped up to make my point and found our producer was fast asleep and had been for quite a while. Still, I thought, Martin Hannett asleep is better value than most producers awake.

We got some players in from the BBC Symphony Orchestra to do the strings. The session was overseen by Strawberry's resident boffin Richard Scott, who had overseen countless orchestral sessions at the studio. The BBC SO strings tuned up and had a bit of a scrape and it didn't sound that lovely to me. I asked if they were in tune and he assured me they were. The following day we played their tracks back and the strings were as flat as a Steve Howe backing vocal. It would have cost too much to bring them back in but Caroline provided a solution. She'd previously worked with some old chap who specialised in reproducing string backings using his vast array of electronic keyboards. It was agreed we'd give it a try. We'd run out of time at Strawberry so we brought him along to Amazon Studios in Liverpool, where we'd booked some additional time to record the guitars and backing vocals. It took Pete, who was a dead ringer for Captain Birdseye, about twenty minutes to salvage the string tracks. We had our mate 'Voodoo' Viv Dixon record the 'la-la-las' of the original song. The Alarm's massive guitar collection was lying around so I requisitioned one of their acoustics to record the rhythm track. The lead was produced by sitting a Mesa Boogie amp on its own in the huge live room. It was so loud it was impossible to be in the same room to play. The end result was a bit on the straight side but that was no reflection on Martin Hannett's involvement. I think we'd have made more records with him (and Liam), given the opportunity. I don't know if the 'She's a Rainbow' recordings were Martin's last ever session, but shortly afterwards Martin became ill. He died the following April, aged only forty-two.

We attended the star-studded funeral. Martin's massive coffin was a formidable centrepiece. When the 2002 Tony Wilson biopic *24 Hour Party People* was released, the world was reconnected with the Hannett legend, played brilliantly by Andy Serkis. But this was the gun-toting 'no fools' Hannett. I feel grateful we were part of a select few who saw another side to the great man.

World of Twist's gig at the International on 11 August was the evening we went from being just another Manchester band to the band most likely. This was the Stone Roses HQ – their manager Gareth Evans owned the venue. We'd seen the International packed out previously for the Roses, the Mock Turtles and countless out-of-town acts but we never seriously expected to sell the venue out ourselves. We knew there was a buzz about us and had been since the *Home* album had been released. We'd featured prominently in *The Face* magazine's recent Manchester and Acid House special. The cover star of the July 1990 issue was the unknown Kate Moss, starring in her first ever photo spread. On its website, *The Face* describes the moment thus: 'Instinctual . . . totally organic . . . A seminal, defining moment in fashion and music, the zeitgeist of the Nineties. Everything changed.' Kate's boundary-pushing moment, her *new democratic freedom to express herself* in this *iconic, personification of youthquake*, entailed sporting a pair of flip-flops, an Indian head dress and whipping her tits out for a couple of shots, thus preserving her status as the most important indie cupcake of the '90s. Me, I was more of a Sam Fox kind of guy.

The International was Julia's first gig with the band. She and Tony had met at the Hacienda and they'd been going out for a few months. I can't remember if her joining was ever discussed. She wasn't there one moment and then she was, but it wasn't a decision anyone objected to. She looked great – particularly on stage – and even if she didn't contribute much to the sound, Julia made an enormous contribution to the band's image.

The International was also the first time Jim Fry got involved with the shows. Jim was the house photographer, obviously, but he was keen to take charge of the staging, too. In our previous life he'd flashed the lights for working men's club act Geisha and gone on to work with the influential ClockDVA as their lighting guy. Jim got everything straight away. It was all about flash bombs, glitter and revolving hypnosis wheels. We'd both grown up with not just the post-punk theatre of the Human League, ClockDVA and Throbbing Gristle but also with Bowie, Kraftwerk, Sparks, Alice Cooper, Hawkwind and Genesis. It wasn't just about having a big fuck-off light show, it was about creating a mood. *Quark, Strangeness and Charm*.

Simply Red's Mick Hucknall, ever in search of the 'new sound', was in the crowd for the International show. Now perhaps the evil face of Manchester music, let's not forget he was also present at the first Sex Pistols gig in the town fourteen years earlier, so give the lad his dues. For some reason that no one can remember, the band were introduced by Vic Reeves and Bob Mortimer, whose *Big Night Out* on Channel 4 was the televisual phenomenon of 1990. Tony wasn't too chuffed about this but everyone else thought it was a bit of a coup and, sure enough, it merited a photo and a few lines in the *NME*'s gossip column. You just can't buy that kind of publicity! The gig itself was beset by technical problems but nobody made much of that – the whole thing looked so darned exciting.

After the International gig, big things were expected of World of Twist. We looked good, we could put on a show. But did we have a great record in us? This wasn't in the bag by a long stretch.

Although Circa seemed more than happy with the recording, we were still very unsure about 'The Storm'. The 'She's a Rainbow' recording was marginally more successful but we had major reservations about releasing that one, too. Spencer from Intastella asked if he could do a remix of 'Rainbow' and, since Circa would have farmed the job out to almost anyone, it made sense to offer Spen the gig. I was no fan of remixes but he did a pretty good job and his arrangement was the one we always played live at future shows.

Adge and Ange got their hands on a proper grown-up budget for 'The Storm' video, which was filmed at a number of locations across the city. The video was made up of four fantasy sequences à la *The Song Remains the Same*. In keeping with her new on-stage sobriquet, MC Shells, Julia appears as a mermaid, relaxing inside a marine cave fashioned meticulously out of plaster by our set-designing wizard Ian Rainford. There's very little movement in this delightful aquatic tableau, but a great deal of beauty. Tony's sequence is fairly straightforward: he is wrapped from head to toe in aluminium foil in a mirrored discotheque. As the other Twisters dance about, Tony O breaks out of the Bacofoil and tries to get in step. He falls. Adge features as a great artist producing a new work, *Lady with a Bunch of Grapes*, for an important client . The grape lady is Ange, who looks very alluring sat astride a Victorian rocking horse, her hair twisted into Medusa curls. For the reveal, the painter displays his work to the client. It is clearly the work of an imbecile but the client is delighted with the piece. The painting in this sequence was borrowed from Tony's flat in Withington. The landlord had produced hundreds of these atrocities and they populated every spare inch of the building. For our sequence, Andy and I appeared in a very extravagant set-piece filmed in the yet-to-be restored Victoria Baths near Rusholme. We filled the place with smoke, strobes and disco lights and filmed Andy and me playing football. As I had the longest hair I got to wear the red of Manchester United. It was great fun to shoot but looked a bit shit in the video – scant return for the amount of effort that went into filming it. But on the whole the video was a success and we felt a little more confident about the single release. It was indulgent nonsense of course but it looked way more interesting than most promos at the time.

In the next few weeks, we'd make our first TV appearance on a north-west 'what's on' programme. We were all a bit nervous and it looked a bit mannered but, again it would do us no harm. We genuinely didn't resemble any other band out there. In October, we'd do our first show in London since signing to Circa, headlining day four of the Irn Bru Rock Week at the ICA. At the end of our set some exuberant young lads in baggy gear got up and danced on stage and we let them. It was that kind of night. Supporting us were Dr Phibes and the House of Wax Equations, one of the great unsung 'head' bands of that era. A power trio from Crewe, their front-man Lawrence Howard King Jr was a fabulous guitarist and showed me how to take my Cry Baby wah-wah pedal apart so I could get a more expansive 'wah'. We really liked Dr Phibes and there was talk of us doing some gigs together. The band never got the success they deserved and split up in 1995, while King Jr was jailed for life two years later for murdering his mother at their home in Wales.

We were back in London a month later at ITV Studios to record *The Word*. It would be our first appearance on national television. We were performing 'The Storm', which had been in the shops for four days. The show was going out live. The next day was Saturday. If the kids dug us, they might go out and buy the record. Even with the added pressure, everyone seemed strangely relaxed about this one. Terry Christian was the presenter of this much-maligned show and we knew him pretty well. He'd been a big supporter of the band since the beginning when he covered us in his weekly pop spot in the *Manchester Evening News*.

Terry's co-presenter was 'It girl' Amanda de Cadenet and she wasn't very good. You could see the crew getting progressively more irritated as she struggled with her links. Having said that, she was barely out of school and, as Cloughie would say, 'Give people time . . . in all things.' Terry Christian, on the other hand, was as polished as a young Bruce Forsyth. His familiar Manc twang never faltered and every cue was bang on the nail.

Also on the show that evening was young carnival hypnotist Paul McKenna, making surely one of his first appearances on national TV. McKenna's act was yet to venture into unctuous life-coaching and he was happy merely to make monkeys out of a handful of spellbound volunteers before the appalled de Cadenet intervened and brought the show to an abrupt halt. Dave Hardy and our driver Paul Gunning could be seen in the background, finding the whole thing hilarious.

We ran through 'The Storm' three times, so by the time we went live we were all pretty confident. It was a great performance. Tony O was utterly captivating, like a day-release Tony Christie. Julia, our Amazonian Barbarella, dazzled in her latest ensemble as she bashed away lightly on a tambourine. My two-tone velveteen strides worked really well on TV and my Sorento 6 stayed mercifully in tune. The director had projected Adge and Angie's *Storm* video behind the band and it all looked suitably psychedelic. Again, if I'd seen this as a fourteen-year-old I'd have been mesmerised. That three minutes on *The Word* was possibly our finest moment on the small screen, marred only by the street dancing dudes whom the director kept cutting to. It was all very 1990. Holly Johnson was on the show: we didn't get to meet him but he was a bit of a hero and was very complimentary about the band, particularly Julia, likening us to 'The Velvet Underground on acid'.

23

Storm in a Teacup

Things were happening very quickly for the band. We were garnering a lot of press and still being touted as the next big thing.

On the phone one morning my mum asked: 'Are you ready to be famous?'

It was an odd but not unreasonable question. I was a jumble of neuroses, innately shy and prone to paranoia, so maybe fame, in whatever guise, was not the wisest career path. But in my head I was a full-on synthetic extrovert. It was the classic introvert rock-star problem. Fuelled by drugs and booze you can entertain the Coliseum; without them, you couldn't entertain the cat. So the introverted aspirant rock star reaches for the personality-changing class As. It's all very simple really.

During the recession of 2009 and conscious that I might need to switch jobs, I tapped my credentials into an online job generator to find out the type of profession I was most suited for. The top answer was librarian. Of course it was. With a fairly delicate id it's clear I was ill equipped to operate, or even cope with, the very complex machine that was World of Twist. I was as God made me and He had made me in the Syd Barrett mould.

In terms of profile I was perhaps the most famous King in our family to date. My dad had been on the cusp of selection for the British dinghy-racing team in 1968 in the Heron class. I also have good reason to believe I'm distantly related to Jack 'The Lad' Shepherd, petty criminal and famous Newgate escapee who was hung in 1724 in front of a capacity crowd at Tyburn (200,000, or one-third of London's population at the time). That's honest-to-goodness infamy right there.

Of all the reasons I wanted to be successful in music, money was never very high on my list. I'd never had expensive tastes. I liked buying CDs but then I'd get most of them free eventually. Of course, I harboured ambitions to own the most monstrous hi-fi system known to man, but that (and possibly a Bentley Continental) would be my only extravagance. I'd never had any interest in clothes and shoes. I hadn't really liked any men's fashions since 1974. I'd only ever worn desert boots and the last time I wore trainers had been around the mid-1970s. I wasn't that arsed about travel, either.

Of course I'd have a music-biz celebrity girlfriend – either Marcia Schofield from the Fall or Betty Boo. At the height of my fame I'd have a brief fling with the singer from the Cardigans, but I'd have to knock it on the head after I developed the early symptoms of Stockholm syndrome.

I couldn't see myself having too many celebrity pals, but I'd have struck up a friendship with Jason Pierce from Spiritualized. A discussed future collaboration would come to nothing, although we'd write a marginally successful Christmas record for astrologer Patrick Moore called 'I Saw Three Spaceships'. I'd be on friendly terms with Talk Talk's Mark Hollis but I'd respect his privacy and wouldn't pester him in the hope that he'd let me play something on one of his future creations. Writer Kurt Vonnegut would be an unlikely pen pal and confidant. I would turn Kurt on to non-League football and the films of Mike Leigh. Years later I would be asked to write his obituary for *The Guardian*.

It was sometime just before 'The Storm' came out that our radio plugger Marc Riley asked me to do a promotional tour of radio stations in Scotland. *That'll be a nice trip*, I thought, and we flew up to Glasgow from Manchester. Marc was really good company, as expected, regaling me with funny stories about the Fall and heavy-metal gurus as we drove up north to Tay Radio in Dundee and a couple of other destinations. It was going very well: the DJ would ask me a few questions about the band; I'd plug the single and do a little ident for the station. We got back to our hotel in Glasgow and I felt quite pleased with myself – I'd been chatty, knowledgeable and fun, a good ambassador for the band. We were going out that evening with a few friends of Marc's, including Josef K's Paul Haig, so I was really looking forward to the evening ahead. I'd gone back to my room to spruce myself up when Marc rang me. He'd managed to blag an interview on a BBC Scotland 'what's on'/music programme. I didn't have to do it but it would be a great opportunity to plug the record.

So, having twisted my arm, Marc escorted me to the University of Glasgow student union bar, where a sizeable crew were readying the set. I was introduced to the interviewer and offered a seat. There were about thirty people staring at me intently, I realised. So naturally I froze. The guy asked a question about 'The Storm' – what was it about? Of course I didn't have a clue what 'The Storm' was about as I hadn't written it. Suddenly Tony was there on my shoulder and, anxious about saying the wrong thing, I said nothing. I just stared at the man, for five, maybe ten seconds. I apologised and asked if we could go again. He repeated the question and I tried to say something meaningful but dried up mid-sentence. I looked over the interviewer's shoulder at Marc, who was looking a bit worried, and behind him at the crew, who were just staring at me in disbelief. Who is this clown? He comes in here and he can't even plug his own single. We tried it a third time and I just put my hands up and said sorry, I can't do this. It was crazy, but all very polite. The interviewer nodded and everyone packed up in silence, thinking this moronic nobody had just wasted an hour of everyone's time.

Marc, bless him, said nothing more about it and we went out for the evening as planned, but I was absolutely crushed. I couldn't speak. My first try-out at being a pop star had failed, magnificently. What hope did I have? I've watched interviews we did as a band prior to that and we were always shrinking behind Tony, so maybe none of us was ready for it. Having said that, the pose of the time was to put your head down and pretend you didn't want to be interviewed. The Stone Roses had turned this into an art form, but in truth I never wanted to be one of those groups; it didn't look clever to me. I wanted to be chatty; mysterious, but clever and effusive – a bit Julian Copish. Tony was great in interviews: a bundle of nerves but always naturally funny. So that whole shoe-gazing, difficult Mancunian thing really didn't suit us. But I had no answer because, unless I'd been drinking, that was me. I thought about that incident a lot. It was a real eye opener. I could see why so many people in the music business get into problems with coke. It's not necessarily a recreational thing – they're just trying to get from A to B, to turn themselves into a functioning, media-comfortable pop star. It's fascinating to watch Bowie's journey through the media machine, from the coke-fuelled twitchy space cadet of the early '70s through to his cheeky cockney barrow boy of later years.

But no, Mum, I wasn't ready for stardom. Not one iota.

Our first tour was fast approaching. I wasn't really looking forward to it. We'd rehearsed a lot but it didn't look right to me. The synthesiser wash always sounded very unrehearsed and never reached the *Space Ritual* textures that were playing in my head.

'The Storm' was released in mid-November 1990. By that time we were on tour. We'd been told beforehand it would get single of the week in the music papers and so it came to pass. There was certainly a massive amount of love for the band and people didn't seem repelled by the hype, but then we had the songs and the live presence to back it up, which doesn't always happen. The gig reviews started coming in and they were all pretty good. I remember the first time we heard 'The Storm' on the radio. We were driving around Edinburgh. Gary Davies played it on daytime radio and it was an amazing feeling. We hadn't made the Radio 1 playlist, which dictated what songs would be played in rotation throughout the week, so it was down to an individual producer's selection. If we made the top forty the next week we'd automatically make the playlist; if we got to number thirty, *Top of the Pops* would be likely.

To give the record another push we'd netted a place on the re-launched *Juke Box Jury*, presented by Jools Holland. This was a funny day. I had been a huge fan of Joy Division in my late teens. I was besotted with the group. As a card-carrying member of the raincoat brigade, they were my main reason for being from 1979 through to their premature demise on 18 May 1980. As I came to terms with my anxiety issues, Joy Division would provide the soundtrack. So here was World of Twist on *Juke Box Jury* with the guest reviewers: Bootsy Collins; Linda Hartley (aka Kerry Bishop from *Neighbours*); tennis deity Pat Cash; and Joy Division/ New Order guitarist Bernard Sumner. They played the 'Storm' video and inextricably Jools Holland voiced his support. Bootsy Collins was a bit noncommittal: 'It didn't really . . . turn my bird, I guess.' The Australian *Neighbours* puppet-girl hated it; she thought it was depressing, 'a bit zen', but her compatriot, hand-some Pat Cash, resplendent in an electric-blue blazer, really liked 'The Storm'. Pat was an old rocker at heart and when he wasn't winning Wimbledon he liked nothing better than rocking out on guitar with the likes of John McEnroe, Roger Daltrey and various members of Iron Maiden. So Pat's opinion mattered greatly. It still does. And Pat liked the song *and* the video.

And so to Bernard Sumner. As part of fellow Mancunian band New Order and one of Manchester's most famous sons, Bernard was surely a reliable ally for the World of Twist. He would like us. Surely? But Bernard didn't like us, the video in particular. He described World of Twist as 'a bit "we are weird"' – by which he meant: a pompous display of feigned idiosyncrasies, delivered with a marked lack of humour with the intention of appearing mysterious and interesting. It was a trait far more prevalent in the early '80s.

Bernard's was a throwaway comment and possibly a reaction to being introduced as a potential ally by virtue of his geographical connection (most of us were a bit weary of the 'Manchester' thing by this point). But it really stung.

World of Twist wore its influences on its chest. They weren't that hard to get. The video – Adge and Ange's first foray into big-budget video making – was intended to be funny, loosely influenced by the fantasy sequences in Led Zep's *Song Remains the Same*. Like New Order's Michael Clark videos, or the monks lugging Ian Curtis's portrait across the sand dunes in Anton Corbijn's *Atmosphere* video, we didn't expect anyone to take it too seriously.

So my opinion of Bernard plummeted that day and, even though I still acknowledge that he's been responsible in part for some of my favourite songs of the past forty years, he's my least favourite Joy Division member.

Handsome Pat Cash, on the other hand, I adore. I still get a warm feeling when I hear him co-commenting at Wimbledon. I loved the moment when he jumped into the crowd and scaled the boxes at Centre Court to hug his wife after winning Wimbledon in 1987. Imagine how much I'd hate that clip if he'd subsequently described my band as 'we are weird'.

'The Storm' got an ironic 'Hit' vote: sort of yes, it's shit but it will be hyped to the top of the hit parade. But we had the last laugh because 'The Storm' wasn't a hit. It stalled resolutely at number forty two and dropped out of the charts a week later.

There was no post-mortem. Nobody suggested (at the time) that Circa might have dropped the ball by releasing the record so close to the traditional Christmas stampede. That all came later, but for now the chart disappointment was a minor blip in what had been a steady start for the band. We'd come a long way in ten months.

24

The New Derek Leckenby

I distinctly remember a meeting with our new tour promoter a month or so after we'd signed to Circa.

'Could we try to move away from the standard gig circuit, play fewer colleges and universities and try to find some more interesting venues and towns to visit?'

We weren't asking to play on Mount Rushmore or alongside the Great Pyramid at Giza. Just some old bingo halls, cinemas or theatres that had fallen off the venue radar. Pavilions, civic halls, assembly rooms, working men's clubs, the odd deconsecrated church. And not the union bars and deluxe pub circuits. Maybe we could contrive some ley-line nonsense that could link all the gigs together. I recall the representative from the tour promoters being very enthusiastic about this idea – you could hear the cogs whirring. Of course, this sort of thing was not without precedent. We remembered going to see Echo & the Bunnymen at the Pavilion Gardens in Buxton on a freezing cold night in January 1981; three years earlier, the Cramps had played a now legendary show at the Napa State Mental Hospital. Spike Island, too, was hardly on the beaten track. We went off to record 'The Storm' and forgot about the conversation until our first tour was announced in October: Leeds Warehouse, Newcastle Riverside, Cambridge Junction. Radical.

We had new flight cases with WORLD OF TWIST stencilled on them. It was all very exciting and Status Quo-like. The band would travel in its own minibus, with the equipment travelling separately. Our road crew were hip and happening, some of the coolest guys in Manchester. Doing the on-stage sound was Mark Coyle who, four years later, would become a household name for producing *Definitely Maybe*. Martin Moscrop, our old pal from A Certain Ratio, took care of the front-of-house sound.

There's very little documentary evidence of the first tour but I'd venture that, had I witnessed it as a punter, I'd have preferred it to the second. A year later the presentation was super slick and the cock rock had been turned up a notch. But had we lost a little of our intrigue? MC Shells was gone by then. Adge and I had foolishly cut our hair so we no longer had that cavalier swagger. We definitely looked more unusual, more Roxy Music, the first time around. Centre stage was the giant hypnosis wheel flanked by two projection screens. If we could get the TriLite on stage we'd have two 9-foot mirrored barber poles on the left and right and hanging off the horizontal beams would be the strobes, UV tubes and the rotating heads of me, Andy, Adge and Tony (Julia never got a head for some reason and they'd been all but decommissioned by the time Nick Sanderson entered the fray). For selected gigs we'd commission random props, usually constructed by our friend Ian Rainford. In time, the hypnotist's wheel would be repainted with the words 'Rock and Roll' and, at some point, it featured a recreation of a Supermarine Spitfire flying over the South Downs. It ended its days after we'd commissioned an artist – at great expense – to recreate *The Crying Boy 'Alfie'* painting on the 7-foot disc. *'Alfie'* was a drawing-room trash classic. Unfortunately it was a reference very few understood. There was some talk that the painting was cursed and that the band's lack of success and ultimate demise could be traced back to the moment we foolishly attempted to lampoon Bruno Amadio's ghastly picture. I believe this to be true.

We'd had some new clobber run up for the tour. I'd had some loons made out of a beautiful two-tone crushed velvet. They never really fitted that well but in the right light they shimmered like moon beams dancing softly on rippling water. I never really got the top half of my ensemble right, but I was pleased with my hair, now unfashionably long and always meticulously ironed. Although I'd bristle if anyone dared suggest I might be wearing make-up, I liked a bit of eye-liner in the Twist days and would fly into a panic if I didn't have my stick of Rimmel in my toilet bag. Tony had a new selection of fitted lurex and PVC shirts knocked up by our tailor. Usually he would coordinate these with a crisp white loon pant, freshly pressed, with the shirt always tucked into the waist. The look would be topped off with a jumbo belt buckle and assorted bling. Tony was one of life's great clothes horses so there was never any worry about his look. Julia too looked sensational and if I hadn't been in the same band as her I'd have surely had a massive crush on her.

So World of Twist looked as cool as a mountain stream, but how did we sound? Our newest signing, Pete Smith (another Strawberry Studio veteran) had been brought in to take care of the sequencing side of the operation and had tightened up the backing no end. He was also a lovely fellow to have around and added hugely to the good vibrations. Pete would need to be on his toes as Tony was always alert to a missing sample or an under-performing sound module but, generally speaking, the elements of our sound were starting to coalesce nicely. The vocals, guitars and synths were live; the rest was sequenced. Some would call this miming and by and large they'd be correct. The synths were very easy to mix in and out and, if Adge, Andy or Jules were generating any offensive frequencies, the offending player could be intercepted before the noise could make it through the PA.

The guitars were more of an issue. Owing to my inability to control my new Mesa Boogie rig, they tended to sit on top of the mix, so if I was having a stinker it sounded very obvious, on stage at least. Still, I put the hours in and by the time we were heading off for our first date, I was in pretty good shape.

Whether he'd done any rehearsing, I couldn't tell you, but Tony was very reliable out front and rarely let us down. The main concern was to make sure he didn't shout too much between gigs.

We all knew World of Twist live was a bit of a spectacle, so if the sound was good we knew we'd be putting on quite a show. The highlights for me were always 'Sons of the Stage', 'On the

Scene' and our usual finisher, 'Kick Out the Jams'. On the first tour we had an instrumental called 'Fire', which I loved playing, a two-note wah-wah fest. It was a constant torment that my playing skills fell a long way short of what I wanted to do. Attempting anything too ambitious would often result in a jarring cascade of bum notes. I tended to go round in circles on the guitar neck, relying on a couple of simple pentatonic shapes drenched with loads of wah-wah, delay and feedback.

For some reason, possibly at the insistence of the record label, the band were assigned a personal tour manager. He was a bit of a straight and looked like he'd have been more comfortable on the road with Mike & the Mechanics. We didn't care for him overmuch and I get the idea the feeling was entirely mutual. On the one occasion he deigned to catch one of our shows, he seemed genuinely surprised that it was, in his words, 'quite good'. There was some issue over our personal allowances and we jettisoned his deadweight somewhere around the Fens. Thereafter, we left Quent, our driver, to take care of the money side of things. It made sense as much of the money was going straight back to him for 'services rendered'.

Wednesday 28 November 1990. Today the stars are beautifully aligned. Buoyant after a great gig in Leeds the previous evening ('Malevolent, infectious, succulent!' writes Ian Cheeks in *Sounds*), we arrive in Newcastle to the joyous news that Margaret Thatcher has resigned. The Iron Lady left Downing Street in tears after assuring her people that she was 'happy [to] leave the UK in a very, very much better state than when we came here'. Try telling that to Sqwubbsy. The *Wizard of Oz* good vibes overflow into the evening: the venue's catering is superb and I eat swordfish for the first time. It's a taste sensation.

The gig itself is a triumph. The sound is tip-top and the visuals look amazing. A young couple are snogging in front of my monitor throughout the gig and their passion clearly rubs off as I play like a demon. After the show, we learn that United have beaten Arsenal 6–2 in the League Cup with a Lee Sharpe hat-trick. Such a wonderful evening is rounded off by a visit to a really cool West Indian club where the vibes are beyond mellow.

Newcastle will be a hard act to follow and Dundee is sadly way off the pace. Dundee's the coldest place I've ever been and will remain so until my next band, Earl Brutus, visit Aberdeen in 1997. I'd been to Dundee a month earlier with Marc Riley, but that had been in placid October. Scotland is the windiest country in Europe and the Tay is in furious mood for our arrival. *Who the fuck's going to come out in this to see us?* I can't remember if anyone did actually bother. My only recollection of Dundee, apart from the awful weather, is walking into a glass-fronted panel at the hotel that really should have been covered with Access and Diners Club stickers. The incident leaves a large bruise below my right eye that temporarily spoils the Twist aesthetic.

We leave Dundee to do battle with the Beaufort scale and head for Glasgow. As we approach the outskirts of the city, Radio 1 are playing 'The Storm'. It's impossible not to love Glasgow. Unless, of course, you are stupid. The place just makes me smile every time I visit. This evening we're playing at King Tut's Wah Wah Hut, so I needed to be sure my Cry Baby does it justice. Quent drops us off in the city centre and we go in search of souvenirs. Adge wants a genuine tam-o'-shanter and I'm after a tartan scarf in Dress Gordon. Naturally, we get a royal fleecing in one of the city's many outfitters. King Tut's will enter rock 'n' roll folklore a few years later as the venue where Oasis are discovered. Tonight it's just going through the motions. A number of venues in the UK have particular quirks that stay in the memory. For instance, the Forum in Tunbridge Wells, set in the middle of a municipal park, is memorable for having no load-in parking, so you're required to shunt all your equipment across a field to reach the venue. At King Tut's, the band has to walk around the back of the building and down a fire escape to get to the stage. There must be many a rocker who's lost their way during this procedure. The venue is half empty, which is a bit disappointing, but all our local mates have turned up and apologise for the indifference of their Glaswegian peers. We return to the city twelve months later and play a storming, packed-out show at the university but, for the time being, the city is stubbornly impervious to our charms.

After Glasgow, we rest up in Manchester for no reason before zigzagging our way down to London for the final show. We are back at Subterania in Notting Hill. It's nearly Christmas and I've just turned twenty-nine. Jimmy Page had had an entire career as a session musician, a Yardbird and released most of his Led Zep albums by the time he was my age.

This time, everyone is here for us. It's the evening's hot ticket in the capital and we have a full house. Maybe it's the fact that Subterania is a bit dingy compared to some of the venues we've been playing, or maybe there's just too many media types in the crowd, but the show never gets going. It's clear 'The Storm' hasn't exactly set the charts on fire, but it feels like a lot of bets are being hedged this evening. Nobody wants to back a loser.

The year 1990 has one further engagement for the band. Two days before Christmas, we are due to play a show at the Ritz in Manchester. The 1,500-capacity ballroom is Manchester's oldest surviving music venue. According to their website, the Beatles and Frank Sinatra both played here, although I can't find any evidence to support either claim. Certainly the Smiths made their first live appearance at the venue, gatecrashing a Blue Rondo à la Turk gig in 1982. Famed for its fabulous sprung dance floor, the Ritz is the best place in Manchester to go dancing. I've seen quite a few bands here in the past two years – the Fall, Happy Mondays – but I've never seen the place full. That thought keeps nagging away as our gig approaches. We sold out the International in the summer but this is a big step up for us and it's so close to Christmas. Will anyone be arsed to come out and see us? The past twelve months have been a steady climb for the band but there is genuine worry that the bubble could burst on 23 December. Anything less than 300 in this place is going to be embarrassing. For the first time, all our bits and pieces will fit on stage, so it will be the full show. There's also a curtain. This is a genuine novelty, so we have to plan something special. Intastella are supporting, which makes perfect sense, both emotionally and logistically. We are best buddies and they travel light, so we'll be able to pack their gear away quickly.

We decide to open with a song called 'Deadline', which we've never played before and will never play again. It's actually a very

old tune, predating 'The Storm', but I've managed to convince
Tony of its worth, saving it from the Ogden song pyre. We run
through it at our final rehearsal and it sounds great. On the night
it's a fucking shambles, but nobody seems to care – such is the
festive atmosphere in the room.

The soundcheck's at six o'clock, so I ring for a taxi and arrive
at the Ritz in style. As the car rounds the corner into Whitworth
Street, I'm astonished by the sight of a hundred or so people queuing already. I'm recognised as I walk up to the front doors. Fuck,
this is like the Beatles. Or Herman's Hermits at the very least. Dave
greets me inside and is feeling buoyant. He's been told it looks likely
the gig will sell out, which is exciting news but presses my panic
button immediately. Tony is here already and is his usual manic
self. He's desperate for this to go well, so he's on top of everything.

It's two minutes to curtain. Tony looks brilliant. He's covered
from head to foot in tin foil, in homage to 'The Storm' video. I
was a bit sceptical about this idea at first, but backstage the lights
catch his foil suit and it's dazzling. He's Tony Mercury.

I've been using batteries in my guitar effects for the tour to cut
down on mains hum. Dave's brother Mike changes them every
couple of gigs and it's been working well up to now. Tonight my
effects will be in front of the curtain and I don't want to go out
front and check them before we go on, not in my shiny tonic
pants and freshly ironed hair. So we fit some new batteries and
leave them all plugged in. I'll just stroll on, the curtains will part
and – kerraang – away we'll go.

We are all in position, ready and charged. It's a full house –
friends, family and the converted. We are well rehearsed and

confident. I can't remember being this excited about a gig. 'Ogdens' Nut Gone Flake' bursts into life and the house lights dim. There's a huge roar, eclipsing any reception we've received to date. The intro to 'Deadline' takes me by surprise, as it's not our usual opener, but I remember it's all choppy wah-wah, a nice easy introduction.

The curtains open and there's a palpable gasp as Tony lights up the stage. I wind up my volume, click open the wah pedal and hit the strings. Nothing. None of the effects have power lights so there's no telling if they're getting any. I crouch down, making sure all the leads are plugged in, and stare over at Mike, who's looking as anxious as me. He joins me on stage and we frantically start unplugging and plugging everything back in, but it's a dead rubber.

Fortunately, the crowd don't notice the guitarist in the middle of a waking nightmare. Their eyes are locked on the Bacofoil tableau. Tony, a born frontman, is stealing all the focus as he punches his way out of his aluminium bondage.

All the excitement has neatly diverted attention away from the song we're supposed to be playing. 'Deadline' sounds absolutely dreadful. I know − I've heard the desk mixes.

Mike finally bypasses my effects and plugs me straight into the amp, but without the effects units down front the levels are all wrong. It's either the deafeningly loud distortion channel or a more acceptable Duane Eddy twang. I opt for the Duane Eddy setting, but it sounds bloody awful so I decide to mime. Apparently this is a very common move employed by orchestral players. It's called 'faking' and is practised when the musician meets a passage they've either not bothered learning or which is fearsomely difficult to play. So I fake it for the entire gig.

The show ends with rapturous applause. I sulkily pack my guitar and useless effects away. By the time I get backstage for a not-very-well-earned beer, the dressing room is swarming with well-wishers and the beer's all gone. Someone offers me a swig of Cinzano but it's not what I'd had in mind.

It's funny that the Ritz gig is regarded by many, particularly our Manchester brethren, as Twist's finest show. I'm glad that the lack of guitar didn't ruin it for everyone but I'm also riled that no one cared or even noticed.

There's an after-show party at the Railway Arch but I'm too pissed off to attend. I get a cab home and watch *The Sandwich Man* while contemplating my first year as a professional musician.

25

Brighton Rock

1991. Will this be World of Twist's year or has that bird flown? Will our quest be thwarted by the inevitable Manchester backlash? If not, we must be front-runners. We have some great material. We have one of the most exciting live acts on the circuit – if more people would come out and see us. We have the best frontman in the business. On paper, it appears to be a clear path. The Stone Roses are still locked in a court battle with their former record label, they've only played three shows since Spike Island as the world grows impatient for their second album. The third Happy Mondays album, released in November 1990, is very good, but the band have gone off to break the States and will only perform three shows in the UK this year. In theory at least, the stage has been set for someone to sweep in and steal their abandoned thunder . . .

We reconvene after the Ritz debacle and air our grievances. There's no doubt the show was a huge success, but the sound was messy and lacked punch. We all agree we need a drummer, definitely for playing live. We all agree it should be Nick Sanderson. Nick has spent the preceding four years in the Gun Club and, prior to that, after the demise of ClockDVA, he'd played with the likes of Pete Shelley and Tom Verlaine. When he gets Tony's call, Nick doesn't hesitate and is on the train up to Manchester the following week.

Inviting Nick to join is a masterstroke, initially. He's always got on really well with Tony and he'll be staying at mine so it's inevitable we'll all go out as a band more often.

The record company didn't seem unduly bothered that 'The Storm' wasn't a hit, so neither were we. There may have been frantic payola meetings going on behind the scenes, but Circa just let us get on with it and assured us we'd score with our next release.

In the third week of 1991, we headed to Brighton to record the next single. It had been decided long before 'The Storm' was released that 'Sons of the Stage' would be our second single. 'Sons of the Stage' is probably World of Twist's best-known song for a number of reasons, all of which involve Oasis. Noel Gallagher had been a fan of the band since our early days and we'd often see him around at gigs. Liam I'd never met. He'd have been one of a bunch of young dudes with mod haircuts and retro Man City shirts who always seemed to be at the same parties as us. Working as a roadie for Inspiral Carpets, Noel had given an interview to a fanzine in which he enthused about

World of Twist, even suggesting that it was his intention to join the band. He never formally asked us but I think if he'd played us a few tunes we'd have given it some consideration. It was reported in some circles that the band had toyed with the idea of calling themselves Sons of the Stage before deciding on Oasis. The band's tenth anniversary tour was called 10 Years of Noise and Confusion, a quotation from 'Sons of the Stage'. Then, in 2010, Liam Gallagher paid us a huge compliment, covering the song with his new group, Beady Eye. If they'd put the song on their debut album it would have been a far greater compliment, possibly paying for a new car. As it was, it probably paid for a new fridge. It appeared as the B-side of their first single which, sadly (from a strictly fiscal point of view), was a limited edition. On their first tour, Beady Eye usually played 'Sons of the Stage' as their encore. I caught the band at their Roundhouse gig in London, going along as Stuart Boreman's guest, which included an after-show pass – although I had absolutely no intention of going backstage. Stuart caused me huge embarrassment during the gig by alerting a couple of young lads that I'd written the song they were tapping their feet to. Stu may as well have told them I'd invented Oasis, such was their incredulous reaction. We couldn't shake the boys off and once they discovered we had backstage passes I was forced to go and meet the band. Liam had left the building (to my veiled disappointment) but their guitarist Andy Bell was there and was friendly and charming. Liam's version of the song was a full-throttle rocker with a larynx-damaging vocal. I liked it and it brought World of Twist to the attention of a few younger fans.

The YouTube count for the Twist video went from 20,000 to over 100,000 in a few days.

The song itself had been written eighteen months earlier, after a Happy Mondays gig at Manchester University. I'd seen the Mondays a few times but this was the best show I ever saw them play. They were promoting the *Bummed* album, which had been playing on a loop in Affleck's Palace all year, so those songs were embedded in our brains.

They had a track called 'Do It Better', which had this fabulously incessant rhythm, and when they played it live the place went mad – 1,200 people bouncing up and down in sync. I thought, *We have to have a song like that.* I rushed home and banged out some chords on my Casiotone MT-40 and thus was 'Sons of the Stage' born. It wasn't a direct steal from the Mondays but that was definitely the starting point. The lyrics were inspired by 'Kick Out the Jams' in homage to the MC5. They weren't a piss-take but they certainly weren't meant to be taken seriously. 'Kick Out the Jams' was always World of Twist's finisher when we played live and journalist Simon Reynolds nailed it when he described our version as revealing the song to be 'pretty much on the same level as the Sweet's "Teenage Rampage": a gloriously vacant blast of insurrectionary hot air'.

MC5 were a pivotal influence on World of Twist. The art came from Roxy Music, the bubblegum from Love Affair; the dance beats came from northern soul, the theatricals from Genesis, the Human League and Hawkwind. But the rock 'n' roll came from MC5. Had YouTube been around when we formed they'd have been an even bigger influence. We'd never seen any film of the band live and they were quite phenomenal. Rob Tyner is one of my favourite singers and my favourite ever frontman. Wayne Kramer was – and remains – not only one of the finest rock guitarists but also one of the greatest guitar showmen ever. So the homage, though tongue in cheek, was entirely genuine.

We'd recorded 'Sons of the Stage' during our first visit to Strawberry, demoing songs for Warner Chappell. We kept the bones of those recordings, so there wasn't a great deal to do on it when we got to Brighton and the bulk of those sessions was spent producing a B-side for the record. Chairmen of the Board was another band we all loved. They'd produced some of the greatest bubblegum soul hits of the early '70s and in General Johnson had one of *the* great soul voices. The song we chose, 'Life and Death', was a ten-minute epic that had appeared on one of their final and less successful albums, *Skin I'm In* (sometimes referred to as the 'Lost Funkadelic album', as it featured several of the *Maggot Brain* players). It was actually two songs tacked together – 'Morning Glory/White Rose' and 'Life and Death in G&A', written by Sly Stone. The original (performed by Joe Hicks) is a very strange record and I think if we'd heard that one first that's how we'd have covered it. Tony worked day and night producing a sort of electro version of the Chairmen of the Board cover, which was an astounding feat of programming, although we'd both admit it sounded pretty wooden next to the Chairmen's. Nick joined us in Brighton for the sessions but, for reasons I still can't recall, didn't drum on the track. Maybe he'd forgotten his kit. He famously turned up at his Jesus and Mary Chain audition hungover and without any sticks. When the Reid brothers asked him if he knew any of their songs he confessed he didn't. Miraculously, he got the gig and stayed with them off and on until he died.

Brighton was very out of season and very cold. We went exploring but found it pretty dull. There were a few clubs open but nothing exciting going on. I recall Norman Cook was DJ'ing at some club and we childishly pestered him all evening, asking for records we knew he wouldn't have. What cards we were back then! We wandered around, bought some shoes, some new kecks and took some photos on the beach, but it was all a bit dreary. I didn't rate the place and certainly wasn't dying to return there. Ironically, I've now lived in Brighton for fifteen years and I love it.

Back in the studios we looked for a few things to kill time that didn't involve making any new music. One evening we came across a room full of master tapes, which was very exciting. We found Renaissance's 'Northern Lights' and someone suggested we re-record the vocals. Fortunately, we weren't drunk enough to see that particular jape through to its conclusion. Later that evening we decided to raid Julia's wardrobe, which was always full of very sparkly outfits. We all picked out something nice, although there were a few arguments about who got what. I was delighted with my figure-hugging glittery leotard with gossamer sleeves and Tony looked very chic in a sort of *Space 1999* lounge suit, but I recall Nick and Adge being disappointed with their selections. I think it was Mick Jagger who once said, 'Leave a group of Englishmen together for long enough and they'll start dressing up as women.' For a possible album launch, Tony and I had thought about having a men-only party at *Transformations*, a cross-dressing boutique opposite Euston station where you could have a full makeover (hair, make-up and clothes), have some photos taken, then spend a few hours drinking champagne and getting pampered 'as only a lady can', so this evening was possibly a trial run. We all piled into the control room and Jim got some lovely shots of us 'mixing' the new record in our evening wear. Somehow these photos got into the hands of the record company, who were very eager to get them into the press. Tony found out and went absolutely mental.

The song was finished and Circa seemed happy enough with the results, although in truth it wasn't a patch on the demo we'd recorded with John Pennington twelve months previously. For me, it was another trek down to London to oversee the artwork, a process I absolutely loved. We'd found a photograph in *Nova*, a '60s magazine, of some psychedelic nymphs sitting naked in a forest. It was decided to re-create this image for the single cover but with our genitals air-brushed out. Once again, Jim Fry was recruited for the job and his marvellous photo taken at Poynton Coppice can be seen on the cover of this book. To me it stands up with the great rock photos, like the cover of The Ramones' first LP, *Aladdin Sane*, Iggy Pop's Cincinnati crowd-walk, the cover of *The Man-Machine*.

After all the we-are-weirdness of 'The Storm' it was agreed we'd film a fairly straight performance video for 'Sons of the Stage'. Straight, but with a few World of Twist flourishes. Adge and Ange had filled this warehouse with several hundred metres of fun fur with the help of our friend Ian Rainford, who constructed a magnificent plaster of Paris oyster shell for Julia to sit in. I remember the make-up lady went a bit overboard with the fake tan and hair straighteners and I wound up looking like a brunette Fabio Lanzoni (look him up) or perhaps his weedy English cousin. A few beers allowed me to execute some of my northern soul/ballroom dancing moves that I wouldn't have dared attempt on stage. Certainly not without the aid of a safety net.

'Sons of the Stage' was released on 11 March and a frantic week of promotion ensued. An interview the band had recorded for BBC's Snub TV went out the same day. Filmed in Withington baths at around 10 a.m. on a weekday morning, we were interviewed in pairs as a school swimming lesson took place behind us. Quite why this was picked as a location escapes me, but it was a two-minute walk from my house so I wasn't complaining. Tony and I gave one of the worst interviews in the history of broadcasting, but our monotone, monosyllabic grunts were cleverly edited together with the new video and we came over as quite witty. A huge thank you to the director on that one, who could have stitched us up a treat.

We also recorded the Saturday morning TV show *Eggs 'n' Baker*, presented by former Bucks Fizzer, the wonderful Cheryl Baker. The show's format was suitably surreal: a kids' food-centric pop show featuring two live (or mimed) performances, some studio cooking (by Cheryl) and some food-related VT inserts. Blur had made their national TV debut on the show a few weeks earlier, so it was a well-trodden path to pop stardom or otherwise. The show was filmed in Liverpool, near the docks. When I heard we'd be performing to an audience of Scouse school kids my mind immediately conjured up scenes from Willy Russell's *Our Day Out* and I was fully expecting us to be confronted by dozens of cheeky, in-your-face scallywags, cadging ciggies and trying to nick your fuzz pedal while your back was turned. But no, they were lovely – and completely awestruck. It made you realise what responsibilities us pop stars carry.

The theme for this week's show was vegetables and the VT that preceded World of Twist's performance was a bit of TV gold. Cheryl was interviewing the market traders on Berwick Street in London. She spoke to Bill Bean (possibly a pseudonym), whose vegetable stall was really quite spectacular – or Bill certainly thought so. What the film crew had neglected to notice was that Bill was coked off his nut. He'd obviously ducked down behind his cart for a sniff just before the cameras started rolling and was struggling to keep all the toot up his nostrils. World of Twist gave another solid performance on *Eggs 'n' Baker*, but the laurels surely must go to Bill Bean on this occasion.

As an addendum to this, one of World of Twist's favourite days out. Andy got a lovely signed photo of Cheryl Baker with the following inscription: 'Dear Andy, I was bewitched by your smile. I'll never forget you. Love, Cheryl x'

26

Under the Volcano

On the Saturday *Eggs 'n' Baker* aired, Twist were back in Sheffield to play a show postponed from the November tour.

Driving through the town, it was difficult to believe we'd lived here and for so long. I felt like Pip returning to Miss Havisham's house in *Great Expectations*. Nothing had changed but it just looked ten, twenty, thirty years older.

Pulp were supporting us that evening. It was a situation they weren't particularly happy about apparently. I think it's possible World of Twist didn't give them enough time to soundcheck properly. The show was being filmed for TV so we were a little jumpy and may have run over a tad. What I didn't find out until later was that Pulp's set was also being filmed to go out on the same show a few weeks later, so they too would have been anxious to get all their technicals sorted.

After Pulp had become enormously successful during the Britpop era, some commentators started to mention the two bands in the same breath. World of Twist had long folded by then but, without denigrating Pulp, some viewed them as the band that had stolen WoT's crown. I never saw much of a connection between the two bands, other than starting in Sheffield around the same period and being regarded as something of a novelty act on the local scene.

It was quite a surprise when a Pulp/World of Twist rivalry was first suggested, but suggested it was – by Pulp biographer Martin Aston and previously by Jarvis Cocker himself in a 1994 interview with *Record Collector*: 'The first concert we did then was supporting World of Twist at the Leadmill, which is ironic – they nicked loads of our ideas, like tin foil on the stage.'

I've never met Jarvis. I once stood behind him at a Hawkwind gig but that's as close as I've got. He seems like a good type, though. I loved how he tried to disrupt that appalling Michael Jackson performance at the Brit Awards and I thought he looked good in the Harry Potter film. I wish they'd cut more of that in – he's a very sharp and witty commentator and he's obviously a man of taste. He once played the theme to *The Man Who Haunted Himself* on one of his radio shows.

I probably know more about Jarvis Cocker the man than I do about his band. When Pulp supported us in 1991, I probably couldn't have named one of their songs and it's highly unlikely they'd have been on Tony's radar at all. Tony's mast was set pretty low at the best of times.

It was strange to be back in the Leadmill, the location of so many memorable nights and shattered dreams (cue Morrissey lyric about miserable nightclub experiences). I can talk at length about World of Twist's fabled live show but the only evidence I have is a very poorly lit obscure film of us playing live in Rotterdam and the recording of the Leadmill show. Neither does the band justice.

There was a dispute with the director and camera operator about the excessive lights the TV set-up required on stage. Tony won, but it was a pyrrhic victory: It was so dark that ITV were unable to film the gig properly. The whole exchange put Oggy in such a bad mood that he refused to dress up for the show and gave an uncharacteristically moody performance. The TV sound was also appalling. This was Nick Sanderson's first gig with us. We'd brought Nick in as we felt the live performances lacked punch. He was a very powerful drummer in the John Bonham mould but on the *New Sessions* he sounds as if he's banging away on some biscuit tins and a rubber tyre. As far as the filmed performance went, it was too dark to see what was on offer, although we did a characteristically rocking version of 'Kick Out the Jams' to finish and there's a nice moment when a member of the audience jumps on stage to land a smacker on Julia's lips.

It wasn't one of our better gigs but Simon Dudfield was very generous with his praise in *NME* and promised huge things for us in the coming months.

The week after the Leadmill show, 'Sons of the Stage' charted at its highest position. Again, we were a whisker away from the top forty but this time we couldn't blame the Christmas rush.

WHEN DOES THE MIND-BENDING START?

We got single of the week again, the features were getting bigger, our adverts were all over the place. So what was the problem? There was a great deal of head scratching, but it was quite simple really: our target audience would rather own records by EMF, Morrissey, That Petrol Emotion, Inspiral Carpets, James, Jesus Jones, Ride, the Railway Children, Ned's Atomic Dustbin, the Charlatans and the Mock Turtles than one of ours. I was pleased to see Chesney Hawkes at number one, though. I'd met him at a crap party in London's Shepherd Market a couple of months earlier and he was very sweet. And of course his dad had been in a proper pop band that had proper hit singles in an era when half the country needed to own your record to have any chance of getting it in the charts. Circa remained undaunted. They had a plan. Their ace in the pack was to release the nude-in-the-woods photo on a 12-inch picture disc and admittedly it did look rather grand. You can still pick up a copy in reasonable condition on eBay for around £10, including postage and packing. The photo got us a little publicity but not enough to push us any further up the charts. *Never mind*, we thought, *we'll be an album band*.

Our final gig of the season was a return to London to play the Astoria Theatre on Charing Cross Road. This was our biggest show so far. Saint Etienne were supporting us for what would be Sarah Cracknell's first appearance with the group.

Julia, in celebration of her Italian ancestry and at Tony's prompting, had decided to change her stage name from MC Shells to Julia Vesuvius. She was going to perform tonight in front of a 10-foot volcano blowing smoke and synthetic lava. Once again, Ian Rainford, the man behind the underwater grotto in 'The Storm' video and the 'Sons of the Stage' clam, oversaw the build and he really surpassed himself. The volcano was in three parts and arrived on its own truck. It was still plaster of Paris colour, but Ian would get to work with his aerosol cans once it was in place. Already you could see it was going to look amazing when he'd finished. The super structure was still a little wet and lumps started falling off as the band, the crew and the Astoria crew began the tricky job of manoeuvring the base into the building. Even though it was drying out it was still very heavy and no one could work out how it had been loaded on to the truck back in Manchester. Everyone had gone a bit soft hands around the structure but finally we were all round it and inching towards the load-in bay. The stage manager appeared and he was unhappy. It seemed he hadn't been informed accurately about the size of the volcano and his crew were not insured to bring the piece in.

'That's okay, we'll get it in ourselves,' we said.

There was a bit of a face-off between the managers but we needed to put the thing down as it was so heavy. Everyone leaned on their shovels for a few minutes while a solution was found, but as more clumps of plaster fell off, it was clear the manager didn't want this thing in his building.

Finally, he saw a way out: 'Has it been fire tested?' Of course it hadn't been fire tested. 'Okay, there's no way you can bring that in.'

The stage crew gave a big sigh of relief and we resigned ourselves to taking the volcano back to Manchester. Maybe we could offer it to the city as a peace statue. Everyone gave a big heave and we tried to pick up the base to get it back on the truck. But we'd stopped working as a team and someone lost their grip. Then everyone lost their grip and the thing fell heavily to the ground. It was no longer the base of a fabulously sculptured volcano simulation and instead a big pile of plaster of Paris, wood and chicken wire. We did our best to clear it up but there were bits everywhere.

Three years later, when I'd moved to London, there were still traces of it behind the venue.

27

The Guaranteed Eternal
Sanctuary Man

Martin Moscrop, our trusted front-of-house soundman, had
been an integral part of the team for quite some time. He mentioned he'd like to have a crack at recording some tracks with
us. We hadn't yet decided who'd produce the album so we
booked ourselves and Martin into the Pink Museum in Liverpool to try out a couple of songs. 'The Scene' and 'Jellybaby'
were the two oldest songs in the set. 'Jellybaby' was probably
the tune that had benefitted the least from having real drums
on it. We'd tried recording this one countless times and it had
always been difficult. It had never really sounded as good as
Tony's demo – the one where he plays everything. We were
pleased with Martin's efforts, though. He did a pretty good job
and we earmarked his recording for the LP. 'The Scene' also
sounded pretty good, except for the guitars, which sounded

rubbish (the fault of the player, not the producer). Sadly, those were never fixed.

At some point between the Astoria gig and our recording session at the Pink Museum, I decided to have all my hair cut off. The haircut was a terrible mistake and probably broke the spine of World of Twist. What possessed me to do it I'll never know, though, admittedly, the hair had become very high maintenance, very uncomfortable and was costing me a fortune in products. Although it did the band no favours, as a measure of how well our press department was operating around this time, my new hairdo made the gossip page of the *NME*.

We were in a bit of a stew about how to proceed with the album. Circa were anxious to get us into the studio, even though we didn't feel ready. The fact that our first two records – our best two songs – had stiffed hadn't done our confidence much good and we'd have liked a couple of months off to work on some other tunes. It wasn't that we didn't have any material – we had tons of it – but very little was finished. If we went in the studio straight away, then we'd have to put both singles on the album, which we didn't want to do.

The decision, it turned out, was not in our hands. The album needed to be recorded in the next month to meet the release schedule. Circa wanted it out in October, when they would get us out on tour again to promote it. If things worked out we could start looking at some European dates in the New Year. Possibly some US dates. Now you're talking.

We were loath to jeopardise our relationship with Circa by sticking our necks out, so it was agreed we'd record the album throughout June. We liked Martin Moscrop's mixes, but there was something nagging away at us. We kind of wanted a Bob Ezrin or Todd Rundgren-type producer – someone who'd really get involved in the music, someone who did arrangements and could work with strings, brass and choirs even. Our heads were still full of great themes and the way we'd sounded on record up to then wasn't the sound we had in our heads.

It was Nick who suggested Dave Ball, formerly of Soft Cell and now, with Richard Norris, one half of the Grid. Tony wasn't at all convinced but I really liked the idea. Dave would get all the reference points, the film themes, the fake soul, the trashiness and the darker stuff. He was also a genius with melodies and might even lend us a couple. I realised I was basing my judgement on Dave's work with Soft Cell and, to a lesser extent, the stuff he did with Nick and Jim in English Boy on the Loveranch. I hadn't been paying much attention to his most recent projects – electronic dance stuff wasn't really my cup of tea. Nevertheless, Nick organised a meeting and it was all very positive. Dave would take his Grid hat off for a few weeks and we'd approach the thing as though it were one of the great lost psychedelic records; as though the Electric Prunes, the Turtles, the Left Banke, the Seeds and the Nazz had all booked themselves anonymously into Sunset Sound in 1969 to make an LP with the Wrecking Crew and Brian Wilson at the controls.

So a deal was struck. We'd record the World of Twist album at a residential studio just off the Fulham Road in London. There'd be six new songs, new versions of 'The Storm' and 'Sons of the Stage' and we'd keep the two tracks we recorded with Martin Moscrop in Liverpool.

We had a plan, but it was deeply flawed. There were various reasons this wasn't the ideal time for us to be recording the LP, but, most significantly, my working relationship with Tony Ogden was now virtually non-existent. Although we got on okay, Tony and I weren't really close. We connected on a musical level – we always had. We liked the same '60s and '70s music and there was definitely a mutual respect for each other's talents. We liked going out dancing together and we had a laugh sometimes, but there had always been something missing. I think he found me a bit intense and I found him a bit intimidating. Maybe it was a sexual thing. He was about the best-looking person I knew, he was a great mover, he was funny, he was fearless and he was unbelievably talented. He wasn't the greatest singer out there and I think that bothered him, but, as far as writing pop tunes, I'd never met anyone who came close to Tony O.

From Tony's perspective, I knew he liked being in a band with me: I was tall, weird, quite rock-starry, I could dance, I could write a tune and, like him, my idea of a great rock band was not conventional. There was no obvious reason we didn't connect. I got on well with Jim, Nick, Andy, Adge, Julia and everyone in our circle, and Tony did, too. We just didn't click with each other. To me it was really important and ate away at me all the time. For Tony, it was almost as if he accepted and actually liked the situation. He was a great rock scholar. He'd read about Jagger and Richards, Townshend and Daltrey, Lennon and McCartney, the Beach Boys and the Davies brothers. While Tony wouldn't have been arrogant enough to place us in that company, our counterfeit 'difficult' relationship perhaps satisfied his sense of rock mythology.

There was also a monetary side to this that idled away in the background. Tony didn't have to give me half the publishing, I knew that. The songs certainly weren't half mine, so it was enormously generous. Maybe he saw it as a down payment on my future industry; maybe he viewed it as 'I write the first album while Gordon sells second-hand clothes, then Gordon writes the second album while I embark on a massive drugs binge'. It was never mentioned, but I think he was always a bit peeved that he was bringing much more to the table than anyone else.

Since the band had signed to Circa, I hadn't spent a lot of time in Tony's company, which had brought our relationship into sharp focus. Dave Hardy was very aware of this and was always trying to engineer situations that would throw us together. We'd meet up when necessary, to record music, shoot a video, do an interview, but somehow I'd reached the point where the prospect of spending two weeks with Tony filled me with dread. Not because I didn't want to spend two weeks with him, but because I knew that while I was trying to record my parts and offer up opinions, his coolness and lack of communication would set my paranoia levels to eleven. So I elected to stay in Manchester while Tony and Nick put down the basic album tracks. I'd hang back and work on my guitar parts. I told everyone it was because I hated being in the studio and they believed me, but that wasn't the full story.

I worked really hard on the guitar parts at home, particularly on 'The Lights'. When I joined up with Tony and Nick in Fulham, the atmosphere was surprisingly relaxed. Straight away I regretted not having been there when they'd recorded the brass parts for 'Lose My Way' and, in particular, 'The Spring'. They didn't sound right. They were really half-arsed and flat but it was too late to rectify them now. Also, the live bass was nothing like we'd discussed. What had happened to that Ladi Geisler 'knack-bass' sound we'd promised ourselves?

Nick's drums, however, were sounding great and both he and Tony had been very impressed with the engineer Nick Hopkins. One evening we stayed behind with Nick and listened to what had been put down so far. We all sat facing the giant studio monitors and Nick pushed the faders up, nothing more than that. We agreed it was sounding ace, much more powerful than anything we'd done previously, and we all dared to imagine this would be a great album. Sadly, listening to Nick Hopkins's desk mixes that evening was the best *Quality Street* ever sounded.

It had been decided, though not by us, that we'd finish off the recording and mix the album at Peter Gabriel's Real World studios in Box, Wiltshire. It had also been decided for some reason that Nick Hopkins wouldn't be joining us.

The journey to Box with future train driver Nick Sanderson is the greatest rail journey I've ever been on and probably the most fun I had during my entire music career.

3 August 1991. Nick loves a train journey and he's planned our route down to the finest detail: Manchester to Bristol Temple Meads, Bristol to Bath, and a taxi from Bath to Box. The journey will take around five hours door to door so we're going to get absolutely rat-arsed. Train journeys and booze, they were made for each other. There is nothing so pleasurable as whiling away the miles, with a good pal, some pleasant scenery and a

nice can of beer – and it has to be cans, wine bottles should be reserved for the *Orient Express*, the Flying Scotsman, the Transcantabrico Gran Lujo – bought preferably from the buffet as that will introduce a pub-type vibe to the proceedings.

Underpinning this desire to get totally wasted is a nervous excitement, unspoken but growing by the minute. We are going to meet Peter Gabriel of Genesis. We were twelve and thirteen years old when *The Lamb Lies Down on Broadway* was released, a record that shaped our youth. We both vividly recall the day we picked up our *Melody Maker*s from the newsagent in August 1975 with the heart-stopping 'Gabriel Out of Genesis?' headline. We both have a lot of history with Peter and, try as we both did to exorcise his presence during the punk wars, he never really left us. In less than six hours, we will be enjoying Peter Gabriel's hospitality at his lavish West Country retreat and we will be trying to remain cool while realising we owe it to our teenage selves to be on the verge of hysteria. For Nick, this will not be his first visit to one of PG's homes. As an eleven-year-old Genesis fanatic he'd broken into Gabriel's house for a walkabout, an episode celebrated in the Saint Etienne song 'Over the Border'. This will be the first time he's visited chez Gabriel fully invited.

One of Nick's public-school protocols was to give everyone nicknames: Tony was Tobes; Andy was Hodges; Jim was Flames; Adge was Hadger (always pronounced with a deep West Country accent). My name, 'Ken', derived from my fantasy football career name.

It is on the journey to Real World that Nick and I properly flesh out our imaginary football careers.

WHEN DOES THE MIND-BENDING START?

Kenny King comes to professional football fairly late, aged twenty-five, having been plucked by Oldham Athletic from non-league Stalybridge Celtic for £18,000. The *Oldham Chronicle* describe me as 'an intelligent, quick-thinking midfielder with a deceptive turn of pace and an eye for goal'. As a youth player mindful of its *Ripping Yarns* associations and not wanting to be nicknamed Barnstoneworth, I'd dropped the old-fashioned-sounding 'Gordon' in favour of the more football sounding Kenny. Oldham fans are quick to adopt the Bower Fold mantra, sung to the tune of Chicory Tip's 'Son of My Father', and soon the terraces are ringing out to the sound of my name, 'Oh Kenny, Kenny . . .' I become a folk hero at Boundary Park with my long hair and extra-long sleeves (in honour of 'The King', the great Denis Law). After four outstanding years with the Latics, which see them rise from the fourth to first division in consecutive years, I am scouted by Manchester United as a possible replacement for the lethargic Neil Webb. And so it is that, at the age of twenty-nine, I make my debut under Sir Alex Ferguson in the 1991–92 season. I only play fifty times for the Reds but score the winning goal in the FA Cup final against Liverpool, before a horrific tackle by Manchester City's Ian Brightwell the following season brings about early retirement. Latterly, I spend a couple of seasons at Stockport County but never regain my form and then retire from the game in 1994, opening a successful Man United-themed diner in Chorlton-cum-Hardy called Breakfast of Champions. I am an occasional pundit on Piccadilly Radio and a popular after-dinner speaker on the north-west sporting circuit. I regularly provide matchday hospitality at Boundary Park where I'm something of a legend and I'm remembered with great fondness by United supporters, many of whom believe Paul Ince would not have got into United's Premier League-winning sides of the early '90s had I remained fit.

Nick Sanderson's imaginary career was altogether grander and he represented United and England for many years as captain, going on to break the all-time goal-scoring and appearance records for both club and country. After lifting the World Cup at consecutive finals in 1990 and 1994, he was knighted in the New Year's Honours list for services to football. A 2000 poll conducted by the BBC would name him as the most popular English sportsperson of all time.

By the time we get to Bristol, we're on to designing football stadiums. Nick wins with his design for Scunthorpe United's new ground, which resembles Albert Speer's 'Cathedral of Light' from the 1936 Nuremburg Rally. The ground has been rebuilt following a military coup that sees the country placed under the command of right-wing dictator, 'Iron' Jack Brownsword, an avid Scunthorpe United fan.

We finally reach Bath but decide we'll go for a few more pints and order a taxi after last orders. Driving over to Box, we get chatting to the driver who speaks with a very acute Bristol (or 'Brissle') accent. He's very interested that we're visiting Real World. 'So have you met this Peter Gabriel then?' 'No we haven't.' 'I've been told that he's a very boring man.' 'Is that right?' 'Yeah, I've never met him myself, but that's what they tell me.' The driver, who's obviously forfeited his tip by bad-mouthing our host, finally arrives at PG's place, which we note is only a mile or so from Solsbury Hill. *Let the magic begin* . . .

Dave Hardy, who's very excited to see us, meets us at the gate and asks us to close our eyes. He leads us across the car park and into a building that smells like straw. He sits us down on some hessian mats and we open our eyes. We are sitting in the main control room at Real World, which looks like the command deck of the Starship *Enterprise* but three times bigger. It's an absolute mind-fuck. The studio monitors are the size of pool tables; the three-sided mixing desk looks like it could control Greater London. Everything is acoustically designed to the last millimetre, although our engineer Richard tells us subsequently it's the worst sounding 'live' room he's ever worked in. Peter Gabriel is nowhere to be seen but we're reliably informed he'll be around tomorrow. 'We told them you'd be arriving late and they left some sandwiches for you.' Dave leads us out of the Starship *Enterprise* and into the living room of the adjoining house where under a glass platter is a selection of the tastiest sandwiches we've ever tasted. We're going to like it here. In the next five days, we take lots of walks (Nick is particularly anxious to see the Box railway tunnel), we go boating, we play croquet, we go to Moles Club in Bath, we play table tennis and we watch the procession of celebrities come and go. Tom Robinson arrives in his sports car one afternoon; international drum wizard Manu Katché is seen wandering about; Nick thinks he's seen bald Chapman Stick-playing bassist Tony Levin. As for Gabriel, I meet him only once at breakfast by mistake. I'm overwhelmed and don't know what to say. Nick, on the other hand, beats the great man in a table-tennis competition and, hearing that his old Genesis masks are on the premises, asks PG if we can borrow them for a photo shoot. Peter's response is, 'Ah yes, the masks. That was a long time ago,' which Nick takes as a no. One evening, we're sitting outside the mill housing PG's personal studio and listening to him bashing out maudlin tunes on an electric piano. He's working on his 1992 album *Us*, which documents his divorce, his subsequent and recently terminated relationship with actress Rosanna Arquette and the growing distance between him and his first daughter. It's fair to say that the music we're hearing, though rather beautiful, isn't particularly jolly.

We leave Real World not 100 per cent sure why we'd gone there in the first place. I'd put some guitars down, we'd recorded some vocals and eaten lots of delicious homemade soup. But we achieved nothing we couldn't have accomplished had we stayed in Fulham. I certainly don't regret going there, meeting PG and all that. It's something to tell the kids, but it didn't contribute one iota to producing a great album.

We get back to Manchester and review our labours. We play the album tracks forwards, backwards, side to side, but it's obvious to us and to all that we haven't made a great album. Friends ask to hear it but the reaction is never more than polite, although Gordon Mackay, a guitarist I used to work with in Affleck's Palace and whose opinion I respect, describes it thus: 'An album that doesn't get any louder no matter how much you turn it up.'

There's no time to dwell on our shit recordings, however; we need an album cover asap. We've decided to call the album *Quality Street*. It's since been suggested that it was a reference to the Quality Street Gang that operated in Manchester during the '60s and '70s, but it definitely wasn't and, had we heard of them, we wouldn't have called it that. 'Quality' was just a word Nick and I overused, originating I think with the football commentator John Motson, who described everything in terms of quality ('A quality goal by a quality player' – Tony Currie, 22 March 1975, Sheffield United v. West Ham). There was also a post-match interview with Gary Lineker during Italia '90 where he kept saying 'quality'. That was important. The idea of recreating the illustration from the Quality Street confectionary tin came later, but it was an easy sell to Tony, who fancied dressing up in a hussar jacket like David Hemmings in *The Charge of the Light Brigade* or Terence Stamp in *Far from the Madding Crowd*, with Julia as his Julie Christie. We scouted a few locations for the shoot and the Pantiles in Tunbridge Wells, which I remembered from my youth, looked like the best option. It took a bit of planning. Jim would take the photos, of course; his girlfriend Judith, a BBC make-up artist, would handle all the slap and stick-on facial hair. We'd have to spend an afternoon down at Angels Costume Hire on Shaftesbury Avenue getting togged up. There was a bit of an argument during that procedure when Julia returned with the Polaroids from her Angels fitting having eschewed the dress we'd requested in favour of something a bit more alluring. Her wings were severely clipped and she was ordered to wear the period-precise crinoline monstrosity in which she appears on the album cover, thus explaining her miserable expression.

28

A Good Day in the Wells

The day in Tunbridge Wells was great fun. Everyone got into costume and character very quickly and soon we were parading up and down the Pantiles in full period bluster. On the downside it was swelteringly hot and the famous Georgian walkway was teeming with Spanish school kids.

Tony looked wonderful. He *was* Captain Nolan and Sergeant Troy. There couldn't have been a woman on the Pantiles that afternoon who didn't want a feel of his sabre. Nick was in the costume of a nineteenth-century peeler and was particularly enjoying the authority/respect that came with the position. Andy was a cheeky barrow boy/Charlie Peace-type character who'd do well to avoid the attentions of Constable Sanderson and his whistle, cosh and mobile phone. Julia looked sensational in her hated pink crinoline. If only she'd smile. Adge's outfit included a wig, moustache and the requisite mutton-chop sideburns. He looked very distinguished – a member of parliament (a Whig, naturally), a surgeon or perhaps a man of letters. Adge was filming the day's events, breaking off from time to time to load and unload the film stock. Jim has a wonderful photo of him sitting in a room at the hotel in costume and trying to change the camera film in a special light-sealed case. It looks like a strange Victorian gynaecological operation.

We may have been dismissive about the finished album but the *Quality Street* cover was something we were all extremely proud of and, to our huge delight, it got voted one of the worst covers of the year in *The Guardian*.

'Sweets' would be the single from the album and Jim and I had a lot of fun putting a live collage, *Andy Hobson's Pockets*, together for the cover. We were delighted with the result but a little of the shine was taken off when we were wrongly accused by Central Station Design of ripping off their ideas. It was a pity as I really rated their stuff. Circa came up with their own promotional gadget for the single, a Wrangler pocket containing a picture CD. I hated the idea, but you have to go along with these things.

Circa wouldn't trust us to make a third video ourselves and pulled in talented young director Walter Stern for the job. Five years later, Walter had awards coming out of his ears for his work with the Prodigy, but for the time being he was busy making sense of this unusual combo from the north-west of England who'd been foisted upon him. The video featured our old friend Bob Stanley from Saint Etienne as the central character. Bob plays an obsessive World of Twist fan whose misguided devotion is his only escape from a home life dominated by his mother's migraine attacks and his full-on twat of a brother.

The video gave us the opportunity to shoot a photo I'd had in my head for years: a group of young men and women pose for a photo-journalist in some remote backwater where culture and fashion are in short supply. With limited resources, this gang has pieced together what their idea of 'cool' looks like and in their small world they're the cock of the block. I gave the costume and props department very specific instructions for the shoot. The gang's bikes had to be Honda 50 Super Cubs with the round headlamps. Imagine my horror when they delivered two virtually new Honda 50s with the new square headlamps. I had my customary strop while Jim soldiered on to produce what I consider the greatest rock band photo ever shot. Two years later, the young Oasis hunted him down to do their first ever photo shoot on the basis of that photo. And thirty years on, taking pride of place in my hallway, the clothes, the bikes and the photo look perfect.

29

A Night in Vienna

One of the big disappointments was that we didn't travel abroad much with the band. I'd have particularly liked to go to the US, as I'd never been there, but how we'd have fared in that den of iniquity is anyone's guess. The Japanese would probably have been interested – the cartoon nature of the group would have appealed to them, I think. Our only trips abroad as a band were a mini tour of France and, preceding that, a crazy festival in Rotterdam called, somewhat misleadingly, 'Ein Abend in Wien' (A Night in Vienna). We'd almost certainly blagged this gig because of Nick's connections with the promoter Willem Venema.

Chris Whitehead was a handsome, granite-hewn, deep-spoken northerner. He looked like Leonard Cohen's better-looking brother. He spoke with a deep authentic Mancunian drawl and his background was engineering. Chris was an old friend of

Tony and Dave's from the Cheadle Hulme days. What not everyone knew at the time was that Chris had been an androgynous glam rocker back in the day, the lead singer in the Inadequates, featuring Dave Hardy on bass and the ubiquitous Tony Ogden on drums. Chris had always harboured a deep longing for a life in rock and left his father's engineering firm to come and tour-manage World of Twist. At the time it probably seemed like a smart career move, based on the assumption that the World of Twist trajectory would be ever-upwards.

Chris's first assignment was to chaperone the band to Rotterdam for the Sigmund Freud-themed festival, but really it was Chris who needed looking after. He was quite frankly out of control. He was a seasoned climber and had promised to walk me up the Matterhorn when all this was over. On the crossing, the band and crew got absolutely annihilated in the bar. I have some lovely photos of Chris and our road crew flailing around in the kiddies' ball-pit. We all calmed down for an hour or two and watched *Terminator II* in the ferry cinema. An hour later we were back on the booze and ushered up to the top deck for some group photos. The mood was very buoyant and as the designated photographer for the trip, I did my very best to document the joyfulness. I still curse myself for losing interest by the time we were in Rotterdam. Photo opportunities missed included the band hanging out with Sonic Youth, Nirvana, Frank Black and the sight of the World of Twist girls getting chased around the venue by amorous Dutchmen.

'Hey Gord, get a photo of this.'

WHEN DOES THE MIND-BENDING START?

I spun around and witnessed the most frightening thing I've ever seen in my life: there was Chris Whitehead (tour manager, experienced climber and father of two) hanging by his Herculean fingertips off the side of the ferry with only his very strong grip and alcoholic anaesthesia standing between life and a cold, watery death. The fact that we were up on deck would suggest it was a calm evening on the North Sea, but really the North Sea is never that calm and Whitehead was drunk beyond words.

The Rotterdam venue was in stark contrast to the insanity of the ferry crossing: a post-modern conference hall, populated by polite, efficient young men, who studiously went about the task of unloading our gear and bags and taking them into the venue.

We'd been booked to perform in the main hall, the Heldenplatz, ahead of the Smashing Pumpkins, Frank Black and Sonic Youth. We hadn't been able to bring our usual regalia with us but we performed pretty well, then enjoyed a very bizarre evening.

Andy had his heart set on seeing a new band I'd never heard of called Nirvana. They were up and coming and scheduled to play one of the smaller rooms at the venue. The place was packed to the gills and Andy shoehorned himself inside, but I couldn't be bothered and consequently never got to see Nirvana. Still, redemption of sorts was just around the corner, if you're looking for a story arc. It was a fantastic evening and I was determined that we should have more artsy engagements like this. At the swanky hotel we were staying in with all the other bands, we were sitting together in the bar later that evening on some nice old Chesterfields and there was a great band spirit. We'd done a pretty good gig and felt like fine ambassadors of north-west indie pop.

We noticed this great lanky column, who obviously couldn't hold his drink, tottering around the lounge, stumbling into passers-by and apologising. He swayed up to our table and asked if he could 'hang' with us. The man was clearly off his tree so would no doubt be very entertaining. He introduced himself as Kris and told us he was the bass player in a band called Nirvana who earlier that evening had played a chaotic show in the intimate Trabanthalle. He was particularly aggrieved that the stage manager had given his band a bit of a roasting for trashing their own gear, as well as most of the hired-in rig and in particular the microphones.

'Fucking guy wanted us to eat shit.'

'Well, they were his microphones – you shouldn't have smashed them up.'

'Err, yeah, but he wanted us to *eat shit*.'

'Well, he's got a point, hasn't he? It was very disrespectful.'

'Yeah, but this *fucker* wanted us to EAT SHIT.'

Kris stuck around for a bit, but he gradually became quieter and quieter until he was just a nodding sleepy head on the end of a flagpole. We were wondering what we should do with him, as he obviously needed a lie down, when the singer from his band and the girl from Sonic Youth turned up. They were very charming, checking to see if Kris had been bothering us. We said no, he'd been great fun. They picked him up and pushed him into the lift. I never really got Nirvana, it all sounded a bit like the Police to me, but Kurt Cobain, for the few seconds I spent in his company, seemed like a nice lad. What happened to him was really sad.

Ahead of our trip to France for a three-date package tour with Ocean Colour Scene and Ride, our third single, 'Sweets', is released. It's definitely the poppiest number in the World of Twist canon, so it could do well. The early signs are promising. Walter Stern's done a great job on the video and everyone agrees that it's a cert for *The Chart Show*. The anticipated backlash has been put on hold, it seems, and once again we get some great reviews in the music weeklies, although Right Said Fred give the single an absolute hammering in *Smash Hits*.

'Sweets', one of the better tracks on the album, is another of my tunes, or one of the two that were probably more mine than Tony's. It was inspired by a Freda Payne B-side called 'Suddenly It's Yesterday' and contains my favourite World of Twist lyric: 'Life is rushing by and I can feel it leaving, / We're all going to die and I can't take it baby'. We were pissing ourselves laughing when we were coming up with lines for the song. Similarly, the lyrics to 'Sons of the Stage' and 'Blackpool Tower', which were also collaborations, were exercises in trying to write the trashiest, most insincere bollocks we could come up with.

As you've no doubt guessed, 'Sweets' didn't get us a hit. Stalling at number fifty-eight, it came in ten places lower than our previous single, 'Sons of the Stage'. If Circa weren't panicking earlier in the year, I'm sure they were now. Quality Street was due for release two days after our return from the French dates and three before we embarked on our second UK tour. It felt as though we'd only just arrived at the table and already the album was beginning to look like our last throw of the dice.

16 October 1991. The French trip starts badly. We leave England much later in the day than scheduled and head to Lille in northern France. We don't get to the hotel until after midnight and they've given our rooms to one of the other bands. Adge is the angriest person in the party and is about to leap the counter to confront the concierge when Ellie, our onboard linguist, averts an international incident. Her fairly fluent French ensures we get alternative accommodation instead of a curt '*Va te faire enculer!*' with a *bras d'honneur*.

The 'Capital of Flanders' is an interesting place. Twinned with Leeds, West Yorkshire, Lille is the home of Pelforth Brune, my all-time favourite tipple, and birthplace of Charles de Gaulle, Louis Pasteur and Didier Six. We're playing at a 2,000-capacity music venue called l'Aéronef. I recall nothing of the show, but I do remember the municipal gardens having a crocodile in a pond no bigger than a kid's sandpit. That's not right, surely? In the town centre there's a fair going on and lots of people are in national costume scoffing Flemish tart and knocking back gallons of the Brown Pelican. It would have been nice to stick around but the following day we're bound for Paris and a show at La Cigale, the legendary venue in the 18th arrondissement.

We're in the capital as part of the Inrockuptibles Festival. Ride will headline by virtue of their superior fan base. Ocean Colour Scene will come on second and Twist will kick-start the party. Ocean Colour Scene are from Solihull and they're quite serious.

We've met them before when we were recording our album in Fulham. I recall the singer coming up to me in the bar to tell me I looked like him and then not saying much else. He reminded me a bit of Manfred Mann's second singer Mike d'Abo but he looked nothing like me. It was an odd introduction. Ride and OCS are a fair bit younger than us and they're all better musicians (or the guitarists are). It's quite intimidating. Both bands have guitar roadies and Ride have a particularly impressive set-up. They've got about twenty guitars waiting in the wings and a table where this chap tunes them all and changes the strings. I remember I've got a big box of Super Slinkys back at the flat but I can't recall the last time I changed my strings, certainly not recently.

Paris is memorable for some exuberant disco dancing in the hotel bar and a bagful of budget vibrators Nick has purchased from a local sex boutique. Again, I remember nothing of the show. I'm sure without our usual props, lights and slideshow, we feel quite exposed, but then we have Tony O out front, something neither Ride nor OCS can compete with.

Tony and I haven't been getting on, though. We've barely spoken since I got back from London. It bothers me greatly, although Tone doesn't seem arsed about it at all. Things are about to come to a head in Lyon.

The way the album's turned out has really got to us. As one of the most hyped bands of 1990, it feels like there's a whole world out there willing us to fail and we've handed them all the ammunition they need to sink us. Rather than close ranks, rifts are starting to develop. It began with Julia. Splitting with Tony made it hard for her to stay with the band. She was the second most noticeable thing about us and we didn't replace her, just congratulated ourselves on becoming a gentlemen's club. Tony, rather than taking the opportunity to Ziggy Stardust himself, has moved in the other direction. His stage-wear has started to resemble his civvies and there appears to be less of an appetite to *mach schau*. He's still utterly captivating as a frontman but it's as though he's made a conscious decision that it's not his job alone to sell the band any more.

There was a disagreement before we headed off about Cath Berry coming along for the trip. Tony had argued that we couldn't afford to bring someone just to sell merchandise. Dave and I overruled him on the premise that we'd never made those kinds of decisions with an eye on the budget. It was always about the vibes and everyone liked having Cath along. It put Tony in a difficult position. It probably didn't help that my girlfriend Ellie was joining us, too.

What Tony and I really needed was to start writing together again, to get ourselves back to the place where we connected most. But that seemed such a long way off. We had nearly two months of gigging ahead of us. Death by a thousand slights.

My head's been okay for a while. I've been self-medicating with my usual cocktail of booze and Valium, but now things don't feel right. The paranoia levels are rising and I can sense I might be heading for one of my 'do's. The trip to Lyon is a nightmare – seven hours of motorway driving and possibly the shittest service stations on the planet.

I've definitely done something to upset Tony, but I don't know what and will never find out. He's stopped talking to me completely and won't even meet my eye. I handle this the only way I know how: by imploding. As soon as we get to Lyon I hit the beers and it's a miracle I can actually stand up, let alone play, by the time we get on stage. Ocean Colour Scene have very kindly agreed to let us go on second. Perhaps they've realised we're a tough act to follow or maybe they're just dying to get home. The paranoia hits its peak when I'm on stage. *Why is everyone staring at me?* It's the worst show I've ever done and all I want to do is hit the booze again the minute I get off.

After the show I strike up a conversation with the singer from Ride and tell him how much I hate the band I'm in. He's very pleasant and appears sympathetic but no doubt is just willing me to fuck off. We get back to the hotel, which looks like an office block on a trading estate in Leigh. Everyone's in the bar and Tony is holding court. He couldn't look happier. I take this as my cue to explode. Nobody in the band sees it as I'm back in my room, but Ellie witnesses the full ranting mess.

'I've just played my last gig with that cunt,' I tell her. 'I fucking hate him, I hate the band, I hate our album, we're fucking shit. I'll be handing my cards in the minute we get back to Manchester, that's a promise.'

Somehow I calm down and get some sleep, but I wake up with a raging hangover and the events of the previous evening come flooding back. I realise I have a day's travelling to get through before we are home. My heart plummets.

We assemble for breakfast to the thrilling news that the van's been broken into and the guitars have been stolen. They've also taken Andy's Fender Amp head and my Mesa Boogie MkIV. I'm heartbroken about the Les Paul but I'm not too bothered about the Boogie and actually the Gibson Firebird I got recently is a bit shit so, when the insurance comes through, I'll get something better. However, this is World of Twist land and our claim will be turned down by the insurance company as the van in which our gear was stored wasn't parked in the gated underground car park we had use of. *Putain de shitbags!!*

I'm determined not to travel back in the company of Ogden, so I volunteer to keep Chris Whitehead company in the equipment van. This is a huge mistake. As a consequence of the break-in, my side window is missing and I spend the next eight hours freezing my tits off listening to Whitehead moan about how we're all a bunch of lazy soft twats who wouldn't last a minute in engineering or any other proper job. How right he was.

On returning to Manchester, I have four days to get my head straight before we go out on tour but I'm still in descent and worse is to come. It's about three in the morning and I'm absolutely fucked but I can't get to sleep. I lie there for hours worrying, panicking, worrying. All I can think about is getting out of the band. There's no fucking way I want to do this tour. I want some time alone, away from Tony fucking Ogden. Sleep comes, but not for long. About an hour after drifting off, I wake up to find the bed absolutely soaked – the sheets, pillows, everything. At first, I think I've pissed the bed – I used to be good at that – but I'm dripping in sweat. I'm covered in it even though the flat's freezing. I take some more Valium; I've been guzzling them like Tic Tacs since we left France. It takes the edge off but it doesn't get me any sleep so I stop trying. I get through the day somehow, but my mood is pretty bad. The telephone hasn't rung all day and I realise I haven't spoken to a soul since I said goodbye to Whitehead.

Normally I'd get a Chinese and a bottle of red and watch some film I'd seen fifty times, but I don't want to do anything. I just sit there; even moving's an effort. The next night I don't sleep at all, so I've had about six hours in the past seventy-two. Finally, the phone rings and it's my mum asking how the French trip went. I can barely speak. She asks me to come over for some food. Maybe the change of scenery might help me relax.

She can see I'm a total mess from the moment I arrive and suggests I get an emergency doctor's appointment with her GP. So, later that afternoon, at the age of twenty-nine, I find myself sitting in a doctor's surgery, with my mother doing most of the talking. The doctor thinks it could be depression, which I'm dismissive of. I've been a bag of nerves for the past twelve years, but depression is something I've never suffered from.

The GP gives me some sleeping tablets and a course of anti-depressants to start the following day. The sleeping pills do the trick and I sleep most of the evening through to the morning. Mum drives me back to the flat but I'm still feeling like a total zombie – just numb. If someone had walked in and chucked my record collection out of the window, I wouldn't have batted an eyelid.

The tour starts the next day. Dave Hardy calls to tell me the minibus will pick me up at nine o'clock and we'll be heading off to the first show in St Andrews, Scotland. I tell him I'm not feeling too good and he starts laughing (which is typical Dave

Hardy). It's not the reaction I'm after, but it's strangely reassuring. Pull yourself together. That's something I hadn't considered. I don't know how I'm going to get through this, but I start to pack. It suddenly dawns on me I don't have a guitar. I'll have to use my old Framus, so I get it out of the case for the first time in months and see it's got no strings. *Where are those Super Slinkys when you need 'em?* All the enforced activity is slowly pulling me out of my trough.

I'm sort of ready but not looking forward to tomorrow. I really don't want to see Ogden. I pop another sleeping pill and an antidepressant and get an early night. I have a good sleep and I'm awake at seven o'clock. I don't feel too bad so I decide I'll just have a quick shower, a shave and start work on the hair – things are definitely getting back to normal!

I glance in the mirror and nearly jump out of my skin. My eyes! What's happened to my eyes?! They look fucking mental. I stare into the mirror and Peter Lorre stares back at me. I splash water over my face repeatedly, but to no avail. My eyes look like they're being held open with fuse wire. I look absolutely crazy. I try smiling but it makes it worse. Fuck, what am I gonna do? I can't let them see me like this.

The bus turns up and everyone, including Tony, is very smiley and welcoming. Everyone's in a great mood. I notice Paul Gunning's at the wheel, which is a surprise but a nice one. As the day wears on, the drugs wear off and my bug eyes return to normal. I decide to ditch the antidepressants and rely on the general bonhomie to steer me through the next few days. There does seem to be an improved mood in the camp, something to suggest this might even be fun. I told Nick about the preceding three days and the pills I'd been given and wondered if anyone had noticed how crazy I looked when they picked me up. Of course, everyone had mentioned it.

30

Grotesque (After the Gramme)

We had a pretty big crew for the second tour. They'd all be travelling in a massive tour bus, which looked like several tons of fun. Martin Moscrop was back on front of house and there were a few new faces. 'Gentle' Ben Knott had been enlisted to help out with the equipment. Ben was the most chilled person I'd ever met and he was a bit of a looker in a couldn't-give-a-fuck sort of way. It was good to have him along.

Mike Healey had joined the team as roadie and general Man Friday. We all liked him and he was very protective towards the group, which was fortunate as he was a big lad! We all made a mental note not to upset him. I felt sorry for Mike when the thing eventually folded, as he loved the band. The following summer he invited us all to his wedding. It was the last time World of Twist were all in the same room together.

Cath was with us again doing the merchandise. She was already looking worried about the amount of testosterone on show and I could tell she wasn't too thrilled about the tour bus situation.

Joining us as support were the Clouds – five super-talented fellow south Manchester musicians, mostly called Simon. Their song 'Dude Electrical Cell' from their 1992 EP *Bingo Club's Millennium Ball* is the greatest song of the 'Madchester' era. Fact.

I can never work out if the Clouds arrived too soon or too late for the party. They certainly ploughed the same sonic furrow as Spaceman 3 and Loop but, for my money, they had the edge on all those guitar-army shoe-gazer bands that emerged from the Home Counties around 1991. If I hadn't been otherwise engaged at the time I'd have loved to manage the Clouds, develop their showmanship, their stage show, introduce an exotic dancer here and there. That's assuming they would have accepted being fashioned into a Hawkwind circa 1972 tribute band.

I interviewed the Clouds while researching this and they were refreshingly philosophical about their career curve. They had not a trace of bitterness for the hand they'd been dealt. I mean, I'm poisoned by bitterness regarding World of Twist and we never recorded anything that came close to 'Dude Electric Cell'.

24 October 1991. After our turbulent gallic experience, the St Andrews show goes surprisingly well. When *Quality Street* gets an expanded release in 2013, we include the encores 'She's a Rainbow' and 'Kick Out the Jams' from this gig. They're both desk recordings but show what the band was capable of on a

good night. After the show, Paul Gunning announces he won't be driving us back to the hotel (what we're paying him for) because he's pissed out of his head. 'Sorry lads, nothing I can do about it.'

Paul's an old friend of Dave Hardy and Tony. A rabid Man City fan, he's particularly proud of a sports annual he owns in which he's pictured at Old Trafford cricket ground in the 1970s being drunk and disorderly. The photo is captioned 'The Ugly Side of Cricket'. Gunning is a big fan of 'The Lights' and always positions himself in the audience during the song to make sure I'm playing the guitar solo correctly. I don't let him down – I wouldn't dare.

The following morning, we go for a walk on the hallowed greens of St Andrews. It's about 9 a.m. and a party of elderly players have made an early start. As we approach them, this short cheerful American fellow gives us a broad smile and tips his cap. 'Hi there.' 'Alright,' we collectively grunt, barely looking up. It's a bit too early for pleasantries. We walk on a few steps before Gunning says, 'That was Lee Trevino, wasn't it?' None of us are golf fans so we wouldn't have recognised the Merry Mex, but it's made Gunning's day and for that I'm very happy.

After a few nights in hotels, I swap with Cath so she doesn't have to sleep on the stinky tour bus. It's not a totally altruistic gesture as the tour bus looks way more fun than the band's minibus and travelling while you sleep is an added bonus.

My first ride on the bus is a cross-country trek from Colchester to Bristol, so we'll definitely still be on the road by the time we hit the pillows. Everything's loaded up so it's time for the crew to relax and they seem to be much better at it than the band. Maybe it's for my benefit but Moscrop puts a tape on of that evening's gig. It's the first time I've heard a decent recording of us live and it sounds amazing – I can't believe what Martin's been doing with the guitars. They don't sound too bad on stage but out front they sound incredible. He's got these massive split delays, that he fades in when I start playing lead. It sounds like I've got another set of hands. It almost disguises all the bum notes I'm playing. Tony as well sounds amazing, so assured, and he's hitting every note. The live drums and bass really make a difference, too. Even though most of the sounds are still sequenced, we definitely sound less like we're miming. Everyone agrees the band is really starting to rock.

This is great. I love travelling by bus. The trauma of France is a distant memory and I can't remember feeling so happy. In fact, I might even take some cocaine. I've only done coke once before and hated the stuff, but everyone's in such a good mood and my brain seems to have returned to normal so let's give it another go! Thirty minutes later and I'm in full grotesque flow. Everyone gets their turn as I tell them exactly what I think of them, supremely confident that it's all they've ever wanted to hear. Thankfully I haven't upset anyone but I sense I've kind of broken the after-gig spell as everyone drifts quietly off to bed. But I'm buzzing, Totally Wired. I stay awake on my own for several hours as the street-light tracers draw a right to left white line across the country.

On my first morning on the Nightliner, I wake up to a very empty bus that doesn't look quite as cosy as it had the previous evening. By the time I crawl out of my bunk, the crew have been up for a couple of hours doing the load-in. I stroll around in my underpants for a few minutes, trying to find a cigarette, and notice there's hundreds of young people walking past the bus. The sight of a skinny, pasty-faced, half-naked pop star in mustard-coloured Y-fronts isn't met with the reverence it surely deserves and there's a lot of pointing and laughing. It's lunchtime on the main campus at Bristol University. *Please God, don't let any of these people be coming to the gig tonight.* I find my kecks and go in search of the crew. Bristol is Nick's old stomping ground and he's promised to show me round the town in the afternoon. Like the rest of his brothers, Nick had been forced to go to Clifton College for his secondary education. The fact that Nick emerged from that particular seat of learning as the fine man he is and not a complete prick is testament to his marvellous character.

The Bristol gig is another stormer. Back on the coach after the show, everyone's chopping out lines again but nobody offers me any. There's obviously been some talking. Martin suggests, with a fatherly smile, that maybe it'd be a good idea if I laid off the coke this evening. That's absolutely fine – I know I can't handle the stuff. I'll stick to speed in future if I want a little pick-up. The drug of kings.

I haven't completely abandoned the group and retire to the hotel when the old barnet needs some attention.

In Nottingham, we've been booked into a particularly strange place. The bar is full of vintage gaming machines, including those ones that double as a drinks tables. Everyone has their heads down playing Asteroids and Pong, but Nick's engaged by the vintage GPO call box in reception and a possible photo opportunity. An hour later, he and Gunning have stripped down to their briefs and are busy recreating the famous 'Tom Jones in his telephone box' photo. They both look sensational and we get some great pictures. I remind myself that the reason young men get involved in this rock 'n' roll caper is largely for the sex. During the first tour we'd convinced ourselves that the total lack of female attention was due to Julia's presence, but we've now been on tour for nearly three weeks, *strictly stag*, and there hasn't been a single groupie incident. Are we doing something wrong, I wonder, as our drummer leans suggestively out of the phone box in his tight nylon briefs?

Earlier that day, *Quality Street* hits the UK album charts. It sails straight in at number fifty and a week later it sails straight out again. We could blame the Christmas competition again but a pattern is emerging. We're told the record company wants to put 'She's a Rainbow' out again. It's demoralising news. Tony's raging about it and I'm with him completely. A cover version at this stage just looks like we're desperate. Admittedly, we haven't written any new material in seven months, but just give us a few weeks after the tour and we'll come up with the goods. But the deal is done and they've scheduled a release in the New Year. We refuse to promote 'She's a Rainbow' but agree to promote the B-side, 'Lose My Way', if they release it as a double A. It's a pretty shit compromise but it's all we've got. There's no video planned and even our graphics man seems to have lost interest:

the cover is just an illustration from the Letraset catalogue. I've had no part in it.

We have a night off just before the London and Manchester gigs and head down to Granada Studios to record a performance of 'Lose My Way' for a regional show called *The New*. It's just a mime and will go out that evening at eleven o'clock. Tony's been watching videos of Manfred Mann that afternoon and decides to incorporate some of singer Mike d'Abo's moves into his performance. Tone's pretty loaded by the time we film our bit and with all the gurning and d'Abo eye-rolling he puts in a very strange performance, but it's great TV. Looking at the film, it's disappointing how ordinary we now look compared to the 1990 Twist. The image definitely needs a rethink.

The London show gives us a huge boost. We get a great turnout at the Town & Country and return as all-conquering heroes for the final show on our native heath. The Academy is the main venue at Manchester University. A purpose-built 2,000-capacity concert hall, which has only been open for a year. Tonight they're charging £6 to get in, − 50p less than Nirvana and 4 quid cheaper than the Ramones, who will both be playing here over the next couple of weeks. The gig's completely sold out. Everyone's coming − mums, dads, aunties and uncles. Our old mates Rig are supporting. Jim is going through the lighting moves after the soundcheck and I stand at the back of the hall and take it all in. The set looks amazing. We've got the podiums, the giant projection screens, the whole shebang. We've come a long way in twenty-one months. Maybe it's all been a little more conventional than we'd planned but we can easily sort that. 1992 can be operation Dada. We'll regroup in the New Year and discuss how to take this to the next level. Songs, obviously – we could use some of those, but I'm not worried about that. I've got about twenty works in progress and Tony about three times that. We'll start making more use of that white elephant of a rehearsal room at the back of Piccadilly Station. We'll get a new set, design some new stage wear. Tony needs to get the glittery shirts going again. Adge and I will grow our hair out – that's a must. Andy can resurrect the Commander Straker look and maybe we can all move around a bit more on stage. There's a lot to think about.

All this positivity, though, is tempered by some serious doubts. There's the age thing, for one. Andy's just turned twenty-five, so he's got a few years left in him, but the rest of us are getting a bit long in the tooth. Adge and Nick are both thirty and I'll be joining them in a month. Tony's twenty-eight. Are we in danger of making middle-aged fools of ourselves? Andy's never going to leave his newspaper job and Nick Sanderson's getting itchy feet. He's a drummer, after all, so he'd like to play his drums once in a while. And the whole set-up is totally inequitable. Tony and I are doing all right with our publishing deal, but Nick and Adge are just scraping by. Then there's the problems with Tony and me. We've reached some sort of detente but we're still not working together and we're not really talking either – not like we were two years ago.

The Manchester show goes well. Dare I say it's a triumph? Tony's not enjoyed it for some reason, though. It's not always easy impressing the locals. Afterwards we throw a party in our rehearsal room. It causes quite a stir and at one point a police helicopter appears to be monitoring developments. The cops arrive in the early hours and turf everyone out. We point out that it's our building but they're not interested. We are in breach of the Entertainment (Increased Penalties) Act. We are raving without licence. I go home and watch *The Sandwich Man*.

31

Lose My Way

1992. The year the cold war officially ends and the Maastricht Treaty is signed. White South Africans agree to political reforms to end Apartheid. The 25th Modern Olympiad takes place in Barcelona and the UK gets a new 10p coin. But, in truth, 1992 is a terrible year. Major earthquakes strike Turkey, Nicaragua and Egypt; war breaks out in Bosnia; there's rioting on the streets of Bombay, Bangkok, London, Los Angeles and São Paulo. On 31 July, 221 people are killed in two aircraft crashes in Nepal and China. The WMO reports an unprecedented level of ozone depletion in both the Arctic and Antarctic – *so mankind is fucked*. Closer to home, Manchester is beset by rioting and, in December, a bomb attack by the provisional IRA rips the heart out of the city centre, although mercifully no one is killed. After three of her four offsprings' marriages end in divorce or separation and the family pile in Windsor goes up in flames, the queen, in a memorable speech at London's Whitehall, declares 1992 her *annus horribilis.*

For World of Twist, too, 1992 will not be a great year.

On 10 February, I pass my driving test on the third attempt. My instructor is convinced I'll never pass in the hostile surroundings of Reddish so he takes me to the leafy environs of Wilmslow, Cheshire. Just minutes before the test begins, the examiner and I break up a schoolboy fistfight outside a newsagent and form a deep bond in the process. I switch on the engine, indicate to pull out and turn on the windscreen wipers. The examiner chuckles: 'I'm always doing that!' *This one's in the bag,* I reckon. That morning, our single 'She's a Rainbow' is released. It's the fourth track taken from *Quality Street* and perhaps our last faint hope for redemption.

We have an appearance on another BBC kids' show called *Hangar 17* and are doing a one-off gig at Camden Palace in London. It has been suggested that the band gets away for a week to come up with some song ideas. Somewhere rural, away from Manchester; somewhere to relax, get the creative juices flowing again. That's how it's sold to us but we know we're on trial. Circa have a month or so to decide whether to take up World of Twist's option or let us go. Staying would be preferable, of course. Circa aren't a bad label and no strangers to success. They don't really get us – but does anyone? The 'She's a Rainbow' thing has left a bad taste in our mouths, but we could turn things around if they back us, get us some better gigs, put us on a plane to somewhere, maybe.

Love is in the air. We're at Elstree studios in Hertfordshire to film our *Hangar 17* Valentine's Day special appearance. We sign in and then go for a wander on the back lot. We find the Albert Square set of *EastEnders* and have a bit of a nosey around. The Queen Vic is locked up, but some of the houses are open so we get some photos. Jim goofs around in Frank Butcher's car lot and Andy steals a leek from Arthur Fowler's allotment, which he actually cooks when he gets home.

We're going to be filmed miming to 'Lose My Way' again. We run through it a couple of times, then they let the kids in. They all cheer and dance on cue. They're brilliant – so uninhibited and just high on life or maybe sugar. We should be paying them to entertain us. On the playback, Tony and Andy look like they're enjoying themselves but I'm just rigid. I remind myself to get very drunk if we ever do another of these.

Then there's the London appearance. We don't know it yet, but this will be our last ever gig. The Camden Palace is an old Victorian variety theatre at the wrong end of Camden High Street. I know it better from my punk years as the Music Machine. I saw Iggy Pop there in 1980. The support was Hazel O'Connor and the live performances were filmed for the movie *Breaking Glass*. She didn't go down awfully well, as I recall. It's actually a great venue for live music but I always preferred the Electric Ballroom up the road. Feet First is a weekly indie disco at the Palace featuring a live PA from a current indie front-runner or, in our case, back-marker. It's always packed out and recognised in industry parlance as an 'influencer'. Circa want us to do it and they pay the piper, so we drag ourselves the 180 miles. We can only play a thirty-minute set and we can't bring the show with us, so it's decided that we'll all dress up to make it memorable. Everyone's dug out their only suit and, strangely, we all look quite good. Not good like the Jam or the Godfathers, more good like we've all come straight from a lo-fi wedding reception.

It might be only thirty minutes but it will be a live performance tonight, no miming.

I've already put this notion in jeopardy by getting paralytic in the few hours between soundcheck and performance. That's twice in three gigs – I'm getting quite good at it. I'll turn down, I tell myself – they'll never know the difference. It's an unnecessary ruse since I knock the lead out of my guitar and don't notice until the end of the set. As we have no light show as such, we rely on the house disco lights. However, Jim has been told that we can programme words or phrases into the holographic laser display that hovers in mid-air as we play and the punters punt. Jim and Andy have decided it might be fun to take some quotes from our recent bad reviews and pop them into the machine, so projected above our heads are phrases like 'pseudo intellectuals' (I don't think anyone ever wrote that about us but it was a nice idea), 'contrived' and so on.

Circa are really pissed off about this and Dave gets it in the neck from our A&R man after the show. Admittedly, it was a bit Gerald Ratner, but I guess it was our little way of saying we're still in control here, even though we definitely weren't.

The Camden gig gets a great review in *Melody Maker* ('glorious'; 'gorgeous'; 'a mirage') but, by the time anyone gets to read it, the curtain has fallen on our concert career. We are but vapour.

WHEN DOES THE MIND-BENDING START?

'She's a Rainbow' stiffed at number sixty-eight in the singles charts, as predicted, so we all felt vindicated in a way. This scathing review from *Melody Maker*, traditionally a great supporter of the band, is probably my favourite ever bit of Wo'T press:

WORLD OF TWIST

SHE'S A RAINBOW

(Circa)

Originally a ludicrously insincere Rolling Stones' song intended as nothing more than a callous, psychedelic cash-in, 'Rainbow' is, at long last, given the treatment it so richly deserves by another bunch of desperate chancers. Sod Fabulous and the Manics, for '4 Real' sluttishness look no further than WoT, a group so devoid of pride they'll do anything, even chuck the kitchen sink at this, in exchange for a sniff of fame. Bubbly beyond belief, cheap, tacky – I can't help but admire their determination. A song for swinging-losers.

(*Melody Maker*, 1 February 1992)

or this one from the *NME* . . .

WORLD OF TWIST

SHE'S A RAINBOW

(Circa)

Packaged in what has to be the worst cover of all time (some Letraset bimbo that some jerk has coloured in with his desktop computer) lurks the crappiest version of a Rolling Stones song to date. 'She's a Rainbow' was a piece of Jagger/Richards fluff that appeared on the Stones' *Satanic Majesties Request* LP. World of Twist have mysteriously decided to update this pathetic song, only they fail to do anything with it or transform it into something special. Later on in the proceedings, they feed the song into some distortion machine and throw what's left of the poor thing into the air. Then they dance around their handbags. Pah! Get thee behind me World of Twist.

(*NME*, 1 February 1992)

In 1961, Nicolaus Silver became the second of only three greys to win the Grand National. He was bought in 1960 for £2,500 by Charles Vaughan, a businessman from south Wales. Thirty years later, his daughter Noreen has turned part of the family stud in north Pembrokeshire into a rehearsal and studio space for the pop industry. The facility has been used by Altrincham's Stone Roses, Blackwood's Manic Street Preachers and later by Stoke's own Robbie Williams. In February 1992, Stockport's World of Twist are spending a week here at the behest of their employers, Circa Records of west London. They have exactly one week in which to write a best-selling long player or they will be out on their post-Madchester ears.

I've just bought a silver Peugeot 205 from County Motors in Davenport. It's my first car and it's an absolute peach, only 15,000 on the clock and it's got a stereo radio-cassette player. 6 March 1992. I'm travelling in convoy with Andy Hobson from south Manchester to south Wales feeling very independent and grown-up. I've made a special mixtape for the journey, featuring, among others: 'Bill Is Dead' by the Fall; 'Boo's Boogie' by Betty Boo; 'The Kaleidoscope Affair' by Swing Out Sister; 'The Adventurer' by John Barry; 'Step Out of Line' by Lucas & the Mike Cotton Sound; 'Lady-O' by the Turtles; 'Backstage' by Gene Pitney; and 'The Folks Who Live on the Hill' by Peggy Lee. Although the record I am currently winding and unwinding to at home is Talk Talk's *Laughing Stock*, the minute World of Twist calls, I slip into easy-listening mode. It's always been the way.

We are taking the whole rig with us to Wales. We'll have two Atari 1040s on the go, two Akai S1000s, two Roland JD800s, guitars, amps, drums, the whole bit. It'll be a pop production line. Except it won't be.

Andy loses me somewhere around Aberystwyth. Fed up driving at convoy speed, he zooms off into the Pembrokeshire darkness. The final part of the journey is a nightmare. It feels like the clifftop drink-driving sequence in *North by Northwest*.

I arrive in the Preseli Hills flushed, flustered and a full forty minutes behind Hobson. The place is amazing, though. The food is fabulous and there's a pub less than half a mile away. Noreen Vaughan is an accommodating host, somewhere around her late fifties, we guess. She's a bit flirty in a Yootha Joyce kind of way and she seems to have more make-up on every time we see her. I don't think she's interested in any of us, although Andy flashes his smile and is allowed to ride on one of her horses later in the week.

The following day, we set up the equipment and settle down to work. We play a lot of pool, table tennis and keepy-uppy. I nominate myself as chief supplies officer and am off in the 205 at every opportunity – to Haverfordwest, Cardigan and Carmarthen, where I see Hawkwind's Nik Turner busking in the town shopping precinct. Tony discovers port after dinner one evening and gets himself a new hobby. We eat lots of nice food, smoke a lot of cigarettes and make ourselves well known at the local pub. But we're finding it difficult to get around to writing any music.

After a couple of days, we eventually switch the machines on, but it's a struggle. I remind myself of all the crap jobs I've ever had, all the crap jobs I'll have in the future and all the crap jobs everyone else has to do. For wasting this opportunity, we deserve to have our eye teeth pulled out one by one before being stampeded by gift horses. But what can we do? The creative spark is the one thing we didn't pack.

I spend a few hours toiling away on my own and think I might have come up with something. I ask everyone to give it a listen, but on playback I realise I've just recreated a northern soul tune called 'Broken Heart Attack'. Tony has a song called 'Misadventure', which everyone likes, but it's difficult to get him to sing it. Nick suggests we plug in all the instruments and have a jam, something we've never done before. The past three months have been frustrating for Nick. Of no fixed abode, he's skint and bored. He loves the band but can't stand the inactivity, the inertia. If we practised once in a while, things might be different. Living at my place doesn't help him since all I ever do is moan about the band. Nick finally explodes in the pub one evening and Dave Hardy gets the full blast.

'Why don't you leave?' Dave asks.

'There's nothing to leave,' is Nick's sad response.

Surprisingly, our experimental jam session sounds very good. We record about twenty minutes of it before repairing, triumphant, to the pub. But we're running out of time. Our A&R man will be here in two days and he'll almost certainly want to hear something. What we need is a cross between Trevor Horn and John Harvey-Jones to whip us into some shape. In a panic, Tony calls Jim Fry. Can he get down here, bring all his unused lyrics and any ideas he might have? It's a good idea: Jim's a doer, Mr Enthusiasm. We need a bit of that. Jim arrives the following afternoon and Tony immediately suggests he take over the singing. Jim's not too keen. Of course he isn't – he's been here before. Tony also asks Nick to have a go. He doesn't ask me. Everyone gets pissed again and we have another go at jamming. We record a bit. It sounds okay, but it's not going to get our contract renewed. Desperation's in the air; it's like opening your textbooks for the first time the evening before the exam. I've had enough and decide to go to bed, but Tony stays up all night – just like the old days – and tries to knock the few things we've recorded into shape. He's still at it when our A&R man turns up after breakfast. We tell him we're just finishing up the mixes. He's driven all the way from London and looks a bit put-out. He's not that bothered about catching up with the rest of us, so he sits in his Lexus playing on his Gameboy until summoned.

Tony's managed to fashion about six tracks out of the previous evening's efforts and the stuff we'd put down earlier in the week. A couple of them sound like songs. The rest sound like they might become songs if we stay here for another year.

32

Remember My Name . . . Tim!

It seemed months since we'd actually sat down and discussed the band: where we'd been; where we were going; if we were all going with it. It was as though we'd all just accepted our roles and were letting this rickety old vehicle drive itself until the wheels fell off. We'd been summoned to the pub for a summit meeting. Whether the disastrous week in the Preseli Hills had influenced his decision or whether it was something he'd been planning, Tony Ogden, the most decisive member of the band, revealed that he didn't want to sing for World of Twist any more. *So that's that then*, we all thought. But no. Tony sincerely believed this could be the start of something positive, the spur we all needed. He was sick of leading the band – and he'd been doing just that for two years. He wanted to take a back seat, play guitar, keyboards, a bit of backing vocals. He was seeing the bigger picture.

He was sick of being Tony O, the spokesman, the main man – so it was his way or World of Twist was finished for him.

Tony was very convincing, but his suggestion wasn't received with any enthusiasm. We all saw it as the most direct route to the Job Centre: 'What the fuck is this? We've got a frontman. He's one of the best there is, everyone thinks so. The only reason we're here is because of him. If he goes – and disappearing into the background will be just that – we're screwed.'

But Tony had thought this through. We'd find a really good singer, someone younger, someone sexy, and we'd rebuild behind him or her. Tony knew we didn't look as good as we had a year earlier when Julia was still in the group. We'd make it work. Get some routines going. We needed to give it a go.

Dave Hardy, who was the least convinced about Tony's proposal, got some adverts posted and set up a stage at the rehearsal room. We'd audition people singing to a selection of karaoke standards. Adge would film it so we could review the candidates by panel at some later date. Tony attended every minute of every audition. Nick and I didn't as we thought the whole thing was a massive waste of time.

Over four or five days, about 150 hopefuls auditioned to become World of Twist's new singer. It was a precursor to *The X Factor*, in that most of it was bad. Some of it was embarrassingly bad, but mostly it was just excruciatingly dull. Everyone's highlight of this ridiculous week-long charade was a spectacularly tuneless performance from a hopeful called Tim who opted to sing a few bars from *Fame*. His inspired chorus ad-lib, 'Remember my name . . . Tim!' had us in tears for weeks. It did the trick, however: I will never forget that boy's name. The only voice we could imagine being the new voice of Twist was owned by an overweight rocker in his mid-forties. If he'd looked like Meat Loaf, David Thomas or even Roscoe Arbuckle we'd have had signed him up in a heartbeat but he just looked supernaturally bland, like Christopher Cross drained of all star quality.

I haven't a clue how the music business works these days, but in 1992 it wasn't about nurturing talent, it was about harvesting success. Most artists and groups signed to multi-album deals didn't make it past the first option period – the point where the record company in effect decides if it's worth continuing to invest money in the artist. If the artist has shown any signs that they might be worth keeping – a decent, if unspectacular, chart performance in the previous twelve months, or some promising material awaiting release – then this decision becomes difficult. The last thing any company would want is to release an artist from their contract only for another company to pick them up and enjoy significant returns for slight investment.

Circa had ploughed a lot of money into World of Twist over the previous eighteen months, so now it was time to gamble on that commitment. It was clear we had some kind of audience out there. We were coming off the back of a near sold-out UK tour, and our chart performances, if not spectacular, were encouraging. On the other hand, it was patently obvious that we didn't have a second album in the wings and word had reached Circa that all was not hunky-dory at base camp. It wasn't a particular surprise that Circa dropped us, but neither was it a decision we'd anticipated.

When the panicking subsided, Dave pointed out that we were in a fairly enviable position. Our debt to Circa would be effectively written off and, though we wouldn't receive any royalties for future sales of *Quality Street* until Circa (now absorbed into EMI) had recouped their investment, we were surely an attractive proposition for any backers. There was still nobody quite like us in the UK. Our live shows were gaining momentum and this present bout of creative inertia, call it what you will, once lifted, would see us making great music again. There was also the question of Tony O: if he wasn't going to sing, what *was* he going to do? Dance, maybe? It was all very intriguing.

The office wasn't inundated with enquiries about our availability, but someone who was very interested was Creation's Alan McGee. Creation were a bit alien to us. They had a very impressive roster but nothing that we really listened to. On the surface, it didn't appear to be World of Twist's ideal domain. But Alan McGee was a persuasive and likeable character and he did seem keen. Tony, Dave and I went for a curry with him in Camden Town. Our old mate Bob Stanley had brokered the introduction and came along for the ensuing fireworks. Alan was a nice bloke and I had a hunch that he and Tony would hit it off. He kept going on about 'Sons of the Stage' to the point where we wondered if he'd heard anything else we'd done. It didn't really matter: it was a buoyant encounter and all that remained, it appeared, was for us to go home and decide how much money we wanted. Alan's secretary would do the rest. It was a strange way of doing business but beautifully simple.

Historically, Dave Hardy got the blame for what happened next, but it was actually Dave (in full Flash Harry mode) in collusion with Tony and me. As I've mentioned, we were all in or approaching our thirties and, conscious this might be the last deal we signed for the band, we wanted some loot. I can't recall what we asked for but it was a lot of money – much more than Creation were used to spending on bands of dubious appeal. Overnight their interest evaporated.

'Dear World of Twist, Thanks very much for your proposal but you may have got the wrong impression of how Creation operates. We wish you all the luck in the future' was how they might have politely worded a response that simply meant: 'Fuck off, you bunch of northern chancers.'

Of course, Alan McGee's stance was absolutely correct and his decision was totally vindicated by his next and most heroic Manchester signing.

The Creation episode pretty much put the tin lid on World of Twist proceedings. The band reconvened, relaxed and in high spirits, at Mike Healey's wedding in Glossop that summer. Tony and I were still writing music, but rarely together.

Tony had started working and hanging around with a fellow called John West, his new drinking buddy – and boy did those two like a drink. They'd call round at my flat from time to time and try to persuade me to work on stuff. It'd be eleven in the morning and they'd have a four pack of lager each. Most of the time our efforts were pointless, but on occasion we'd create something good. Tony had written a new song called 'New Electric Pop & Soul', which was definitely a return to form, and we knocked that one into shape without too much pain. He was also working on songs with other singers. There was some really good material – 'Gimme Your Loving' and 'Your Hair'. I was never sure if he intended these to be World of Twist releases. Whenever we met up we'd talk about carrying on but as time drifted on we got together less and less.

I'd got it into my head that I could write songs for other people and I demoed a few ideas with 'Voodoo' Viv Dixon. I was also trying to write some material for Bob Stanley protégés Golden, whose Celina Nash can be seen holding the 'Fox Base Alpha' placard on the cover of Saint Etienne's debut album. Saint Etienne themselves asked me to remix one of their songs, 'Avenue', which I really enjoyed and put my back into. I felt certain I'd get asked to do more of that kind of stuff, but I didn't. In reality, I was just treading water, waiting for the money to run out. Warner Chappell were still paying us for the time being, at least, so Tony and I were still solvent around this period. But they too would pull the plug in the next twelve months.

Manchester was changing. By 1992, the Hacienda was probably the worst night out in the UK. The music was unspeakably crap and we'd stopped going there a long way back. As far as Factory went, World of Twist had never made it onto the A-list, or even the B-list, so getting into the Hacienda meant queuing for up to an hour, which was definitely not for me. Like everyone else, we'd all decamped to the Gay Village several months before the Hac became intolerable, with coach parties of lads from Wakefield and the like. The pre-G-A-Y Canal Street scene was chilled and great fun. (A few years later we'd have been barred entrance to clubs like Manto under the 'no bisexuals' policy.) However, we preferred the seedier joints on the whole. Our favourite bar was an old-school private members' club called Austin's, which had the old sliding-window routine at the door. If they liked the look of you, and they usually did, you could join the inscrutable clientele therein. There'd be truck drivers in full slap, necking with young boys who looked like they'd stepped out of a Helmut Newton photo. It was like a Soft Cell video come to life. We loved it.

In June '92, *NME* announced that the band had split, but that wasn't strictly true. Nick had returned to London to get some session work and later in the year would rejoin the Gun Club, but technically he never left. Dave was now managing other bands, such as Oldham's wonderful Wonky Alice, but he was still holding out hope that Tony and I would snap out of it at some point and get the band going again. It was a forlorn hope. Nick and I recorded with Tony on one final occasion. We went into a studio in Macclesfield and recorded a very ambitious version of Jimmy Webb's 'MacArthur Park', a song that had provided the final lyrics to 'The Storm'. So the story had come full circle.

Warner Chappell pulled the plug in the next twelve months so the mission was effectively terminated and, bit by bit, we dismantled the apparatus.

33

When Does the Mind-Bending Start?

Early in 1993, I saw a colourful advert in the *Sunday Mirror* magazine, inviting readers to a three-day 'Festival of the Sixties' at Caister-on-Sea. In 1993, the festival situation was not as it is today. Back then your summer was comparatively festival-free. Reading was in its twenty-second year, Glastonbury in its twenty-third. Rolf Harris had emerged as the surprise hit of that year's Worthy Farm shakedown. WOMAD, the alternative Reading Festival, was there for the adventurous and it was the first year of the ill-fated Phoenix Festival in Stratford-upon-Avon. But there was none of this boutique, street food, bands you've never heard of, middle-class family-orientated nonsense. If you went to one of the few pop festivals on offer you expected to eat very badly, get robbed, forego personal hygiene, burn your tent and get home in a bit of a mess.

These days, with unbelievable festival choices to entice us, a 'Festival of the Sixties' might strike one as the worst ticket of the summer and potentially the three worst evenings of the year. Back in 1993, it looked like retro heaven. The first thing that caught my eye were the words L O V E A F F A I R. On further inspection I noticed the Foundations, the Tremeloes, the Fortunes, Edison Lighthouse and White Plains (both technically '70s outfits), Dozy, Beaky, Mick & Tich, Marmalade, Dave Berry, the Ivy League, the Honeycombs. Admittedly, there was also a surfeit of Merseyside filler, but by and large the line-up was dynamite and I'd probably still have gone if it were just the Love Affair and the Foundations.

Andy Hobson was predictably excited and signed up on the spot. He suggested we contact Tony, too. I hadn't seen him for quite a few months but this was definitely up his street and it'd be great to get together for something fun, without the spectre of Twist hanging over us. Jim Fry was easy to persuade and the party was to be completed by the Pole sisters, Ellie and Lizzy.

Due to some transport cock-up we arrived at the camp halfway through Friday evening. Andy, in his home-made 'Doo Wah Diddy' T-shirt, had been there for several hours and thought we'd set him up as a joke. He'd got himself very drunk while he was waiting and gleefully showed us around Neptune's Palace, our venue for the weekend. The place was like a giant working men's club. It was absolutely packed, every table full of middle-aged punters lapping up the watered-down beer and entertainment. All our favourites were playing on the Saturday, so we just eased our way into the festival, sitting at the back of the room feeling superior and stylish. Two hours later we were as much a part of the room as the next table, singing along to 'Needles and Pins' and 'I Saw Her Standing There', a song that every band seemed contractually obliged to perform. What a night we'd had.

I slept in on the Saturday but Andy and Jim were up with the lark and down at Neptune's for the Dreamers, who opened the show at midday. After the first number Jim was dispatched to the chalet to round us all up.

'There's something going down at Neptune's Palace that you can't miss.'

We took some convincing. The Dreamers? And no Freddie? They were bad enough *with* him! Actually, Garrity was a great singer – it was just a pity he never got any decent songs to sing. If I could come back with some kind of singing voice and it can't be Rob Tyner's or Iggy Pop's, then I'd make do with Freddie Garrity's. His trademark split-leg jumps, his endless camera-mugging, the demented cackle, that's why the kids came to see F & the Ds. Oh sure, we'd all chuckled along at the gaucheries of the four squares in the background, two speccy and two not, their byzantine buffoonery at the Palladium, their preposterous leg swinging on *The Ed Sullivan Show*, but the Dreamers? Without Freddie? Are you serious?

But at 12.30 in Neptune's Palace, the Freddieless Dreamers are really going for it. It's hard to tell if there's an original member here. If there is, then vanity's got the better of them as the glasses have been exchanged for contact lenses. But, nevertheless, if these are the Ersatz Dreamers, they are tight, tuneful and relaxed. And they're funny – not unintentionally, although they're also that.

The guitarist/singer delivers a long, drawn-out introduction to the next song and the rest of the band raise their eyes, feigning impatience. The drummer sneaks out from behind his kit and pulls the singer's trousers down; underneath the singer is wearing stockings and suspenders. The band fall apart laughing as the singer finds it hard to hide his embarrassment. How's he going to live this one down? But he gets his own back, pulling down the trousers of the bassist, lead guitarist and drummer. *They're all wearing stockings and suspenders!* This is fucking brilliant. I can think of dozens of indie bands that could benefit from this level of showmanship. In the middle of the next song the band, who are great musicians, all faint suddenly and fall to the floor. While they're lying on their backs on the stage the drummer, who can really play and who is really the star of this act, delivers a very accomplished drum solo, which starts on the kit but ends with him wandering around the audience, paradiddling the tables and beer glasses. He prepares to bring his sticks down on some geezer's bald head, but pulls back with a wink and a grin. His timing is superb. The drummer, who in my mind's eye is a cross between Micky Dolenz and the drummer from the Rubettes, gets back on the stage, where the band are still lying on their backs, and disappears behind the curtains. After a few seconds of Eric Morecambe-style comedy commotion, his head pokes back through the curtains. 'Hmmmm, Betty.' He's wearing a raincoat and a beret: he's Frank Spencer from *Some Mothers Do 'Ave 'Em*. The place goes wild. I look around our table: Tony, Jim and Andy are in raptures. If we could have had nights out like this every week, then World of Twist would have carried on for a hundred years.

We all agree that, if they ever put one of these things on in thirty years' time celebrating the early '90s, we'll put our name forward. Like this weekend, the bill will be full of former superstar bands with one or two original members: Mark Day's Happy Mondays; Dave Rowntree's Blur; Suede with Mat Osman; the Stone Carpets (feat. Clint Boon and Mani). The whole weekend will be an homage to people who aren't there: Ian Brown; Shaun Ryder; Jarvis Cocker; Damon Albarn; the Gallagher brothers. Most of the groups (including Twist) will have to bolster their sets with cover versions of songs by the better-known bands: 'Roll With It', 'Parklife', 'Made of Stone', 'Common People' and 'Wrote for Luck' will receive multiple plays. And, for the minor acts (including Twist), it will be advisable to work a bit of cabaret into the set:

'Madchester' weekender – World of Twist set

1. 'Sons of the Stage'
2. 'The Storm'
3. 'Unbelievable' by EMF
4. 'Common People' by Pulp (before which Tony does a quick costume change and returns as Jarvis Cocker, wearing glasses, tie and Norman Wisdom jacket)
5. 'Kinky Afro' by Happy Mondays (another costume change. Tony comes back on in ridiculously baggy clothes and we invite some kids up to dance like Bez. They each get plastic maracas, a smiley T-shirt and a tub of Haribo)
6. Competition time: we invite ladies from the audience up for a '90s dance-off, while the band plays 'Smells Like Teen Spirit'. The winner gets a bottle of bubbly, a

copy of World of Twist's new covers album, *Twist into the Future*, and a kiss on the lips from Tony O

7. Medley of lesser-known World of Twist tunes (inc 'Sweets', 'Jellybaby')

8. '90s Acieeed medley (incl. 'We Call it Acieeed' by D-Mob and '(You Gotta Get Yourself) Connected' by the Stereo MC's

9. 'Sons of the Stage'/'Unbelievable' singalong finale ('Thanks for coming, hope you've had a great time, we're World of Twist, you've been "Unbelievable"')

We left Neptune's Palace after Manchester's phenomenal Dreamers. Nothing could nor should follow that and certainly not the bovine clatter of Liverpool's Merseybeats. The Foundations, on the other hand, with original singer Clem Curtis, were the absolute nazz. Britain's first and greatest multi-ethnic pop group, the Foundations, were spilling off the stage with a full brass section augmenting a highly syncopated five-piece band. The Foundations put us in a very good mood and there was more where that came from. Dozy, Beaky, Mick & Tich (minus Dave Dee) took us for a whirlwind tour of their very impressive catalogue. There was no 'Don Juan' or 'Wreck of the "Antoinette"', but otherwise the hits were all intact: 'Bend It!', 'Hold Tight!', 'Zabadak!' and, of course, 'The Legend of Xanadu' (complete with synthesised whip-cracks).

Afterwards, we spoke to Beaky III ('I'm not the original Beaky') and asked him if there was anything happening after hours. It turned out there was a party at Wayne Fontana's chalet.

'Will he let us in?' we asked.

'Well, you've got some birds with you, haven't you?' said Beaky, leering at the Pole sisters.

We had a Wayne Fontana and the Mindbenders connection, as it happened. We were all from Manchester and WF lived opposite the Church in Cheadle Hulme, a pub just round the corner from Tony's house. Surely that was enough to get us in?

Back at the chalet, we were joined by Steve Ellis's backing band, who'd been chatting up Ellie and Lizzy. They confirmed that there was a party down at Wayne Fontana's and we should all head off down there. Predictably, the party was as dull as you'd expect from a bunch of '60s also-rans and their less than committed backing musicians, lads our age, who were aghast that we preferred Love Affair to Suede. Wayne held court, a big confident Mancunian who carried himself like a northern night-club owner – part gangster, part stand-up comedian. In his hey-day (1963–66), he projected a scruffy, louche charm and sported the floppiest, most unkempt hair of all of the moptops. From under his substantial fringe he had a cheeky twinkle in his eye and a rebellious smirk, as if he'd just been plucked from a bus queue following an afternoon's shoplifting. And of course, he had a pretty good voice. If he'd got anywhere near some decent material, Wayne Fontana could have been massive. However, the band's dubious legacy was merely to provide Phil Collins with his third and final number-one single, 'Groovy Kind of Love', a song Wayne didn't even sing on.

Now, relaxing in his deluxe Haven chalet in Caister-on-Sea, Wayne had removed the ten-gallon hat he'd been wearing on stage to display a shiny bald pate with long back and sides à la Scouse comic Mick Miller. I thought he looked a bit grumpy. Tony O was busy making new friends and finding out where the drugs were hidden. His distinctive foghorn laugh stood out above the monotonous hum of '60s anecdotes and we'd surely been tagged as gatecrashers. Tony had positioned himself near to our host. He edged closer to Fontana and leaned in to speak to him: 'So Wayne . . . when does the mind-bending start?'

We were asked to leave.

So when did the mind-bending start for World of Twist? Chemically speaking, we weren't a particularly experimental quintet. As the bulk of the band's material was written by Tony, it's fair to say that at least 75 per cent of the songs were written under the influence of some drug or other, but there was no great drug synergy fuelling our creativity.

Tony was the best at taking drugs by a long way. He once visited his GP, revealing that it was his intention to go on a massive drugs binge in a few weeks and was his system up to it? Adge was probably our number two 'user'. As he raved a lot more than the rest of us, he was definitely our ecstasy man. Andy and Nick could take it or leave it. They weren't in the habit of turning anything down, but they rarely went in search of class As, which were never central to a good night out. Coming last was my good self. The only thing I took was the odd bit of speed if I was going to a northern soul function. I'd taken mushrooms in the past and smoked a bit of pot, but taking anything of an MDMA or hallucinogenic nature would have been playing Russian roulette with my adrenal glands.

The *psychological* mind-bending, however, was another matter. Tony and I had been tearing emotional strips off each other for some time and it was fair to say that neither of us came out of it very well.

My innate introversion and normality made it much easier for me to piece everything back together after the band's demise. For Tony, it was far more complicated and not made any easier by his chosen support network.

But the full extent of World of Twist's mind-bending capabilities? Well, that may not become apparent for another twenty years or so when our records become as revered as those of Tintern Abbey, Winston's Fumbs or Rupert's People. Did we blow some minds out there during our brief but feted moment as the late twentieth century's last great psychedelic adventurers and cosmic tunesmiths?

I like to think so.

Underture

'We had an amazing time. We wanted to make the greatest psychedelic dance rock album ever and there was a
lot of coke and E in the studio. But the album came out
at half normal volume. We'd spent £250,000 making an
album with the smallest bollocks in pop history! The band
just fell apart. We were smoking marijuana for breakfast
and that led to communication problems. I didn't wanna
sing, the guitarist didn't wanna play. When the company
didn't get a hit they threw us in the bin. I was devastated –
I spent four years on smack watching Third Reich movies
because the good guys always win. I'm really sorry for letting our fans down. I've got a new band called Bubblegum
and I'm desperate to put something out. But I'd ask anyone to play that World of Twist album twenty times with
every dial on full. If it doesn't rock, come and smash it
over my head.'

– Tony Ogden, *The Guardian*, 2005

The tragedy of World of Twist's demise for the music world was not so much the loss of World of Twist but the loss of Tony Ogden. He was a great star in the making, the greatest frontman of his era and, without question, the most talented person I've ever met.

Tony Ogden died in July 2006, just three weeks after Syd Barrett, and it's tempting to draw comparisons between the two. Each to some extent was the victim of drug-related psychosis; each spent their final years as a recluse. However, Tony, in his self-imposed exile, continued to write and showed some interest in reaching a larger audience with his work. At first collaborating with John West and then with our old friend Martin Wright, Tony had composed and recorded at least four albums' worth of new material by his death, and much of this work bears favourable comparison with anything he wrote during his World of Twist reign. If you search online you'll find evidence of Tony's latter-day genius, under the suitably grand label of the Bubblegum Secret Pop Explosion. 'Pop Wheels', 'Angry Brigade', 'What's Your Name', 'The Lost Parade', 'Electric Dress', 'Girls in Colour', 'Can I Come Over' and 'Escape in the Love Machines' (played at Tony's funeral) are all beautifully constructed songs, full of wit and imagination. The lyrics and inventiveness are pure Ogden, the voice sadly isn't, which makes it difficult for me to listen to them. Gone is the confident Tony O attack replaced by a fragility and nervousness that was never part of the Tony we knew. But then did we ever know him?

Tony's whole make-up was an enigma. Naturally guarded and secretive but wild, open and extremely loud in the right company, Tony never spoke if it was possible to shout. He'd stroll about restlessly, hands in pockets, his head down. In the pub he'd hunch over his pint with the ever-present B&H and the nervous laugh, which came out in sniggers or uncontrollable guffaws. But Tony's demeanour was deceptive. He could be silent, graceful and athletic. He could probably have been a sportsman, and although he had no interest in sport he did like the occasional game of tennis and was very handy with a ping-pong bat. On the dance floor, he could move like a shaolin priest. He never took a bad photo, he looked fabulous in any clothes and he was very funny, exciting and unpredictable. His ability to arrange and his way with a tune was unmatched by his peer group. He was a great reader and a great lyricist, a skill that was ever expanding on the evidence of his later output. And of course he was the face of World of Twist.

As we all lined up behind Tony, I don't think any of us appreciated just how difficult it was to front our band. It was fine when the plaudits were coming our way, and in the first twelve months we received nothing but praise, but as our psychedelic fancies began to grow stale in the eyes of the press and the indifferent reviews began to coalesce, it must have felt very personal. It was easy to see why he wanted to step down. It makes me cringe when I think of how little support we offered him.

Nick Sanderson, the greatest person in the world to be bored with, died from cancer in 2008 and, fourteen years later, I'm still missing him. Sands had this incredible capacity to connect with people. It didn't matter who they were or where they were from. Standing next to the leather-jacketed contingent at his funeral – the Mary Chains, the Parkinsons, Earl Brutuses, friends and family – was a delegation from the local branch of ASLEF. Even in his short time as a train driver he'd made loads of friends on the job. Nick's death decentralised the planet for all of us. It's taken a long time to recover. I'm not even sure if we have.

In the twelve months it's taken to write this book, we've also lost the legendary Dave Hardy (the true alpha male of this adventure) and our beautiful friend Martin 'Lefty' Wright (aka 'The Lad'), both from the same cruel illness that robbed us of Nick. Martin was a cert for any World of Twist reunion, so it definitely won't happen now, I'm sorry to report.

So what was the point of it all – of World of Twist, of 'Madchester', that most celebrated of eras, and of Manchester, that most celebrated of cities? Legacy has become a popular term to describe the preservation and documentation of a particularly important artist's work. Every month for the past twenty years, I've bought *Mojo* magazine and, every month, seemingly on rotation, it celebrates the work of the Beatles (and individual Beatles), the Stones, the Who, Led Zeppelin, Pink Floyd, Bob Dylan, Bruce Springsteen, Neil Young, David Bowie, Kate Bush or Paul Weller. A museum of the increasingly mortal. Why have we developed this obsession with preserving the work and memory of the not-so-distant past? I think there's a clue in a book I've been reading about the history of British music hall.

Marie Lloyd, Dan Leno and Little Tich were the first great stars of music hall. Lloyd was the undisputed queen of the halls, a cheeky, buck-toothed songstress known for her three innuendo-laced signature tunes. 'The Boy in the Gallery', 'A Little of What You Fancy' and 'Don't Dilly Dally' were all delivered with her trademark sauce. The sad-eyed Leno was the clown prince of music hall, a song and sketch man who died of nervous exhaustion at the age of forty-two. Harry Relph, aka 'Little Tich', standing 4 foot 6 high, was known throughout Europe for his comedy 'big boot dance', which he performed to his great discomfort in shoes nearly as long as he was tall. All three are long forgotten and virtually unknown to the wider public, yet they were the greatest entertainers of their era. One of music hall's most enduring hits was 'I Do Like to Be Beside the Seaside', a refrain known by many and still sung today, but has anyone heard of Mark Sheridan, the man who made the song famous? Or does anyone know that Sheridan blew his brains out in a Glasgow Park in the last year of the Great War?

It's my firm belief that, of all the amazing songs the Beatles wrote, one of those most likely to endure through the ages is 'Yellow Submarine', and even then few will know or care who wrote it. Despite our best efforts, I can't help feeling that in a hundred years from now, Armstrong, Ellington, Fitzgerald, Sinatra, Presley and even the Beatles will be as obscure as old British music hall artists, with only fanatics and history books keeping their memory alive. Even now my daughters, who can recognise every tune in the hit parade, have little interest in the people who sing the songs. So if this is the fate of the most iconic artists of the twentieth century, what fate befalls the Happy Mondays, Stone Roses or indeed World of Twist?

At the tail end of punk, a record everyone seemed to own was the *Nuggets* collection, a double LP set compiled by Patti Smith's guitarist Lenny Kaye: *Original Artyfacts from the First Psychedelic Era, 1965–1968*. For many, this was our first introduction into the world of US garage and psychedelia – a Tarantino soundtrack waiting to happen. It was a wonderful mix of one-hit wonders, such as the Castaways and the Knickerbockers, and some of the bigger names of the US underground, like the 13th Floor Elevators and Todd Rundgren's Nazz. Listening to *Nuggets* was a wonderful education, teaching us that the two-and-a-half-minute thrash of punk was maybe not as original as we'd all supposed, and that a whole underclass of Stones, Beatles and Kinks sound-alikes had existed in the US every bit as sexually frustrated as their UK counterparts. Those first two sides of *Nuggets* became as well known to us as the Lord's Prayer, but they were merely the tip of the iceberg, as numerous volumes of the US series *Pebbles* would prove. Just like the UK's northern soul scene, we discovered that the supply of US garage sounds from the '60s was seemingly inexhaustible. Over time, I became far more interested in the UK's second XI take on psychedelia, but the US band I found most intriguing were the Dovers from Santa Barbara. You may not have heard of them – most people haven't, it seems. As far as I'm aware, they recorded just eight songs during their very brief career, released on four singles. All eight tracks are diamonds of the very roughest form, pure garage gems that stand proud with any pop releases on either side of the Atlantic. The Dovers were Jan & Dean crossed with the Byrds, Blue Oyster Cult and Echo & the Bunnymen. Their music is genius and I wish more people knew this.

Perhaps somewhere out in the American mid-west there exists some '90s Anglophile indie nut who gets as much from World of Twist's intriguing but meagre output as I do from the Dovers.

If so, then that's good enough for me.

Acknowledgements

For:
Jane, Jody and Dora

Dedicated to:
David Hardy, Martin Wright, Nick Sanderson, Tony Ogden

Extra special thanks to:
Jim Fry – my co-pilot on most of the adventures herein. Your friendship, wit, imagination and enthusiasm have been a constant inspiration for forty-five years. It's been a privilege flying with you.

Special thanks to:
Bob Stanley; Cath Berry; Ellie Pole; John Pennington; Marc Riley; Martin Mittler; Matt Mead; Mike Hardy; Pete Selby; Stella Grundy; the Clouds; World of Twist (Andy Hobson, Alan Frost, Angela Reilly, Julia Seppi, Nick Sanderson, Tony Ogden)

Thank you to:
Andrew Berry; Andy Robbins; Anthony Green (RIP); Ben Knott; Caroline Elleray; Chris Whitehead; Eric Brooker; Ian Bendelow (RIP); Ian Eastwood; Ian Rainford; Jeremy Deller; John Novak; John Robb; John West (RIP); Jonathan Barrett; Josie Wright; Julia Adamson; Kevin Haskins; Liam Mullen; Mark Pugh; Martin Fry; Martin Hannett (RIP); Martin Moscrop; Michael and

Lesley Pinchien; Mike Healy; Neil Drabble; Nick Phillips; Patrick O'Reilly; Paul Brotherton; Paul Gunning; Pete Smith; Richard Davis; Rory Connolly; Simon Reynolds; Simon Sanderson; Spencer Birtwistle; Stuart Boreman; Terry Christian; the King family; Viv Dixon

Without whom we would not be here:
1910 Fruitgum Company; ABC; Barry Gray; Brute Force; Chairmen of the Board; ClockDVA; Crazy Elephant; Cupid's Inspiration; David Bowie; Dean Parrish; Dexys Midnight Runners; Doctors of Madness; Don Fardon; Don Thomas; Gene Latter; Gene Pitney; Genesis; Hawkwind; Holland-Dozier-Holland; Jimi Hendrix; Jimmy Webb; Joe Meek; John Barry; Joy Division; Julian Cope; Kasenetz-Katz Singing Orchestral Circus; Keith Mansfield; Keith West; Kiss; Kraftwerk; MC5; Mr Bloe; Nazz; Ohio Express; Orange Juice; Pretty Things; Richard Harris; Roxy Music; Sensational Alex Harvey Band; Shadows of Knight; Slade; Sparks; the B-52's; the Beatles; the Buzzcocks; the Fall; the Foundations; the Honeycombs; the Human League; the Left Banke; the Love Affair; the Rolling Stones; the Sex Pistols; the Small Faces; the Steve Karmen Big Band; the Stooges; the Who; *The World of David Bowie*; Ultravox; Vice Versa; Wigan's Chosen Few; Wigan's Ovation; Yes; Yvonne Baker

Photograph credits:
Cath Berry; James Fry; Gordon King; Mark Pugh; Martin Mittler; Richard Davis. Penultimate photo in plate section © David Nixon/Retna UK via Avalon.

Nine Eight Books would like to thank:
Peter Stoneman for additional creative editorial support; Jim Fry for generous access to his photo archive.